Tottie Merry Christmas

MATLOCK BATH

A perfectly romantic place

Christopher Charlton and Doreen Buxton

from all the Elses & Hawks

Published by The Derwent Valley Mills World Heritage Site Educational Trust, a registered charity funded initially by the Derbyshire Building Society and the University of Derby, publishing material relating to the history of Derbyshire's Derwent Valley. The authors have no pecuniary interest in this book and all proceeds from its sale will be invested by the Trust in future publications.

Registered Charity number 1099279

Design and layout copyright © 2019 The Derwent Valley Mills World Heritage Site Educational Trust. Applications for the copyright owner's written permission to reproduce any part of this publication should be addressed to the publisher.

ISBN 978-1-9161609-0-3

Designed by Ian Lane, Mill Design and Advertising, Belper, DE56 2SD

Printed by Warners Midlands Plc, The Maltings, Manor Lane, Bourne, PE10 9PH

For book purchases phone 07784 875 333 or email DVMWHS.EducationTrust@gmail.com

Address for Correspondence (not to be used for book purchases) c/o The Derwent Valley Mills World Heritage Site Partnership Coordination Team, Shand House, Dale Road South, Matlock, DE4 3RY.

Contents

Acknowledgements

This book began in a University of Nottingham Department of Adult Education local history workshop directed by Christopher Charlton. Images were collected and with the permission of the owners, the late Brian Wheatcroft, photographed them. Now, many years later and with more pictures and a text, this work is offered as a belated tribute to Brian's memory and to the members of the class. Thanks also to Trevor Steed who continued the copying process for us.

Many people have contributed their help. Our thanks are due to Ann Andrews for useful cross referencing chats; the late Frank Clay, for many generously shared hours recording details of the twentieth century; Roger Flindall for information from his newspaper and mining records; Hugh Potter for his use of holiday visits to seek out diaries of erstwhile Matlock Bath visitors and to Stuart Band, Colin Goodwyn, Jim Rieuwerts and the Reverend John Drackley for their additions. Throughout, we have benefited from the research and thoughtful interest from our colleague David Hool.

Alongside them are the people who have supplied images, not only those pictures which have been reproduced here but the many more which have been consulted in order to confirm a perspective or date. Particular thanks to Dr John Bradley for bringing to our attention the very significant historical contribution made by the stereograph photographers in the second half of the nineteenth century; and to Tony Holmes and Glynn Waite who have generously shared their image collections. The debt to the late Ken Askew and the late Ken Smith is immense, not least for their enthusiasm for all things Matlock Bath and for their unfailingly positive response to requests for permission to use a copy of their picture of this, or a better picture of that.

We have been helped by consulting the property deeds kindly lent by local property owners and from those available in the Government Property Office archive at Taunton. The collections at Derby Museums and Art Gallery, Derbyshire County Council Buxton Museum and Art Gallery, the Devonshire Collection, Chatsworth House, the Midland Railway Study Centre, the Yale Centre for British Art, Paul Mellon Collection, Derby Local Studies Library, the Derbyshire Records Office and Matlock Local Studies Library have supplied images and records. Pictures from Richard Evans, the late Hazel Greatorex, Peter Miller,

Mrs and the late Mr Higton, the Pidcock family, the late Frank Clay, the late Terry Moore, W W Winter Ltd, the Arkwright Society, Adrian Farmer and Dianne Charlton are gratefully acknowledged.

The trustees of the Derwent Valley Mills World Heritage Site Educational Trust and others who read the text in draft have made valuable amendments.

In preparing this book for publication we have enjoyed the benefit of Ian Lane's design skills and infinite patience; it has been a pleasure to work with him again.

Foreword

There are few places in the world as quirky and historically interesting as Matlock Bath.

Over recent centuries it has seen fashion, favour and fortune come and go and has left us with a unique streetscape reminiscent of a seaside town. Georgian, Regency and Victorian architectural splendour is set within a remarkable geological landscape, a deep cleft within the carboniferous limestone that rings the mighty dome of Millstone Grit that makes up the High Peak.

It's a place steeped in a rich history of industry, commerce and ingenuity, which has shaped Matlock Bath into the place we see today.

Visitors throng the town at weekends, pouring off trains from Derby, or out of their cars and coaches, to enjoy the scenery, the cable cars at the Heights of Abraham, the aquarium and the many cafes, chip shops and ice cream parlours that line the 'Parades'. Also to enjoy the spectacle of the hundreds, sometimes thousands, of motorcycles that come on warm sunny weekends and even some evenings in summer. They may perhaps be oblivious, other than in a passing way, how this once isolated rural location, the smaller satellite of nearby Matlock, came to be such a revered place where people 'took the waters' in the 18th century. More obvious is its lead mining heritage, documented in the excellent mining museum housed in the Grand Pavilion. Visitors are perhaps only fleetingly aware that this place sits within a World Heritage Site, still the only one in the East Midlands; it's a real Derbyshire gem.

Matlock Bath has a captivating air of faded glory and its breath taking landscape speaks to the hearts of many, making it a place that people visit time and again because it inspires a curious loyalty. We all love places like that.

Living in Derbyshire we are blessed with more than a few places that inspire this kind of loyalty. It's important, though, that we ensure that people understand the story of this place, never more so than in an age when people want more and more information, especially in bite-sized social media friendly snippets. To do that you have to have the very best primary source information that comes from excellent research and is expressed in a clear, accessible narrative that people can refer to (and I'll return to this point about narrative in a minute).

The evolution of Matlock Bath is traced through this academically robust and compelling work, and I was delighted to be asked by the DVMWHS Educational Trust to write the foreword. It is a book that has been needed for a long time and is a huge contribution to the corpus of material, not just to the Derwent Valley World Heritage Site, but to Derbyshire.

The world is changing all the time and we, and the places we inhabit, inevitably change too. That is why it is critical to be well informed and to understand the history that shapes a place, to construct a narrative that gives a sense of value of the place. That is what this book does. Matlock Bath is a place that has adapted, survived and expresses its story by its very presence in the landscape and the sheer tenacity of the street scenery that clings to the steep craggy hillsides and the jagged edges of the River Derwent that has carved this place out for us. It is also a story of the people that built this place, that mined it for galena to make lead, ever since the Romans trudged over the hills from the south some 1,700 years ago, to the entrepreneurial characters that turned it into a spa town built around its springs and petrifying wells.

Derbyshire, world famous for many things, not least its contribution as the birthplace of the Industrial Revolution, the humble but globally renowned Bakewell Pudding and great houses like Chatsworth, needs a narrative to make a coherent story for the county, something that many visitors to our county tell us they feel is missing when they come here. This book will be a vital contribution to developing that. The creation of a clear narrative is something that I am keen to see happen for our county, so yet another reason I was pleased to be asked to write this.

The Derwent Valley Mills World Heritage Site Educational Trust is a group of volunteers that are deeply interested in researching and communicating the importance of this amazing and internationally important place to the world. We need people like this, we need their efforts, their research and most of all their high quality professional publications that will help us to understand, tell the story of, and, most importantly, preserve this special valley.

Cllr Barry Lewis
BA (Hons), MA, Leader of Derbyshire County Council

'Matlock Bath', drawn and signed by John Betjeman, January 1959 for Deborah, Duchess of Devonshire.

Introduction

On any warm summer evening in this the second decade of the twenty first century, Matlock Bath is thronged with people drifting along the Parades, the car parks are full, the roadsides lined with cars and motor bikes. A passing onlooker might ask where all these people have come from, why are they here? A hint of the answer came on a fine Saturday morning a few years ago, when a casual query to a leather-clad lady outside a cottage in a Cambridgeshire village brought the response 'We're just taking the bike for a run up to Matlock Bath, we often go that way on a nice day.' It's a habit with a history; motor bikes being only one of the succession of modes of transport that have brought visitors to Matlock Bath.

At the end of the seventeenth century, Matlock Bath did not exist. The area it was to occupy was within the parish of Matlock and known as Matlockwood, a name which survives high on the hillside in that part of Matlock Bath which is still called Upperwood. The valley was sparsely populated by families working in lead mining and farming and was served only by stony, and often steep, footways and bridleways.

Soon after 1700 a trickle of visitors began to arrive. They were attracted by the claims made for the healing properties of water from a natural spring which supplied a primitive bath cut into a rocky shelf in the side of the valley. They sought relief from a variety of ailments. There was no road suitable for a coach to pass through the valley, 'the rocks at that time extending too near to the edge of the river'. Reaching the bath would have presented a sick person with an uncomfortable journey on foot or on horseback, perhaps picking a way downhill on the slippery bridleway from Bonsall. But the infirm were not alone in making the journey to this part of the Derwent gorge. It was not long before this 'new' place began to interest the inquisitive traveller who found the valley's wildness not daunting but a delight. In due course the charm of the bath's setting became an attraction for tourists in its own right and in the service of these two clienteles a settlement grew up around the bath. 'The bath at Matlockwood' gradually became known as 'the Matlock bath' and eventually Matlock Bath.

Many of these new visitors were people who could afford the time and expense to travel for interest and pleasure and were encouraged by the growing popularity of English scenery.

For them the ability to sketch or paint a recognisable scene was a desirable accomplishment and amateur and professional artists recorded their experiences. The tradition for visiting Matlock Bath and documenting what was there had begun.

Over the years the class of visitor and the pattern of visiting changed as did the images taken away. Oil paintings commissioned for Kedleston Hall in the eighteenth century made way in the twentieth century for photographs reproduced in thousands as postcards and the amateur pencil sketches were replaced by Box Brownie snapshots. The leisured gentry of the eighteenth century supplemented their own artistic endeavours or their purchase of topographical prints with personal accounts, journals, letters and diaries. As the nineteenth century ended, the picture postcard provided instant images on which day-trippers recorded their hasty messages to send nationwide. In the years in between, the record was sustained by the many illustrated guide-books and, with the advent of photography, the popularity of stereographic views.

An archive of Matlock Bath material has been created, largely but not exclusively visual, which is now scattered across the country and beyond, housed in museums, record offices and private collections. This book is built upon a small part of this resource. It offers an explanation of why Matlock Bath grew and how it came to look the way it does and provides an obituary for the buildings which have been lost, many of them 'demolished for the A6 road-widening'. It does not include the story of lead mining in the area which began hundreds of years before there was a place called Matlock Bath.[1]

We are conscious of having concentrated our attention more on Matlock Bath in the eighteenth and nineteenth centuries than in the twentieth; a focus which reflects both personal interests and the limitations of space. We also acknowledge our dependence in much of this book on local newspaper evidence; the strengths and weaknesses of these sources of historical information are well known and we recognise the risks we have taken in accepting so many newspaper accounts at face value. Our errors will no doubt be exposed in due course.

Baths spas and hydropathy

To understand the changing fortunes of Matlock Bath in its life of about 230 years as an active spa it may be helpful to outline the national context in which the resort plied its trade. It is our contention that while its growth in the eighteenth century reflects its ability to match emerging fashions in water treatments and the leisure industry associated with them so also its gradual decline as a spa from the middle years of the century that followed is closely linked to its inability to invest in the new facilities demanded by changing tastes in the health and leisure market or to embrace the new water cures that extended the life of some of its competitors.

Matlock Bath entered the spa market at a time of rapid expansion and renewed belief in the efficacy of water treatments. Indeed the Restoration and early years of the eighteenth century were an heroic period for cold water bathing and drinking spa waters. Between 1660 and 1699 at least 39 English spas were developed adding to the 16 already in existence and a further 34 were at work by 1750.[2] Drinking mineral waters was a long established custom but cold water bathing had fallen out of favour. Now reinterpreted and marketed for a new generation it again became fashionable and where high society led, a wider public followed its lead. Its increasing popularity owed much to the advocacy of Sir John Floyer (1649-1734), a physician who practised in Lichfield and who greatly admired the baths at Buxton.[3] Through their persuasive pens he and a number of other medical men presented cold water bathing as a new cure-all remedy. The pre -reformation Church they argued, which had attributed the efficacy of numerous holy wells to the intervention of the saints whose names they bore, had missed the point. It was the mineral content of the water that healed and not the beliefs, the popish idolatry that the post reformation Church, with little success, attempted to stamp out.[4] They also blamed the medical profession for its faith in 'chemical' cures and short sightedness in not recognising the natural resources so abundantly available.

Many of Derbyshire's mineral springs were adapted for public use in this new search for health. And while the success and consequential growth of Buxton and Matlock Bath is relatively well known, by 1733 there were at least 23 other mineral springs in the county being exploited for their health-giving properties, though few enjoyed more than a very modest existence.[5] As a widespread practice the fashion for bathing in cold mineralised water was short-lived.[6] The bracing effect was considered too severe for many patients though where the water was warmer it continued to flourish. The handful of resorts that enjoyed this rare phenomenon of hot spring water, prospered accordingly. No other spa in England could match the warmth of Bath's thermal waters at 116°F and both Buxton at 83°F and Clifton at 76°F were significantly better endowed than Matlock Bath where the water at no more than 68°F was sometimes described as tepid rather than warm. Erasmus Darwin (1731-1802), a frequent visitor to Derbyshire from his home in Lichfield, considered to be one of the best doctors of his generation, was among those who were happy to recommend both the internal and external use of mineral water to their patients while at the same time recognising the risks of immersion in cold water for those who were already in a weakened condition. His advice to his close friend Josiah Wedgwood in September 1772 reveals both his appreciation of the efficacy of drinking Matlock Bath water and his awareness of the risks of bathing in it. Early in that month Josiah's wife had suffered a miscarriage; three weeks later Erasmus writes 'As Mrs Wedgewood's Stomach will not bear any spirituous Liquor at present, and as Water must therefore constitute the principle part of what She drinks, I would in earnest advise her to go for a Fortnight to Matlock or Buxton, as those calcareous Waters are more likely to be useful to her than others. I should be cautious about advising her to bathe, as She is yet so weak, but it might be try'd at Buxton; the Bath at Matlock would be too cold for Her.'[7] Alas the temperature of its water was something Matlock Bath was unable to change and it was a permanent constraint on the development of the resort as a spa centre.

By the end of the eighteenth century the practice of bathing in mineral waters in England had so diminished that a list of the most noted mineral waters in Europe identified only 7 English spas from a total of 119 as having bathing facilities and of those only two were offering cold baths.[8]

In contrast to the decline in cold water bathing the market for mineral waters used internally had grown. Indeed, during the early years of the nineteenth century the English spas were at the height of their popularity as John W. Williams, a contemporary witness, records. 'It has become almost a characteristical fashion amongst the English to unbend occasionally from the cares of business and leave the impure air of the city, to acquire freshness and health by a visit to some natural spring in the country.' He was writing in the 1830s.[9] He deplored the current neglect of both warm bathing and the cold bath which he claimed had arisen from its use for complaints for which it was inappropriate with the resulting failure tarnishing its reputation as a potential beneficial procedure. He believed it was his vocation to persuade the public to rediscover and embrace 'bathing as a part of [the] National System of Living'. For him this certainly included a greater use of mineral water, warm and cold, but above all it had to be the adoption of sea bathing, the new medical panacea; here was mineralised water on a massive scale. It was a competition the landlocked inland English spas were bound to lose. Sea bathing, the seaside and its associated pleasures, in fact the entire seaside package inexorably captured the imagination of the public who made their way to the coast in increasing numbers so sustaining the growth of the great seaside resorts.

While that was to be the picture over the longer term, many years of active growth remained ahead of the traditional inland spa centres. Hembry[10] has identified 20 new spas and 14 significant improvements to existing resorts during the 1830s. These new developments were not based on radical new thinking or departure from the now longstanding spa traditions but they incorporated features that enabled the spas to present a new face to the public. The cold baths had been replaced by warm, tepid and vapour baths heated by burning coal and with them more sophisticated treatments. Later, by the middle of the century more fundamental innovations were introduced with the adoption of hydropathic methods, initially imported from the continent but which soon acquired a British identity. These involved the use of water on the body externally without any reliance on its actual or assumed mineral content. It was this new approach that reinvigorated Malvern and Ilkley and created a whole new resort at Matlock.

Competition in the leisure industry in the nineteenth century was fierce and only the best endowed of the traditional inland resorts flourished. As early as 1806 13 of the 30[11] English seaside resorts provided bath houses with heated and cold baths fed by tidal waters; this and the growing use of bathing machines helped convince the public that the seaside was the place for water therapy and that it could be enjoyed with sea air and fun. At the same time the claims made for the curative properties of mineral water were under scrutiny. The waters at Malvern, Buxton and Bristol were shown to possess no more chemicals than ordinary tap water and in London a number of the wells and mineral springs were found to be so heavily polluted they were unfit for human consumption.[12] Confronted by such issues the medical profession retreated; mineral water treatments were reassessed and a more limited evidence-based appreciation of their application emerged. At the same time there were those who embraced the new hydropathic cures some of whose advocates were medically trained and some of whom were not and before long many of the same extravagant claims that had been made for the spa water treatments were now attributed to this new therapy.[13]

It is suggested that by 1815 there were no more than 40 viable spa resorts.[14] In each of these, underpinning their success, there had been major investment both in specialist services and in the complementary infrastructure required to satisfy the needs and aspirations of their invalid and pleasure-seeking clients. This would involve not only pump rooms and perhaps bath houses but also assembly rooms, lending libraries, reading rooms, coffee houses, shops, lodgings and hotels, a church and one or more chapels, pleasure grounds and ideally a theatre. For a resort which lacked one or more of these components the catch up cost to make good the deficiency would be large and would involve risk; and where there was no single guiding hand as in Bath or Scarborough where councils were the key players; or Buxton with its single dominant landlord, it was a matter of chance whether an individual investor or group of like-minded people would emerge who were prepared to undertake the risk of substantial expenditure with an uncertain return. As in Matlock Bath with its lack of a pump room so in other small spas the years passed while the resort haemorrhaged patronage without a solution being found.[15]

Fortunately for Matlock Bath and many of the older rural spas, no longer in the front rank, and unable to compete with the larger urban and coastal resorts, other attributes, climate, scenery and road and rail links to a larger town or city, made them attractive and convenient places to live and they became essentially residential settlements; small towns with a street name or two as the only reminder of their previous life as a spa,[16] or in Matlock Bath's case a small town with a flourishing leisure business and a lingering interest in spa treatments. The large urban spas which competed successfully with the coastal resorts did so by adopting new treatments and by increasing the range and quality of their leisure facilities. A new breed of 100 bedroom hotels was born catering for a rapidly expanding market; urban parks and winter gardens were created and in Harrogate in the 1870s and in Bath in 1895[17] new theatres were built staging theatrical and cultural events for the growing numbers of middle class visitors. In Harrogate in the 1860s the Royal pump rooms were busier than ever and this encouraged the local authority to open new baths. These opened in 1871. They included 18 bathrooms, 4 shower and 4 vapour baths and 2 swimming baths, and alongside the municipal investments a considerable amount of private capital was committed to further baths and hotels.

Hydropathy, the new form of treatment, was both a threat and a boon to the established spa resorts. A threat because the new hydro resorts it brought into being, such as Ilkley and Matlock, were aggressive competitors; a boon in that both the inland and the coastal resorts could readily absorb hydropathic establishments so extending the range of choice they offered their invalid and leisure clients. By the 1890s Harrogate was home to a clutch of large hydros and several smaller ones and in 1889 Scarborough added its own Hydropathic Establishment to its existing sea baths.

Not all of the hydros that sprang up were quite what they may have seemed to the unwary visitor. So fashionable did hydropathic remedies become that hotels and boarding houses adopted the hydro label despite having little or none of the equipment or trained staff required, operating on the basis that there were bath treatments available nearby. The true hydropathic establishment was entirely self-contained with a trained physician and attendants on hand and bedrooms and treatment rooms in close proximity to suit patients who were convalescent or otherwise infirm.[18]

As the twentieth century began, the inland spas that were still in business faced an uncertain future. Medical opinion increasingly turned its attention towards the benefits of climate and the submission to a supervised regime of exercise and diet as the pathway to restored health; water treatments were now confined to a limited range of medical conditions. The spas recognising the mood of the times emphasised their attributes as health resorts. Where once it had been the potency[19] of their mineral water now their climatic advantages, scenery, golf courses, bowling greens, leisure and cultural life were central to their marketing strategies. Water treatments remained now delivered primarily through hydropathic procedures and even those hydros which had once been more or less sanatoria were forced to dispense with their starched fronts and adopt something approaching a hotel culture. Various initiatives were attempted to breathe life into the stricken body including in the 1930s a national campaign but even such bizarre stunts as cocktail parties in the Droitwich brine baths produced limited results.[20]

With hindsight it is clear the spa market was dwindling. There were so many opportunities for holidays around the coast of Britain or abroad and no amount of clever or witty promotional campaigning could have rescued the inland spas from their terminal decline. After the second world war some of the spas including Buxton and Bath benefited from contracts with the newly established NHS delivering treatments on prescription but after about twenty years or so this business fell away, so bringing an end to a long tradition.

Drinking the waters

The therapeutic use of mineral waters was underpinned and sustained by its own pseudo science, a mixture of empirical observation, myth and practical common sense, a mumbo jumbo from which emerged prescribed rules of behaviour for those embarking on a course of treatment. These covered most aspects of taking the waters and were intended to govern the behaviour of a visitor to the spa. Age, gender, physical and emotional condition, sexual indulgence, diet, the season of the year and the time of day were all to be taken into account. We may be sure Matlock Bath would have had its own instructions for people planning to drink the mineral water but apart from Thomas Short's observations, no such advice has come to hand and we must rely instead on these more general directions which towards the end of the eighteenth century would have been regarded as orthodox medical opinion.[21]

[Mineral waters] 'are found to agree much better with persons in the middle stages of life than with the very old or very young' and should not be taken by those younger than eighteen or older than sixty. 'Treatment should begin with bleeding followed by a gentle purgative such as Epsom Salts.'

The time of day was considered important as was the regime to be observed after treatment. Patients should start early though not too early. Six or seven 'is very proper. Those who go to the wells at three or four in a morning, are exposed to all the injuries of a cold and damp air, which prevents perspiration, and often brings on coughs and other disorders of the breast and head. It was formerly the custom to drink [the waters] in an afternoon but this is at present left off, as found to produce many disorders of the stomach; and such as are desirous of having the utmost effects of the waters content themselves at this time of the day with drinking them at home in small quantities and mixed with wine.'

'The summer is the season in which the mineral waters are to be drunk with the greatest advantage. The months of June, July and August, are more proper for the taking of them' but in an emergency 'treatment may be begun in May and continued till September; and in some extraordinary cases, the use of them may be allowed even in Winter.'

At first the water should be taken in small quantities and drinking is to be punctuated by periods of ten minutes or more of walking about. On the first day [one and a half] pints[22] should be taken in four drafts. On the second day 1 quart. On days three and four 3 pints; thereafter 2 quarts; 'more than this it is not proper to take, unless the person be of a very robust habit.'

Taking the waters should be followed by moderate exercise until dinner which should not be too heavy observing the maxim 'never to eat or drink so much as one can, but always to rise with an appetite.' Certain foods should be avoided 'such as are dried in the smoke, or have been long kept in salt; and the flesh of young animals is in general to be greatly preferred to that of old ones; and in general, a too great quantity of vegetables, especially of the flatulent ones.'

'Lamb, chickens, veal, and the like are most proper for the diet at this time; and to these are to be added the tender river-fish, as trout and pike. Broths also of all kinds are good; and peas, kidney beans, spinach, and asparagus…the bread that is eaten under the course should never be stale; the most proper drink at the time is good wine, and if the person is not over thirsty, it is best to drink this pure, not mixed with water; but in this case it is only to be allowed within the bounds of moderation; half a pint at the utmost, at a meal, to those who have not been habituated to it; and to those who have, somewhere less than their customary quantity. The liquor next proper after wine, is sound and well-bodied ale; but such as is either new or fermenting, or so old as to be stale is by no means to be used. Acids, tea, and other things, which decompose these waters, should not be taken for some time before or after drinking them.' Suppers are to be moderate and the wine diluted.

Violent exercise, 'too much sitting still', or sleeping after meals are to be avoided and 'all people are to abstain as much as may be from venery during the time, lest it too much debilitate the body, already weakened by the discharges occasioned by the waters, by stool and urine.' These discharges were the expected outcome of taking the waters in some by stool alone 'in others by urine singly; but in most they operate both ways together.' The purgative effect, the outcome which was considered to offer demonstrable proof of a spring's health-giving properties, may not always have been derived from the natural content of the water. Curl questions whether the purgative effect of many of the London spas was the result of their mineral content or of pollution. This is a question which cannot now be answered though it is clear that in London, once sufficiently sophisticated analytical skills were available, in the later years of the nineteenth century, a number of springs were found to be so polluted they had to close; and it is not unreasonable to suppose that there were similarly polluted spa waters in other parts of the country.[23]

At the well or pump house

'The great attraction to Matlock Bath is now the scenery, the waters being but little used, owing to the unfortunate absence of a suitable Pump Room, where all might drink.'[24] So Benjamin Bryan writing in 1903, identified the most conspicuous deficiency in the resort's provision for visitors to its springs and a sign of its secondary status among the English Spa towns. For all the premier health resorts, investment in a pump room had been among the earliest steps in their development.[25] Buxton had had a covered well house as early as 1709 and a much larger and more imposing structure from 1782; Bath had a pump room from 1706 greatly enlarged in 1751; and Tunbridge Wells a shelter over its open well in 1720.[26] In London though many of the wells did not have a separate pump room there were notable examples as at Bagnigge Wells[27] where a small circular open sided structure known as the Temple housed pumps from two wells, each with different chemical properties; and at Streatham Spa where a single storey pump room was attached to the main building. At Kedleston there was no pump house but unlike most country spas, adjacent to the bath, seats were provided for 12 or 16 people to drink the water.[28]

In the pump houses water was served by attendants but where the wells and springs were open to the elements it would appear to have been customary for people to help themselves and drink from the basin or spout[29] or for poor women to fill cups and hand them to the clients in return for a gratuity.[30] To his displeasure Dr Granville found this practice still in operation in 1840 when he visited St Anne's Well in Buxton and he compared it unfavourably with his experience of the German spas.[31] Matlock, without a pump room relied on facilities for water drinkers at each of the three baths including the open-air provision at the Fountain Gardens.[32] Certainly the New Bath catered for them and apparently without charge. Granville commends their arrangements; 'the fountain of the tepid stream is placed with a glass tumbler ready to hand, just at the spot where the dwellers have to pass – as if to tempt them with a sight of the salutary spring.'

Whether paid as a fee or a gratuity the price for a glass of water generally appears to have been one penny though at Bagnigge Wells there was an admission charge of three pence for anyone drinking at the pump house.[33] As early as 1651[34] spa water was being traded in bottles and by 1713 there were at least 9[35] selling their water locally and further afield. The wealthy had their favourite spa water sent to them whether they were at home or away and by 1733 there were at least 16 English spa waters available in London.[36] By 1816 at least 36 spas were bottling and trading their water including most of the high status resorts such as Bath, Tunbridge Wells, Buxton and Bristol Hotwells but so also were some of the minor rural spas. Among them was Nevill-Holt in Leicestershire. There the water owed much of its fame to a local resident, Henry Eyre who became a national figure in trading bottled water selling nationally and internationally including importing water from Spa in Germany.[37] In London numerous spas sold bottled water. Not all of it their own, and some, as at Streatham, would deliver to all parts of London.[38] The price varied considerably depending on whether the water was sold at or near its origin or some distance away. London prices per dozen bottles reflected the transport costs and also the perceived quality of the brand. Bath's bottled water sold at 9/- but Bristol Hotwells, a similar distance from London, for a shilling less; and Scarborough much further away than either of them could sell its water for no more than Bath. The most expensive waters were from Bourne in Lincolnshire at 18/- and Holt (near Bath), Harrogate and Nevill-Holt at 12/-.[39]

Bathing

Thomas Short's recommendations for those using the bath at Matlock Bath (there was just the one when he made his study of the warm springs there) are concise but clear. Bathing should last from 10 to 30 or 40 minutes, 'as the Patient's strength will bear' and should always be undertaken on an empty stomach

FIGURE 1. **Martha Norton the Well Woman at Buxton.**

The caricature is by John Dixon (1755-1818). St Anne's Well at Buxton was served by such poor people as Martha Norton who were appointed annually to look after the well and help visitors to it to take the water. Mark Langham, *Buxton: A People's History*, states that these women were not paid but relied on tips. Martha was appointed fifteen times between 1775 and 1820.

Derbyshire County Council, Buxton Museum & Art Gallery.

either early in the morning or late in the evening though the morning would be better 'before Light and solar Rays have too much dissipated the Spirit of the Bath'. After bathing the body should be 'well dried and rubbed' and this should be followed by gentle exercise to promote circulation and perspiration. He advised the use of bathing here for cases of 'Rheumatism, weakness of the Parts, Strains, Scurvy, Itch, Scab and other Diseases of the Skin, as Morphew [a leprous or scurvy eruption], livid Spots etc', a modest list of ailments by comparison with his recommendations for the warmer waters of Buxton[40] which he believed would provide a remedy for a wide range of medical conditions.

Short added to his 'a few general Rules' on the proper use of Buxton water the observation that 'all [the] waters of greater Note are seldom without neighbouring Physicians who are capable to give better Rules upon the spot' than was possible in print; and so it may have been in Buxton. But such services, so far as we have been able to establish were in limited supply at its smaller neighbour. No evidence has come to light suggesting Matlock Bath was able to sustain a resident physician. More likely, given the size of the settlement and the seasonality of its spa, Matlock Bath relied on the patronage of doctors such as Erasmus Darwin[41] who practised in Lichfield and later Derby; or Dr Armstrong[42] of Uppingham. They knew well the properties of the waters and directed their patients to the resort. More local expertise was available in Wirksworth, the only neighbouring settlement large enough to support a medical practice until the growth of Matlock in the second half of the nineteenth century and at least two of the Wirksworth doctors, Dr Goodwin and Dr Webb[43] are known to have served the Spa's patients and there are likely to have been many more.

Promoting the Spa

The successful promotion of a Spa in the eighteenth century depended on word of mouth endorsement, medical advocacy, advertising and where good fortune provided the opportunity, the exploitation of a unique selling point. This might be the long held belief that your spa was sanctified by divine intervention; or for Matlock Bath its awesome scenery. It was word of mouth that helped brand a Spa, identifying it as a suitable place for people of a certain standing to meet and enjoy one another's company;[44] so much is evident in the development of Bath and Tunbridge Wells. The fashionable attracted the fashionable; so also at the other social extreme, rowdy young men, out for a good time, might well bring with them thieves, trepanners and young women luring the unwary and gullible.[45] Endorsement by contemporary opinion leaders and the medical experts of the day was essential both in delivering a perception of spas in general as a part of mainstream medicine and in establishing the social and therapeutic integrity of individual spas.[46] Every spa of significance had one or more medical luminaries promoting its cause. There are numerous examples. Cold Bath Springs in London relied heavily on a Dr Edward Baynard,[47] Buxton enjoyed the support of Sir John Floyer and later, Dr Alexander Hunter amongst many others,[48] and Bath – it basked in almost universal endorsement from those in the profession, though there were some concerns that the water might be too hot for some patients.[49]

Spa advertising took many forms extending well beyond hand bills and newspapers. Many of the London sites became subjects for cartoonists and for satirical sketches which were often laced with innuendo and double entendre; there was also doggerel verse. Here are some lines promoting Bagnigge Wells by William Woty (c.1731-1791), a prolific versifier.

> *Hight Bagnigge; where from our Forefathers hid*
> *Long have two Springs in dull stagnation slept;*
> *But taught at length by subtle art to flow,*
> *They rise forth from Oblivion's bed they rise*
> *And manifest their Virtues to mankind*[50]

Matlock Bath had its own pundits and poetry to support its claims as a spa resort and when the first major investments in accommodation and bathing facilities were made in the late 1720s/early 1730s it had both of these elements, the endorsements and the poetry in place.[51] The poetry, a eulogy to Matlock Dale's peerless scenery, echoed and complemented the visual messages carried by Thomas Smith's art see pages 15-21. We do not know how widely the poems and engravings were distributed but the impression they created of Matlock Bath's unique charms as a wild and secret place, waiting to be explored, forged an image that became the resort's indelible hallmark for the next hundred years.

Why were the spas successful for so long?

A study of the London spas has identified a list of conditions which the medical advisers and the proprietors of these establishments claimed would be cured or alleviated by taking their waters, see page 10 To modern eyes, the list is bizarre. Surely no one believed these cures were possible? Wasn't the likely outcome, for example, of breast cancer, diabetes or leprosy known well enough for an eigh-

Matlock Bath celebrated in Verse

Hail, awful Matlock, Nature's chiefest Pride'
What to all other Places is deny'd'
Thou, thou alone enjoyest Thou keep'st the Form
Which Nature gave thee, nor can Art transform,
Or change thy Beauties which to thee she gave:
When by divine Command, first from the Grave
Of Nothing rose this Earth. In vain shall Art,
Attempt such pleasing Beauties to impart
To our astonish'd Eyes. In vain the Skill
Of Painters, or the Poets forming Quill.
Thy Hills in Horror beautiful arise,
And seem to touch the Summit of the Skies;

And:-
On whose sweet Southern Bank fair Matlock stands,
At once the Valley and the Clift command
Close to its Verge, the sleepy Alder grows,
Nods o'er the Current, that loquacious flows,

The poem continues making reference in turn to the ash, oak maple, holly and below the linden or lime -

That from the jetting Rocks project to View,
Profusely there in fair progression rise,
And animate the Steep with wild surprise,
The jetting Rocks proud Castles seem in Air,
That bold Defiance to Invaders dare'
O'er these, a-top, the Linden waves his Head,
Chaplets[52] the Summit, and o'er looks the Mead.

Extracts from 2 poems described by Thomas Short as addressing 'The Charms and surprising Beauties of this Place'[53]

teenth century audience to dismiss these extravagant claims as false? There is an obvious comparison here with Quack medicine.[54] Its voice was even more strident and its claims as preposterous,[55] yet quacks flourished; their advertisements appeared in all the newspapers and people who might have been thought to have been immunised by their education and good sense to give them a wide berth, bought them and recommended them to others.[56] In fact both persuasions had something in common. Each offered hope; a powerful force when mainstream medicine had failed. As William Wadd observed 'People apply to quacks because like drowning men, when honest practitioners give no hope, they catch at every twig.'[57] And the same was true for some who turned to spa treatments.

That was not the whole story. In a sense many, maybe most of the spa treatments were successful in that they secured the advertised outcome which was, in contemporary professional parlance, 'by stool and urine'. As so many of the mineral waters were purgative and

Water Cures All;[60] the claims made by the London spas.

Arthritis, asthmas, biliousness, blood disorders, breast cancer, cancers, catarrhs, chlorosis, colic, constitutions broken by intemperance, consumption, convulsions, deafness, defluxions of humours, diabetes, dizziness, dropsy, drowsiness, eye disorders, fevers, fistulas, fluor albus [Leucorrhoea – white vaginal discharge], fluxes, giddiness, glandular obstructions, gonorrhoea, gravels, headaches, heart disease, heats and flushings, hectical creeping fevers, humours, hysterics, indigestions, inflammation of the blood and eyes, inward bleedings, jaundice, kidney stones, Kings Evil [scrofula], leprosy, lethargies, liver complaints, loss of appetite, melancholy distempers, nervous afflictions, numbness, palpitations, palsy, piles, quinsy, redness of the face, rheumatism, rickets, ruptures, scrofula [tuberculosis], scurvy, shingles, shortness of breath, skin complaints, sores , spleen, stone, strangury [retention of urine], swelling of legs, ulcers, vapours, venereal distempers, visceral obstructions, vomiting, weak eyes, weakly women, weakness of joints, wind, worms and yaws [a contagious disease of the skin].

in some cases strongly so,[58] how could they fail? Thus patients might easily be persuaded, and fairly rapidly, that their condition had improved. Of course there were also some genuinely positive outcomes; for those with rheumatic and similar ailments the benefit of bathing might well be real and because the spa water however it was used was accompanied by a regime of regular exercise, reduced alcohol, healthy food and in Thomas Short's words, 'Cards, Music and Cheerfulness' it is no wonder people felt better after a fortnight at the Spa.

It is also unreasonable to assume all the clients who filled the Inn and lodging house beds in the Summer months were there because they were ill. They may have been taking a Summer break as the Wedgwood family did annually in the 1790s dividing their holidays between Blackpool, Matlock and Weymouth.[59] These were not visits to a spa; they were visits to a resort. As time passed catering for such visitors, holiday makers rather than patients, became increasingly important for all the English spa resorts especially after the development of a railway network which introduced a new type of visitor, the day tripper. These visitors were never going to be clients for the spa treatments which by design required several days to be effective and in some resorts they became the principal market with investments targeting their needs rather than those of the traditional spa clientele. No wonder Granville was sometimes irritated by the casual delivery of spa treatments he found as he toured the English Spas c.1840, comparing them with the dedicated efficiency of their German counterparts. This was surely as much a reflection of new economic priorities as any failing on the part of the providers of the water treatments. If they were to survive the spas had either to become wholehearted leisure resorts catering for holiday makers as well as invalids or specialise as some managed to do by adopting the new hydropathic treatments imported from continental Europe, or look for a new existence unrelated to the spa or leisure industry.

CHAPTER ONE

The First Baths

In the early eighteenth century William Woolley described Matlock as

'a church town and square steeple…There are three or four good stone houses in the town. It is a pretty odd pleasant place situate along the north-east of the River Derwent, over which there is a good stone bridge. Along the river are very steep high cliffs over against one of which, in a very romantic situation, run into the Derwent several silver springs the clearest I have ever seen – one of the largest of which some of the neighbouring gentlemen have contracted into a very large cistern and built a house over it, with other conveniences for a cold bath which is pretty much frequented.'[1]

The bath Woolley was describing was on a part of the commons or wastes of Matlock called Warmwalls at Matlockwood on the west side of the Derwent valley about a mile south from Matlock church, though still in Matlock parish. In 1730 John Medley[2] commented on the origins of the enterprise 'This WELL, as I have been inform'd by ancient people of the neighbourhood, has been time out of mind, noted for performing divers great cures: for the most part external ones, (and pity it is, that a register of them was not made and kept) which gave occasion to the first thoughts of forming a bath.'

The 'neighbouring gentlemen' were the Reverend Joseph Ferne, Rector of Matlock, Mr Benjamin Haywood of Cromford, Mr Adam Wolley of Allen Hill, Matlock and George Wragg[3] who farmed Hascom Leys Farm on the hillside to the north of the bath. The bath had been built 'at their own expense in or about 1696 and called Wolley's Well, there having been a bathing place which had longe before been cut out of the hard rock by the Wolleys of Riber who were the principal owners and sharers of the Manor.'[4]

The primitive nature of the first bath was nothing remarkable given its remote rural location and its use for the benefit of local people. We are told[5] that Wragg made the spring into 'a little bath' and 10 years later when he had negotiated a long lease at a small rent on it and 'a little ground adjoining' he enlarged it and built several small outbuildings for the convenience of its users. John Macky[6] (?–1726) described the bath as 'a Rural One, and much like the Place it is in; it is Tiled over or Thatch'd, I forgot whether, where is a large Leaden Basin, large enough for Eight or Ten to Bathe in, and if it happens, as was my Case, the Water be too Deep for you, there is a little Sluice which brings the Water to any Height you please.' He describes the water as 'Temperate, neither Hot nor Cold, that is not so cold as the Natural Water nor yet so warm as Milk: It is reported to have done many wonderful cures.'[7] Daniel Defoe[8] noted the spring 'being secured by a Stone Wall on every Side, by which the Water is brought to rise to a due heighth, is made into a very convenient Bath; with a House built over it, and room within the Building to walk round the Water or Bath and so by Steps to go down gradually into it.'

FIGURE 2. **Radium Well, postcard, about 1900.**

The site of the spring William Woolley described is marked today by this tufa grotto in the Temple Road car park. It is more usually called the Royal Well. It bears the date 1696 to commemorate the early use of the spring to supply the bath but the grotto itself was built as a decorative feature in the grounds of the Royal Hotel which occupied the site after 1878.[9] The postcard's title is a reminder that in the late 19th century, radium in the water was promoted as beneficial for health.

Ken Smith collection.

Residential accommodation[10] for visitors to the bath was offered at George Wragg's Hascom Leys Farm, (later known as The Villa and before its demolition in 1908, as Ashfield House) about a quarter of a mile away beside the steep road leading to Upperwood.[11] Better facilities were not provided closer to the Bath until new owners Thomas Smith a former High Sheriff of Nottingham and Marmaduke Pennell, alderman and former Mayor of Nottingham, bought Wragg's lease of the bath and 2 acres of land adjoining in about 1725 for £1000. Soon after they began to build accommodation and stabling at the north end of the site.[12] Smith died in 1727 but Pennell continued the development and supported their investment by improving the horse road to Matlock Bridge and making a coach road to Cromford. It was these developments and the investments which followed over the next 20 years which secured a future for this tiny settlement, transforming it from a hamlet with a medicinal spring serving a local population into a small but virile spa and resort with the potential for growth.

After Pennell's death in 1732, his son in law Stephen Eggington added more buildings and in 1741 when he sold the property to a consortium of mainly Chesterfield men[13] it was described as old and new bath houses, with separate baths for ladies and gentlemen, dressing rooms and apartments as well as stables and stores and the cock pitt [sic]. Abandoning mixed bathing, or the shared use of the bath by means of designated timing, or as here by providing separate facilities for men and women, was another significant step away from rusticity and towards what would have been seen as refined contemporary social and medical practice.[14]

Derby Mercury, 11/5/1738.

Derby Mercury, 27/7/1732.

There are glimpses of the role that the local newspapers in Derby and Nottingham might have played in making the first Bath more widely known in this period. The value of the prizes offered for the cock fight, advertised above, suggest that it was a prestigious event which was expected to attract gentlemen from a wide area.[15]

The sale of Matlock Bath spa water outside the resort is a further indication of the growing maturity of its spa operation. It is evidence that Matlock Bath had joined a select group of spas which included Bath, Tunbridge Wells, Bristol Hotwells and a number of London spas[16] though there is no evidence for how Ezra Bestall's business venture prospered at this early date.

The advertisements which appeared a few years later[17] had a more powerful appeal in the promotion of the resort. They were offering visual images of Derbyshire and Staffordshire scenes which included Matlock Bath, Figures 3, 4 and 5. The artist Thomas Smith was one of the earliest British painters to specialise in landscape. His pictures show travellers at leisure in English settings rather than on the fashionable continental Grand Tour. They advertised Derbyshire as a worthy place of resort and encouraged tourists to come to explore. The engravings of his views made his work more widely accessible and, more importantly, provided visitors with souvenirs of their stay in this hitherto little known part of the country.[18]

FIGURE 3. **"A Prospect of Matlock Bath &c. from the Lover's Walk", after Thomas Smith of Derby engraving with etching by Vivares, published 1743.**

This view is the earliest known picture of the range of buildings housing the Baths from which Matlock Bath took its name. It stood on a shelf of tufa rock on the flank of Masson Hill in an area known as Matlockwood; the hillside above is still called Upperwood. The site is now the Temple Road car park. The spring which supplied the baths is one of a series of springs along the hillside which deposit carbonate of lime on mosses and other materials over which they flow to form tufa, a lightweight rock with the appearance of a petrified sponge. The principal buildings shown in this illustration are the 'two commodious buildings' developed by Marmaduke Pennell after 1727 at the north (right hand) end of the site and Stephen Eggington's additions after 1732. The road through the valley ran directly in front of the hotel buildings then down the hill to the right, now Fishpond Hill, shown impossibly steep in this view. It was not formally re-routed to its present day A6 level until 1819 though this print suggests some travellers had pioneered use of the lower level much earlier. Figures are shown on the bowling green[19] on the terrace and in the foreground, on the east bank of the River Derwent, in the area romanticised in the inscription below the print as Lover's Walk. The stable building, lower right, is on the site of the present Fishpond Hotel. In front of it note the pond and its outfall to the river.

The enlargements, right, taken from two of Joseph Farington's prints, see pages 46-47, illustrate the changes made in about 1800 to produce the layout of the Fishpond Hotel as it appears today.

Private collection.

FIGURE 4. **Matlock High Torr &c., after Thomas Smith of Derby, engraving with etching by James Mason, published 1751.**

Another example of Thomas Smith's enterprise in providing visitors with a souvenir of their stay captures the awesome majesty of the Tor. In case he should be accused of exaggeration, Smith's inscription confirms its essential statistic 'the River Derwent runs at the bottom of this Vast Rock whose perpendicular height above the Water is 354 feet.' The dark adit entrance on Raddle Rake Mine is shown at river level. It is noticeable in this and other early views of the valley how patches of the slopes were used as pasture.

The Bath had new owners in 1741 who claimed they were unable to find a tenant to pay an acceptable rent and for the next 26 years the business was 'managed by Servants'.[20] The arrangement clearly worked well and the owners reported their profits were 'more per ann. than by any rent that had been offered.'[21] The bath became known as the Old Bath when a second, the New Bath was opened for business in 1745, see page 24. The Old Bath proprietors drew attention to the distinction when announcing[22] in 1751 that 'At MATLOCK OLD BATH the LONG ROOM is now ready for the Reception of Company,'[23] and 'a NEW BATH made, larger and more commodious than either of the old ones.'

Guests at the Old Bath were surprised to find that there were

> *'no extravagant Charges annexed; the Company pay nothing for Lodging or Bathing, let them stay ever so long or short a Time; and the ordinary Expenses are Three*

> *Shillings a day for Meals, including Tea in the Afternoon. And though there is no Master nor Mistress in the House, there is found the most courteous and compliant Behaviour from the Attendants, and the whole Business is conducted with the utmost Politeness, Decency, and Oeconomy [sic].'*

The letter writer quoted above provides us with valuable observations on several topics which we have used in this account; one of particular importance is his graphic description of the Old Bath as he found it in 1755, see below. He apologised to his correspondents for 'dwelling so long on the Description of this Place: I admire it greatly, and my Companion left it with great Reluctance; but our Time being fixed, we set forward next Morning.' His short stay allowed no time to provide us with comment on the New Bath to which he either paid scant attention or failed to record his thoughts.

> *'Matlock-Bath consists of one uniform range of Buildings; except an Out-house of handsome Lodging-rooms, nearly adjoining, and with Stables, which are out of Sight of the House. In the first Part of the Building are two Baths; one for Gentlemen, the other for Ladies; the Entrance and Dressing-rooms are quite distinct; the Ladies Bath is arch'd with Stone about ten Feet above the Surface of the Water, which makes the Place cool and renders it impervious to every Eye but their own: Over the Baths are the Lodging-rooms, for the Convenience of those who most constantly bathe. Beyond the Bath, on the Ground-floor, is a Range of Rooms, each capable of entertaining a dozen People; at the further End is a large Kitchen and Servants-hall. In the Middle of the Building, is a grand Stair-case fronting the top of which, is the Music-room; on the Right-hand is the Assembly-room, which is large and commodious, having a passage out on the side of the Hill, which rises to a great Height, and shelters the Back-part of the House. As the Company who come to this Place, are, for the time being, one Family, they breakfast, dine and sup together in this Room. On the Left-hand of the Music-room are Bedchambers, and others on the Floor above.*
>
> *Before the Front of the House runs a spacious Terras [sic]; from whence a few Steps bring you down to a level Grass-plot, convenient for the Company to walk or play at Bowls on, as they like best; and at the Edge of the Green is built a Dwarf-wall, beyond which descends a rocky Shelf to the River Darwent [sic], which is here very wide and rapid, and runs with a murmuring Noise, greatly increased by Repercussion of the Sound from the high Rocks which overhang it... .'[24]*

The way the Old Bath was managed was changed in 1767; it was advertised to let on an 11 or 21 year lease and by 1770, the tenant was Robert Mason. Certainly Matlock Bath prospered at this time and, as Mason himself announced, was 'much frequented by the Nobility and Gentry for its salutary Waters, [and] healthy and rural Situation.'[25] In the 1780s the accommodation for visitors was further enhanced by the construction of a large new stabling complex. It was built on the area where the Pavilion stands today and was made possible by an award of this land in 1784 by the Matlock Enclosure Commissioners[26] to the Old Bath shareholders.[27]

Lover's Walk

At a very early stage in the development of the English spas publicly accessible space for patients and visitors to take exercise, and see and be seen, was recognised as an essential component of a successful resort. Tunbridge Wells[28] acquired a promenade, the Upper Walk, as early as 1638 and by the end of the century Buxton had its first bowling green and walk. Such tree lined gravelled paths were subsequently accompanied in many instances by planned green spaces planted with trees and furnished with seats and refreshment booths and, in the Pantiles in Tunbridge Wells and in Bath, luxury shops.[29] In the eighteenth century in London these green spaces were regarded as essential attributes for spas and wells and they evolved into pleasure gardens with their own walks, arbours, long rooms, breakfast and supper rooms and music venues. Many of them developed their own special attractions, some for music, some for food and wine, some for theatrical entertainments and some for bear baiting and dog and cock fights. They catered for residents and visitors to the city and the best known, Ranelagh and Vauxhall, established international reputations. Those that were associated with wells or springs and most of them were, some of them sinking wells in order to claim a medicinal function, welcomed invalids and health seekers alongside their other clientele. They brought together people from a range of backgrounds though the more fashionable had limits to entry, Vauxhall for example excluding servants in livery and dogs.

It is not clear how far these London pleasure gardens responded to new fashions in garden design and in particular to the growing rejection of formality in favour of a more natural appearance which from the middle years of the eighteenth century was in vogue. Vauxhall gardens, pre-eminent among the London pleasure grounds, had its Wilderness and rural downs with grass and lambs; but for the most part formal patterns of walks and vistas were maintained and it has been suggested that there was no departure from this formula until the Sydney Gardens in Bath were opened in 1795[31] laid out in the 'naturalistic landscape manner'. This was more than 70 years after Matlock Bath's first pleasure ground, Lover's

Singular Rocks near Matlock Bath[30]

Often visitors wrote about their experiences as in this example when Robert Mason was the proprietor of the bath. Mr H Rooke from Nottinghamshire submitted a drawing and an accompanying text to the Gentleman's Magazine which together convey much of the sense of excitement which inspired so many of Matlock Bath's eighteenth century visitors.

'The traveller who wishes to explore this curious country must quit the trodden path, climb the cragged cliff, and penetrate the dark recess; he will there find ample recompence for his trouble. The rocks here represented are on the brow of the hill, directly behind Mason's bath, but the ground is inclosed with stone walls, which, together with the bushes and brambles that surround the rocks make the approach rather difficult. This curious group of rocks evidently appears to have been separated by some violent convulsion in Nature, which has also formed several chasms; the little rock over the great one is very remarkable. From this spot you command a very extensive and pleasing view, I think preferable to any in the neighbourhood of Matlock.

It may be thought extraordinary that no path has been made from the Hallhouse to this romantic spot; but to take off this appearance of neglect in Mr Mason, who is as attentive to the amusement as he is to the accommodation of his numerous guests, it is necessary to say, that the ground behind the house is not his property.'

Walk.[32] The comparison may not be entirely apt; Lover's Walk was carved out of a natural landscape and then dressed with all the fashionable trappings demanded by contemporary taste; it was nature tamed rather than nature contrived. But it does emphasise the novelty of what was achieved in Matlock Bath and helps to explain the enthusiasm with which it was greeted by the visitors who explored its winding paths, rocks and natural vistas. Without the majestic scenery of the Matlock gorge it is likely that Matlock Bath would have joined the scores of places known to possess therapeutic waters but which never grew into fully fledged resorts. It was the promotion of the romantic enchantment of discovering wild nature that sustained it. The inspired and skilful creation of the walk was a significant early step in the achievement of that aim.

Thomas Smith's drawing shows the Bath set in modest grounds but emphasises its position overlooking the dramatic scenery of the valley. By 1742 visitors would have been ferried across the river to the Lover's Walk. It was described by Arthur Young[33] as '[a walk] made along the banks of the river, but parted from it by a thick edging of wood and quite arched over with trees; it is waved in gentle bends in as true taste as I remember any where to have seen; where the wood is so thick as to be quite impervious.' It led south to a spectacular focal point, the Cascade, the natural outfall from another thermal spring see Figure 5. From there another path was engineered which led the visitor 200 feet up from the river bank to the top of the cliff, 'the prospects still varying all the way you go' to reveal, at the top, vistas of the valley and of Riber Hill to the east and High Tor to the north. Bray[34] confirms the essential feature 'an ascent to the top of the rock, by about 220 steps, besides several gradual slopes; this is so well managed by different turnings that though the rock here is almost perpendicular, little difficulty is found in gaining the summit, and the wood grows so close to the edge of the path, that there is no room for the least apprehension of danger.'

It is not known who planned the Lover's Walk but it is an important example of early landscape gardening in the original meaning of the term and worthy of some conjecture about its origin.[35] Whoever was responsible, there can be no doubt as to its significance. The great eighteenth century English contribution to the history of gardening was to forsake the controlled formality of garden design from the century before; to abandon the perception of Nature as something to be kept at arm's length but to embrace it. Horace Walpole (1717-1797) credited William Kent (1685-1748), portrait and ceiling painter, architect and landscape gardener as the leader who 'first leaped the fence and saw all nature was a garden.'[36] The poet Alexander Pope (1688-1744) who in addition to his literary genius was also an arbiter of fashion in architecture and landscape gardening, advised that a successful gardener 'consults the genius of the place' and 'calls in the country'.[37] The desired effect for either was consciously to include the estate park if there was one and the countryside beyond in the planned view from the house. Lover's Walk is of this fashion; an early example of landscaping the natural scene and remarkable because it was achieved, not for a gentleman on his private estate as was happening elsewhere but on leased land for public use. Lover's Walk has remained in continuous use and without significant change since its creation more than 290 years ago and is among the oldest surviving public pleasure grounds in the country.

FIGURE 5. **Cascades below Matlock Bath - oil on canvas, Thomas Smith of Derby, about 1740.**

The fisherman is standing on the east bank of the River Derwent where the Cascade was a focal point at the southern end of Lover's Walk. It is tempting to dismiss this view as a flight of fancy but to do so is to overlook the changes which have taken place in this part of the gorge since Thomas Smith painted the scene in the middle of the eighteenth century. Here the waterfalls flow freely from the same thermal spring which later supplied the bath at the New Bath; now the water is confined in a single pipe beneath the A6 and is reduced to a single plume. The river is wider now, the shore on the west bank and the natural rapids shown in Smith's picture have been drowned and replaced by tranquil water by the later erection of the weir at Masson Mill.

Many of Smith's paintings are known only as prints produced from engravings and though these have often had colour added, as in the print of High Tor shown earlier, the survival of Smith's choices of colour in this view is a reminder of the contrast between the original depiction and the later reproduction. A skilful engraving of this picture was produced by Vivares in 1743.

Derby Museums and Art Gallery 2010.

It was not in the sophisticated style of, for example, London's famous Vauxhall Gardens where Royalty might rub shoulders with any class of society, where it was fashionable to drink, dine and be entertained, to see and be seen promenading the illuminated walks or to arrange a secret, even clandestine, assignation along an unlit path, but rather for the enjoyment of wild nature and as the name suggests for moments of unchaperoned dalliance where a bend in the path hid members of your party from view. Not all the assignations in the Vauxhall Gardens were secret nor were all the visitors in search of high society, culture or wildlife. The words Joseph Addison put in the mouth of his fictional character Sir Roger de Coverly, though imagined, do convey a certain reality, at least for the Spring Gardens phase of Vauxhall's development. 'He should be a better customer to her garden', Sir Roger told the proprietress, 'if there were more nightingales and fewer strumpets.'

Lover's Walk lacked Vauxhall's masked ladies but it possessed many of the same adornments. At each venue visitors enjoyed an initial boat journey and found themselves among man made paths, bowers, balustrades, urns and grottoes but whereas the visitor to Vauxhall walked to an eating place or a music venue, the culmination of the tour in Lover's Walk was the view across the gorge from a summit path or of the Cascade seen across the River Derwent.

The features with which the proprietors of the Walk embellished its paths and vantage points were all borrowed from polite society, from the private parks which were being created beyond the country house and its formal gardens and from the metropolitan and other pleasure grounds patronised by polite society as part of the fashion for an improved landscape. A park that was much talked about and copied belonged to Alexander Pope. He and his villa and garden at Twickenham beside the Thames were the subject of much discussion; for his obsession for his house and grounds and the park for what has been described as its Lilliputian scale which somehow encompassed all the must have elements, a lawn, grotto, shell temple, vineyard, kitchen garden, orangery and garden house. Scattered about were urns and statuary and in pride of place at the furthest point an obelisk in memory of his mother. Lover's Walk never embraced so many embellishments but its adornments were of the same genre. The identity of its creator may be unknown but his aim is not in doubt. Juxtaposing with wild though accessible nature the trappings of current fashion, he sought to create in this remote village a model landscape which reflected the epitome of contemporary taste. Dean Swift (1667-

Sir Arthur's Grotto

Now see how he sits
Perplexing his wits
In search of a motto
To fix on his grotto.
How proudly he talks
Of zigzags and walks,
And all the day raves
Of cradles and caves,
And boasts of his feats
His grottos and seats,
Shows all his gewgaws,
And gapes for applause;
A fine occupation
For one in his station!
A hole where a rabbit
Would scorn to inhabit
Dug in an hour,
He calls it a bower.

From My Lady's Lamentation and Complaint against the Dean, 1728.

1745),[38] the author and satirist, much admired Pope's work at Twickenham but this did not blind him to the absurdity of the contemporary fashion to adorn nature and he turned his mocking eye on this compulsion that so overwhelmed his friends. In this case, see panel, his target was Sir Arthur Acheson (1687-1765) ridiculed for his obsession with his house, grounds and garden in Ireland.

William Stukely, an early commentator on Matlock Dale,[39] described what became known as Lover's Walk, in relation to High Tor as

> *'Over against it about half a mile off is another such cliff, but by the care of a gentleman that lives underneath (Mr Ashe) it's reduc'd into a more agreeabl form. there is an easy ascent up to it by steps hewn out of the rock, and an abundance of alcoves, grotts, summer-houses, cellars, pinnacles, dials, balustrades, urns, &c, all of the same materials. earth is carry'd to the top, and fine grassy walks with greens planted along 'em, upon this hanging terras. whence you have a free view over many a craggy mountain. I was highly pleas'd with so elegant a composure, where art and industry had so well plaid its part against rugged nature.'*

Nothing is known of Mr Ashe. Reference to him as a gentleman suggests that he may have been a man of taste familiar with the growing interest in the natural style of 'laying out ground' and who himself may have seen the potential for such a development which could be enjoyed by visitors to the Bath. He may have been acting for the Bath keeper, or for Wigley Haywood who was a lessee of the Hagg Wood, see also note 35, at the time, or for himself. However it came about, it is likely that the bath owners would have encouraged the enterprise, recognising how essential it was for the growth of the spa that it should have a pleasure ground.

Later accounts attribute the physical creation of the Walk to more humble hands. Horace Walpole, reports 'Matlocke [sic] Most beautiful Scene, rocks, woods, cascades, mines, walks and seats, these last improvements made by a fisherman who rents the rock for £5 a year of Mr Lascelles, and gets money by showing them.'[40] Two years later, in 1770, Arthur Young[41] after a fulsome description of Matlock Bath adds 'But are not these things wonderful, when I tell you, that these walks, the steps up the rock, and the bench at the top, [which elsewhere he calls Adam's bench] are all the work of the boot-ketch at the bath; who has likewise built a pleasure boat on the river; such industry, and at the same time so much taste are highly commendable.'[42] Walpole also drew attention to the economics of the enterprise at Matlock Bath - the creator of the walks 'gets money by showing them' and this was to remain the case into the twentieth century when payment was still made for crossing the river by boat or bridge, rather than for the services of a guide. The practice of charging visitors to explore the valley's natural features became endemic and attracted universal indignation.[43] But how else could there be a return on an investment of this kind? Henry Moore[44] sought to justify such charges, responding to complaints about the cost of crossing the river, by pointing out Richard Walker's predicament '[He] keeps the very extensive, interesting and beautifully picturesque walks in repair... which were originally formed by his father. Being private property, he also pays rent, therefore, when it is considered that the Matlock season is but a few months of the year, with the keeping of the boats in order, the following charges will be allowed to be reasonable. A party crossing the river 3d each, and for rowing on the river 6d each, which includes the charges for the crossing.'

A second bath

In May 1745, the *Derby Mercury,* advertised the opening of a second bath and informed readers that the proprietor was Isaac North whose wife had formerly been Housekeeper at 'the old Bath'. The establishment's simple descriptive title, the new Bath, has remained in use to this day though at some point along the way the word Hotel was added, a sign of its enhanced status.[45] John Saxton of the Mansion House, Crich and described as a farmer, developed the site which Short had earlier described as an agricultural holding where 'a spring twenty Yards North at the back of the Kitchen supplies the house with water.'[46]

FIGURE 6. **View of Matlock Bath, gouache on paper, George Robertson, 1798.**

This view looking south shows the New Bath on the right hand side facing east across what was then the turnpike road running along the front of the building. When it was diverted to its present position at a lower level in 1819-20[48], it cut through the hotel's bowling green. Adam[49] wrote 'the North wing is the last erected…Underneath this wing is the hot or tepid bath.' The sign-board bears the name Saxton. George Saxton, a former postmaster of Chesterfield (reputed to be unrelated to the owner of the Bath), became proprietor in 1788. In his family's 69 year tenure, the hotel was often referred to as Saxton's and the grassy plot fringed by a gravel walk shown here became known as Saxton's Green. This area, now used for car parking, was greatly reduced when the A6 road was widened in 1974. This small watercolour is one of a series of local scenes painted by George Robertson, an artist working for William Duesbury at the Derby China Manufactory.

Derby Museum and Art Gallery.

The New Bath stood some few hundred yards south of the Old Bath on the same shelf of tufa rock and provided both accommodation and a bath served by a powerful spring.[47] It shared with the Old Bath, the advantages of being 'delightfully situated on the Banks of the Derwent, commanding the most Picturesque and Romantic Views, Matlock affords.' It was always popular. Standing a little aloof from the social hub of the Old Bath, its guests enjoyed views of the valley from the comfort of the green in front of the building or from a quiet stroll in the extensive gardens which were much praised. The tepid bath and 'behind the house… the Fountain with a glass tumbler always ready for the visitor to quaff a bumper of the limpid stream'[50] were the spa facilities it offered; there was also a bowling green. As with so many of the principal investments in Matlock Bath over its lifetime as a resort, we do not know how John Saxton came by his money, nor are we able to share his thinking in staking so much at such an early stage in the development of the Spa, but we must assume the success of the Old Bath in the hands of Pennell and his successors gave him confidence to take the risk.[51] It seems the risk was repaid handsomely over the years.

FIGURE 7. **Watercolour attributed to George Pickering, 1811.**

The view from the opposite direction, confirms details of Robertson's image. Picture the Past

FIGURE 8. **The New Bath from the front.**

The pride and glory of the estate was the spreading lime tree already in 1818 so large that its branches were propped giving it, as Henry Moore[52] observed, the appearance of a banyan tree.

Reproduced from William Adam, *Gem of the Peak,* 1851 edition.

FIGURE 9. **The indoor bath, New Bath Hotel, c. 1992.**

The cluster of buildings which comprise the New Bath Hotel has been included on the list of structures of special architectural or historic interest, grade II. The listing description indicates why it is considered important. 'This fine complex displays its long evolution as a tourist hotel with, at its core, a particularly unusual survival of a C18 bath with the natural warm spring supplying it still running strongly.' This snapshot illustrates the essential characteristics of the bath which is approached down steps from the Hotel entrance lobby. The bath basin is sunk into the tufa bank and covered with an arched stone roof; steps in the near right hand corner (not shown) allow a bather to walk down into the water. The bath's dimensions are 18 by 30 feet; it holds 15000 gallons. The mosaic tile decoration and the extractor duct running along the roof on the left are modern additions. Associated with the bath on the same level are cramped changing rooms and a small sauna, facilities which were last in use in 2012. It is assumed this area always served as the dressing rooms for bathers and attendants. The Hotel reopened in 2016 after a period of refurbishment but in 2019 the indoor bath is not back in use.

It was a little further into the new century, in June 1829, when John Ruskin (1819-1900), later to become art critic, social thinker and philanthropist made his first visit to Matlock Bath. He stayed with his parents at the New Bath. His father was fond of saying his son had been an artist from childhood but a geologist from infancy beginning a mineralogy dictionary at the age of 12. Ruskin recalled 'the glittering white broken spar, speckled with galena, by which the walks of the hotel were made bright, and in the shops of the pretty village, and in many a happy walk along its cliffs, [he had pursued his] mineralogical studies of fluor, calcite and the ores of lead, with indescribable rapture when [he] was allowed to go into a cave.' When he returned to the New Bath in 1871 it became the scene of one of the darkest episodes of his life; it was thought he was close to death. He appears to have suffered a complete mental breakdown heralding his later periods of insanity. Local treatment failed and Henry

Acland (1815-1900) an eminent medical authority and friend of many years was sent for. He judged the situation so serious he caught the first express train he knew would pass through Matlock Bath and pulled the communication cord when he judged the train to be near his destination leaving his card with the guard. During the many weeks of convalescence at the New Bath several of Ruskin's artist friends came to stay and at his instigation explored the caves and the countryside sketching what they saw and bringing him their work for his approval.[53] His study of the spray of wild rose he was painting when he became ill is among the drawings held by the University of Oxford.[54]

FIGURE 10. **Saxton's Green, Matlock Bath drawn by W Brough, published 1850 and half stereograph.**

This lithograph looks north across Saxton's Green towards the church. The building on the left hand side of the picture was Walker's Hotel, later renamed Walker's Bath Terrace Hotel FIGURE 59, and after the family sold the property in 1886, Bath Terrace Hotel. It was established in 1798 as Fox's Lodgings and extended in the 1850s.[55] For some years including 1814, it housed the Post Office.[56] In 1824 the office was moved to the building later known as Woodland House FIGURE 141. On the right hand side, the cottages include a house with a spar shop displaying goods on an outside stall.[57]

Private collection.

The half stereograph on the right shows the cottage in the late 1850s. The sign over the door reads Smedleys [?] Grand Cavern, referring to the Cumberland Cavern.[58] The pile of stone in the right foreground is tufa for sale. It was fashionable to use it in garden landscaping schemes.

John Bradley collection.

CHAPTER TWO

Discovery

Spreading the word

By the middle years of the eighteenth century Matlock Bath began to be favourably reviewed in comparison with other better known spas as in this recommendation of the resort in 1755 from an unnamed source.

> '*MATLOCK BATH is indeed a most beautiful Place; happy in its Situation, for those who love a peaceful Solitude, or would divide their Time betwixt that and agreeable Society: It seems calculated in the due Medium between the gay Flutter and Extravagance of Bath and Tunbridge, and the dull, dirty lifeless Aspect of Buxton and Epsom; abounding with every thing which tends to Health and rational Pleasure: Further than this it has not to boast; and beyond this, Happiness is sought for in vain.'* [1]

In the footsteps of Thomas Smith of Derby came other professional artists, Alexander and John Cozens, William Gilpin, Joseph Wright of Derby, Zuccarelli, de Loutherbourg, a young J. M. W. Turner and the Derby china illustrators. Alongside them many of the visitors also found worthy subjects here. They came from the strata of society for which drawing and writing skills were required accomplishments; they produced their sketches and accounts sometimes for public sale, more often for private enjoyment or as part of military training. Matlock Bath's writers and artists dispersed their interpretations as they travelled on and returned home. Philip de Loutherbourg conveyed his impressions to a London theatre-going audience. He produced dramatic oil paintings of Derbyshire scenes and in 1779 in his role as chief stage designer for Richard Brinsley Sheridan at Drury Lane Theatre, he used sketches from his visit to the Peak District to inspire stage sets for a pantomime, *The Wonders of Derbyshire*. The opening scene was 'A View of Matlock at Sunset'. Poets were inspired too - from all walks of life including, on a visit in 1814, the eight year old Elizabeth Barrett, (1806-1861), later Elizabeth Barrett Browning, the famous Victorian poet. Many of the poems, even allowing for changing fashions in appreciated style, are of questionable quality but often add pithy and amusing details about topics still of interest to tourists today – the weather, fellow guests, the accommodation and the food, for example -

'The dinner good could scarcely cause
The epicure to wave applause,'. [2]

This publicity was beneficial for Matlock Bath and may have served it well when the French Revolutionary Wars which began in 1793 had made touring abroad difficult. Would-be foreign travellers were obliged to explore nearer to home.

As early as the 1770s there were complaints of a shortage of accommodation at the Old and New Baths and some visitors were obliged to seek lodgings elsewhere, at the Boat-house in Matlock Dale or the Temple, the recently built Black Greyhound at Cromford or inns in Wirksworth. Such was the experience of the sculptor and architect William Tyler RA see Panel. In 1782, a similar problem faced Frederick, Lord North (1732-1792), who had been the country's Prime Minister from 1770 until his resignation earlier in that year. At the end of August it was reported that in the previous week the Right Hon. Lord and Lady North and their family 'arrived at Matlock Bath; but the principal places of public resort were so full of company, that his Lordship and family were obliged to go to Wirksworth for lodgings. The next morning they visited the cotton-mill at Cromford, the property of Mr Arkwright, and expressed their highest approbation, in viewing the intricate machines employed for spinning cotton, &c.'[4]

William Tyler's search for lodgings, 1774[3]

[The travellers found] *'no accommodation for us at either of the Houses. This disconcerted us very much, especially as we were informed no Beds could be got nearer than Wirksworth, this was about five miles distant, and from thence we must return back, this was losing time of which we had so little to spare. We had therefore a consultation, for what was to be done, and had nearly determined on going thither, when Forrest, who was so wonderfully struck with the sight of so many beautiful spots we had passed in this place, declared that he would stay here till our return tho' he could expect no better lodgings than such as he might find among the Peasants, and was resolved to take his chance with any of those to indulge his curiosity. I was glad to hear his resolution, having the same inclination to stay, and therefore proposed our going back in search of lodgings at a village a mile from the Baths where a poor woman hearing our debates, told us we might get beds at a little Alehouse.*

Thither we went and thought our accommodation good enough to put up with for one night, and indeed we were pleased both with our entertainment and lodging which was much better than we could have expected in such poor habitation. Here we first dined then devoted the afternoon to ramble about the enchanting scenes that had delighted us so much at first view.'

FIGURE 11. **The Boat House, watercolour, attributed to George Pickering, 1811.**

In 1752 Joseph Spence (1699-1768) visiting his 'great Favourite Matlock' described the Boat House as 'a publick [sic] house kept by honest Tom Tisdale'. Spence, an acclaimed scholar, friend of Alexander Pope and apostle of the 'new taste in gardening' considered the view from the Boat House, as the most beautiful in the place, and much the more delightful than the view from the Bath, describing it as 'very much like some pieces in Gaspar Poussin's Landscapes'.[5] He urged his patron, Lord Lincoln, not to miss seeing Matlock.[6] Three years later visitors to the Boat House remarked upon the 'neat Assembly–room where Company from the Bath frequently come to drink Tea, and have a Concert; there being a handsome Orchestra furnished with a Harpsichord and divers other Instruments. Sometimes the Company go in the Pleasure-boat on the River, and have a Concert of French Horns, &c, which must make fine Harmony among the Rocks.' On this day the landlord explained that 'his Company of Performers was at present but thin; but that, if we liked Music, his daughter and himself would endeavour to entertain us; accordingly she on the Harpsichord, and he on the Violin play'd us half a Dozen Pieces in a very agreeable Manner.'[7] More than a hundred years later, Thomas Rawson, was still offering his clients 'Boats for a row on the river may be had at one minute's notice.'

Chesterfield Local Studies Library.

ON the 7th of June, 1775, (being Wednef-day in Whitfun Week) there will be a
C O N C E R T
Of V o c a l and I n s t r u m e n t a l
M U S I C,
at the BOAT-HOUSE, being the Sign of the White Hart, near Matlock Old Bath, in the County of Derby. The Evening to conclude with a Ball.

¶ ♭ ¶ JOHN JOHNSON, Landlord at the above Houfe, begs Leave to inform the Nobility, Gentry and others, that he has fitted it up in a genteel Manner for their Reception, and the Favor of their Company will be greatfully acknowledged.

N. B. Coffee, Tea, and Chocolate drinking as ufual; with a good Boat, and Mufic attending on the Water, if required.

Derby Mercury 19 and 26/5/1775.

The Temple

The advertisement below makes clear that the Temple had been established well before 1773 and certainly long enough to have already been extended and refurbished, though when it was opened is unclear. The name is surely a rather clumsy attempt to create a classical identity. For many years it was run as an annexe to the Old Bath.[8] By 1783 it had stables, coach-houses and gardens and was owned by Anthony Lax Maynard, who was a major shareholder in the Old Bath.[9]

The Enclosure Commissioners authorised the creation of a road between the Old Bath and the Temple to be called Temple Road[10] though more usually referred to as Temple Walk, a promenade between the two establishments.[11]

MATLOCK-BATH, DERBYSHIRE.

JOSEPH FLETCHER, (Head-Waiter from the Tilt-Yard Coffee-House, London) begs Leave to inform the Nobility, Gentry, and Others, That he hath taken and entered on, that Houfe at Matlock-Bath, which was lately occupied by John Turner, Efq; commonly known by the Name of Solomon's Temple, fo called from its fine Situation, elegant and neat Building; and alfo for its Command of the moft pleafant and delightful Profpects at Matlock.

The late additional Buildings, new and genteel Furniture, with good Beds, has made it elegant and compleatly fit for the immediate Reception of Company.

Thofe who pleafe to honor him with their Favors, may depend on good Ufage, as he is determined to make it his entire Study to oblige his Company, and merit their future Favors.

Tea drinking in the Afternoon by the Company from the other Houfes, in the Coffee-Room, as ufual.

N.B. A circulating Library of BOOKS, that are lett out to read.

The LONDON, YORK, DERBY, and other PAPERS, taken in during the SEASON.

Good STABLING and COACH-HOUSES.

July 1, 1773.

Derby Mercury, July 16th, 23rd, 30th and August 6th, 13th, 20th, 1773.

In March 1807 there was another change of management and possibly of focus. The Temple was now in the hands of Aeneas Evans who had a lodging house near the Crescent in Buxton. He advertised that he had taken the Temple, Matlock Bath for the reception of company. His new kitchen and cook would provide 'for those Families who may wish to have their Victuals dressed in the House'. Alternatively they might eat 'at the Public Tables'.[12]

A generation after the first major investment in the thermal springs these advertisements confirm the progress that had been made in the range of diversions offered to visitors towards the end of the century. Still with limited accommodation and without the pump room and an assembly room[13] of the quality of its more sophisticated and wealthy neighbours, the Spa was nevertheless equipped to cater for a fashionable clientele. It atoned for any lack of style through its awesome scenery tamed and made accessible by paths and grottoes and by its temperate climate. It offered music at the Boat House or in a boat on the river; there were establishments selling tea, coffee and chocolate and a circulating library where books might be borrowed and with the London, York and Derby papers to be read during the season. In the summer of 1794 with the 'village very full of company' a Mr Hamilton extended the range of pursuits available to the visitor, opening a theatre. We do not hear of it again and doubt it took root.[14]

There remained the problem of a shortage of accommodation for visitors which could only be resolved by major investment and this did not materialise until the end of the century.

Tea, Coffee and Chocolate

The tea, coffee and chocolate[15] the Temple and the Boat House offered the visitors no doubt enriched their leisure but we must not overlook contemporary views of the medicinal value of these drinks. Tea was regarded by some authorities as 'a very powerful aphrodisiac'; indeed there was speculation that this explained China's large population. Other claims were no less extravagant. 'Tea is extolled as the greatest of all medicines: moderately and properly taken, it acts as a gentle astringent and corroborative [strengthening agent]; it strengthens the stomach and bowels, and is good against nausea, indigestions, and diarrhoeas. It acts also as a diuretic, and diaphoretic [promoting perspiration]. The immoderate use of it, however, has been very prejudicial to many, who have been thereby thrown into the diabetes.' But used in moderation it is 'for the most part innocent'.

Coffee also had its strengths and dangers though it too had a place in the medicinal arsenal as an emetic and purgative. It was said to 'carry off fumes and disorders of the head... dissipate megrims[sic], absorb acrimonies of the stomach; whence its use after a debauch of strong liquors.' It promoted circulation but was best used by people of 'a pretty corpulent habit' and was considered 'hurtful to those who are thin, lean, dry and of a bilious temperament.'

Of the three, chocolate, described as 'dusky [in] colour, soft, and oily; usually drank hot', carried the least risks being an 'excellent food', 'nourishing' and a 'good medicine' for keeping up the warmth of the stomach and assisting digestion.

Travelling to Matlock Bath

Descriptions of the Peak District such as that from Charles Cotton in 1681[16] were not encouraging for travellers.

Environ'd round with nature's shames and ills
Black heath, wild rock, bleak crags and naked hills.

Celia Fiennes[17] documented the hardships of travelling there [By] 'reason of the steepness and hazard of the Wayes – if you take a wrong Way, there is no passing – you are forced to have Guides as in all parts of Darbyshire, and unless it be a few that use to be guides the common people know not above 2 or 3 miles from their homes.' More than a hundred years later in 1801, Richard Warner still considered that the 'intricacy of the road from the Dog and Partridge [on the Ashbourne to Ilam road] to Matlock rendered it prudent to take a guide'[18] to conduct them through Tissington, Bradburn and Hopton to the Via Gellia. Such difficulties had isolated many parts of Derbyshire.

One of the earliest champions of the original Bath and its surroundings, John Macky,[19] expressed regret that the proprietor had not spent the £30 considered necessary to make the road along the valley 'passable for a Coach, which at present it is neither Way, and which prevents some of the better People of the County from coming here.' Soon after, Daniel Defoe[20] echoed the sentiment, 'This Bath would be much more frequented than it is, if two Things did not hinder; namely a base, stony, mountainous Road to it, and no good Accommodation when you are there.' The road through the valley was improved by Marmaduke Pennell in or soon after 1727 and sometime before July 1736 the road from Cromford to Swanwick had been improved 'mostly at Mr Turner's expense for the encouragement of his cole [sic] trade'[21] though it also benefited visitors to Matlock Bath. Nevertheless the third edition of Defoe's 'Tour' published in 1742, eleven years after his death, despite these improvements repeats an earlier description from William Stukely warning travellers of the dangers they faced in making their way to Matlock Bath.[22] Such comment was true of travelling in other parts of Derbyshire and it was not for the benefit of visitors to the baths alone that the road through the valley was turnpiked in 1759 as part of a route from Wirksworth Moor to meet the Chesterfield to Chapel-en-le-Frith turnpike near Longstone.[23] In 1759, 1766, 1804 and 1817 respectively, Turnpike Acts were passed to improve roads from Chesterfield to Matlock, from Cromford Bridge to Langley Mill, from Cromford to Newhaven and from Cromford to Belper so linking the valley to the existing turnpike network in several new directions. The toll-bars associated with the stretch of turnpike through Matlock Bath are shown in Figures 14 and 15.

FIGURE 12. **View in Matlock Vale, after J. Smith, engraved by S. Middiman, published 1785.**

The print shows a rather ghostly looking horse and lightweight carriage travelling down the road which crossed Scarthin Rock on the way from Cromford towards Matlock Bath. This rock barrier presented a high, steep obstacle to wheeled traffic for many years despite the advantage being taken of the natural dip in the ridge, known as the Scarthin Nick and of such improvements as were made when the road was turnpiked in 1759. In the picture the figures are standing on the turnpike road looking down over an alternative, longer but more level track from Matlock Bath to Cromford, known as the Roundabout Way,[24] running between the river and the foot of the cliff along the line of today's Church Walk before looping round the end of Scarthin Rock to cross the Bonsall Brook over the bridge which is now enclosed in the Cromford Mills' yard.[25]

Adrian Farmer collection.

FIGURE 13. **Pass into Matlock Dale, sketchbook watercolour, Reverend John Swete, 1795.**

The sketch shows a rider dropping down towards Matlock Bath from Cromford through Scarthin Rock. Swete was one of those visitors to Matlock Bath for whom sketching was a pastime.[28] Note Matlock Dale today refers to the length of the valley to the north of Matlock Bath, not as here where it refers to the southern end.

Devon Heritage Services Z19/2/19.

When Richard Arkwright built his second cotton mill in 1776, the building blocked the Roundabout Way mentioned at Figure 12, but he improved the shorter alternative route into Cromford by lowering the level of the turnpike over Scarthin Nick. Several travellers testified to his success including Bray in 1777[26] who commented on the passage cut through the rock. When the turnpike from Cromford to Belper was constructed in 1817, this passage was cut down a further 30 feet.[27]

The visitor's problems were not confined to reaching Matlock. As late as 1821 a resident at the Old Bath[29], though delighted with the scenery and sheltered setting of the resort which 'would render it a most desirable resort for invalids' qualified his praise with 'were not these advantages in a great measure counterbalanced by a deficiency in regard to certain accommodations' and in particular 'the want of a good Causeway on each approach to the place.' This shortage meant that for visitors and parishioners alike 'communication

FIGURE 14. **Warmwalls Toll-house and gate, photograph, 1880s.**

This view looking south towards Cromford along what is now the A6, is difficult to reconcile with the present much widened highway. The photograph was taken from close to the original Matlock Bath Holy Trinity School building. It shows the Warmwalls (sometimes Warmwells) toll-house on the east side of the road opposite the bottom of the Wapping. It was built in 1820, when the turnpike road through Matlock Bath was diverted from its original route over the top of the tufa bank close to the New Bath to its present lower position.[30]

Private collection.

FIGURE 15. **Holt Lane Toll-gate, photograph, 1880s.**

At the opposite end of Matlock Bath, the northern entrance to the resort was marked by this toll-gate and two-storey toll-house shown on the extreme right in this view. The gate was originally on Holt Lane but was moved here in 1833. The old toll-house was pulled down and the materials were incorporated in the new one.[31]

Ken Askew collection.

between Matlock Bath and its Parish Church [then St Giles' at Matlock] was completely interrupted in rainy weather by the dirty state of the road.' Attention was drawn to the widespread 'practice [elsewhere] of making raised Paths along the public roads' and 'with the materials being at hand, the expence of forming good Causeways would be but trifling, particularly when compared with the advantages resulting from them to the Parish.' The letter highlights an often lamented trait and recurring failure in the management of Matlock Bath, the slowness to recognise a problem and to act upon it.

Some eighteenth century visitors

Matlock Bath was a spa resort but it is clear from letters and diaries that it also became a popular stopping off place for travellers on a tour and for county wide journey-makers like Dr James Clegg, Presbyterian minister of Chapel-en-le-Frith on his preaching circuit and medical round. He sometimes broke his journey here and stayed over, bathed or took the water, met friends and once in 1730 took a short holiday to explore the area and to fish. It was a meeting place too for local friends and business associates as Edmund Evans' letter to William Strutt in June 1777 anticipated. 'We shall make a numerous sociable Dance, Mr Arkwright, Simpson's, Evans', Toplis' and families will be there as also will be the pretty Miss Mather of Derby.'[32] It became a place of business and culture and the Old Bath and to a lesser extent its younger rival hosted many important meetings which otherwise might have taken place in Wirksworth, traditionally the local administrative centre. Turnpike Trustees, Enclosure Commissioners, members of the Old Bath Association for the Protection of Fish and Game and the promoters of the Cromford Canal met here. There were also concerts and sales of property - land, houses and lead mines. It was this trade supported by neighbouring residents and travellers rather than visitors which sustained the infant community during the long months out of season.

Among the more frequent visitors to Matlock Bath in the second half of the eighteenth century were some of the most prominent members of the Lunar Society, the most important group of scientists outside London.[33] Jenny Uglow[34] has described Derbyshire as their playground. Mathew Boulton (1728-1809), Josiah Wedgwood (1730-1795), Erasmus Darwin (1731-1802) and John Whitehurst (1713-1788) all knew the county well and their expeditions to Matlock or further into the Peak to explore, provided them with the opportunity to develop their friendships and pursue their scientific and philosophical investigations. Dr Erasmus Darwin, a founder member of the Society and instigator of the Derby Philosophical Society, was a regular visitor and a pivotal figure in each group generously welcoming and encouraging members. He was in Matlock [Bath] in 1780 with Richard Lovell Edgeworth (1744-1817), also a member of the Lunar Society from Ireland, investigating the source of the hot spring and in February 1788 sent a scientific paper[35] on the origins of Matlock Bath's thermal springs to James Pilkington who published Darwin's findings the following year.[36] Darwin had many other links with the area which grew once he moved to Derby late in 1783.[37] He was fascinated by the cotton spinning machinery invented by Richard Arkwright (1732-1792) and came to know him well and also his business partner Jedediah Strutt (1726-1797) though he never became close friends with them as he had with Matthew Boulton in Birmingham. His shrewd diplomacy overcame Watt's dislike of Arkwright so that both he and Boulton supported Arkwright at his first patent trial in February 1785.[38]

The publication of Darwin's *Botanic Garden* secured his place as the leading poet of the age. *Part II, The Loves of the Plants* appeared in 1789 to universal praise and it had reached its third edition by 1792 when it was joined by *Part I, the Economy of Vegetation;* in each the poetry is accompanied by long narrative notes explaining the classical and other allusions and often the science concealed within the couplets. Had Matlock Bath commissioned Darwin, as today a travel writer might be persuaded to promote a hitherto unknown resort, it could not have expected more of him. His love of Matlock Dale, his belief in water treatments,[39] his knowledge of the area's scenic, geological, thermal and mineral riches and, as an inventor himself, his interest in the Arkwright machinery at Masson Mill, all find a place in his major work. The starting point for his description of cotton spinning is Gossypium, the cotton plant.

So now, where Derwent guides his dusky floods
Through vaulted mountains, and a night of woods,
The Nymph, Gossypia, treads the velvet sod,
And warms with rosy smiles the watery God;
His ponderous oars to slender spindles turns,
And pours o'er mossy wheels his foamy urns,
With playful charms her hoary lover wins,
And wields his trident, - while the Monarch spins,
First with nice eye emerging Naiads cull
From leathery pods the vegetable wool;

With wiry teeth revolving cards release
The tangled knots, and smooth the ravell'd fleece
Next moves the iron- hand with fingers fine
Combs the wide card, and forms the eternal line;
Slow with soft lips the whirling Can acquires
The tender skeins, and wraps in rising spires;
With quicken'd pace successive rollers move,
And these retain and those extend the rove;
Then fly the spoles, the rapid axles glow; -
And slowly circumvolves the labouring wheel below.[40]

The narrative text which accompanied these lines contains as good and succinct an account of the Arkwright spinning process as can be found. Presciently he forecasts 'the clothing of this small seed [cotton] will become the principal clothing of mankind.' Less well known are his lines depicting Matlock Bath's warm springs, limestone cliffs and fissures, its woods and its mineral riches.

Where, as proud Masson rises rude and bleak,
And with misshapen turrets crests the Peak,
Old Matlock gapes with marble jaws, beneath;
Deep in wide caves below the dangerous soil
Blue sulphurs flame, imprisoned waters boil.
Impestuous streams in spiral columns rise
Through rifted rocks, impatient for the skies;
Or o'er bright seas of bubbling lavas blow,
As heave and toss the billowy fires below;
Condensed on high, in wandering rills they glide

From Masson's dome and burst his sparry side;
Round his grey towers, and down his fringed walls,
From cliff to cliff, the liquid treasure falls;
In beds of stalactites, bright ores among;
Crusts the green mosses, and the tangled wood,
And sparkling plunges to its parent flood.
O'er the warm wave a smiling youth presides,
Attunes its murmurs, its meanders guides,[41]

It is not possible to measure Darwin's contribution to the discovery of Derbyshire by those wealthy enough to travel and explore but it was surely considerable. He wrote at a time when there was an unquenchable thirst for travel books especially those which discovered new regions of Britain to explore and for verses evoking the beauties of British landscape. But while much of what was published was palpably trite and derivative the originality of Darwin's work in the themes it explored, its erudition and accomplishment marked it out from the tide of travel books flooding the literary scene.[42] His reputation as a literary giant was short lived[43] but while it was at its height his poetic works delighted a wide audience, drawn from far beyond his personal circle of scientists, inventors, philosophers and medical men, extensive though that was; this was an audience of the fashionable and the literati, all from the same class and persuasion as the visitors who we know, in the last years of the century, patronised the resorts of Matlock and Buxton.[44]

Some of Matlock Bath's more prominent visitors are known by name and the personal links which brought them to Derbyshire can be identified. In May 1771 Benjamin Franklin[45] (1706-1790), scientist, statesman, founding father of the American State and of the American Philosophical Society which may have been the model for the Lunar Society and perhaps the Derby Philosophical Society, made a tour of Derbyshire travelling via Matlock to Castleton and on to Manchester. A friend of Darwin's and of the Lunar Society, particularly John Whitehurst the inventor and clockmaker, he was also acquainted with Anthony Tissington (1703-1776) the Duke of Devonshire's mine agent, an authority on minerals and a member of the Royal Society. Franklin famously experimented with electricity but he was also interested in many of the same scientific issues as the Lunar Society members.

Josiah Wedgwood, another of Darwin's intimates, was a regular visitor. His letter to his nine year old son John, below, dated 19th October 1775 provides us with a delightful flavour of a stay in the resort. Wedgwood with his wife and daughter Sukey (Susannah) had travelled from Etruria, his pottery works in Staffordshire via Leek and Calden [sic] Low on October 8th and returned home via Derby. During their stay they visited Darley and the Gregory mine at Ashover. Sukey's keepsake for her brother from the trip was 'a beautiful specimen of polish'd Spar in the Form of an Egg'.

'We have been near a fortnight in Derbyshire with Mr & Mrs Bentley and other company which altogether made up a party of thirteen. The time pass'd away very agreeably and when we made a Fossiling party we wished you could have been one, to partake of the pleasure we receiv'd in these excursions.

We slept at Ashbourne that night, & after a pleasant ride to Matlock the next morning we met our good Friends Mr & Mrs Bentley there, with Miss Oates from Chesterfield, & Mr and two Miss Stamfords from Derby. These were of our particular party but there were many Gentlemen and Ladies besides which we knew, & a good sociable dance in the evening united the whole company together as one & made the place very agreeable to us all.

Tuesday 20th…After dinner - crossed the River to Adams walk, & the weather being fine had a delightfull view from the seat in the Cliff, & the top of the Hill. – All were full of praises of Adam for enabling them to climb the once inaccessible Rock, & rival the Birds in their view of the enchanting scene below, & let me stop here a moment to tell you, my dear Boy, that this poor Man – this Adam of Matlock, by a well tim'd exertion of his ingenuity and industry, had acquir'd more real fame than many noble Lords, & his name will be remember'd with gratitude and respect, when theirs are totally forgot.

We were joined by Mr & Mrs Kenyan & two Miss Birches who very properly inquir'd after you. They stopped a day or two here in their way to Town. We took a walk by the river side at the bottom of the Cliff to the Mine you were in when you first heard of the Old man having done this & the other.

The Engines you & I saw unfinish'd are now at work, & throw up a vast quantity of water, & the Ore they raise is pretty considerable.

Mr Whitehurst, Mr & Mrs Brock have now join'd us, & a Mr Williams from Chelsea who is taking a young gentleman he has care of to Warrington Academy. We cross the River again, and drink tea at the New Bath, & spend a chearfull [sic] evening afterwards on our own.

Wednesday we took an early breakfast, & made a party to Chatsworth a seat of the Duke of Devonshire ten or eleven miles from Matlock. You will not expect me to describe this truly noble seat, but I hope sometime to have the pleasure of shewing it to you.

Thursday being a dull rainy day there was no stirring abroad, so the Ladies & Gentlemen sang, and fluted, & played, making their confinement to the House as agreeable as possible. The evening was concluded with various songs, & so well was the want of fine weather abroad, made up by the good humour & harmony within, that the company declar'd it the most pleasing and elegant day they had spent at Matlock.

Friday morning – walk'd to Cromford & attempted to see the Cotton Mills but were disappointed, Mr Acwright [sic], the inventor & superintendant of the mill permitting very few to have the pleasure of viewing his ingenious performances.

Mr Bentley & I had contriv'd a Concert to entertain the company with this evening. They knew nothing of the matter 'till the Band struck up altogether in the Long Room – I have forgotten the piece but 'tis no matter, it was a very full one, accompanied with voices, & very agreably surprised the whole company. Our band was picked out of Blacksmiths shops, Coblers [sic] stalls, & the mines in the neighbourhood, but notwithstanding their humble situation in life it would be paying them no compliment to say that they made better musick than we had heard from Brothers of the string much finer Dress'd than themselves.'[46]

Matlock Bath suited the Wedgwoods. Adam's Walks, and the congenial company of their friends supplemented by visits to mines, mills and engines and the 'fossiling' and their ability to make their own pleasures; this was enough to declare their visit a success. But others may have been aware of the lack of more sophisticated entertainment, the absence of an adequate Assembly Room and of a Pump Room and the limited accommodation and shops. It was the lack of this infrastructure which enabled Buxton with its superior facilities and wealth to outbid Matlock in attracting tourists as the number of visitors to Derbyshire grew.

The discovery of Derbyshire and the growth of both Buxton and Matlock was not welcomed by the Lunar network.[47] Jenny Uglow suggests that by the 1790s those who had known the county in earlier years felt it was no longer the secret place they had enjoyed as young men; for Boulton this would have been the 1750s. Probably this was no more than a difference in perception between the generations and not a feeling shared by the younger members of the circle. Patty Fothergill,[48] whose father had been Matthew Boulton's business partner for 20 years before his death in 1782, holidayed with the Boulton's and Edgeworths in 1793 and found Matlock 'one of the most romantic places' and Bonsal Dale 'one of the finest rides in England'. Her diary reports visiting Castleton caves, card parties and balls and for August 30th 'After supper we danced as usual and as it was the last night we kept it up a good while and danced Over the Hills and Far Away which is the most romping dance I ever saw...' Despite its lack of sophistication and the growth in visitor numbers, clearly for her, Matlock Bath had retained its charm. Later in the early years of the nineteenth century Matlock Bath's most publicised visitors were the young Lord Byron (1788-1824) and Mary Chaworth (1786-1832) who came to the Old Bath where we are told he sulked because his lameness prevented him from dancing with the beautiful Mary.[49]

Writing in 1777 Bray[50] confirmed Wedgwood's relaxed style of a visit 'The company dine together in a large room, at two, and sup at eight, after which there is music for those who choose dancing, or cards for those who prefer them; everyone drinks what he likes.' Hembry[51] in *The English Spa* considered this custom of eating together as peculiar to

The Members of Wedgwood's Party

Thomas Bentley (1731-1780) had been a general merchant in Liverpool when he met Josiah Wedgwood. They became close friends and business partners, with Bentley moving first to Staffordshire and then to London to manage the firm's showroom and workshop there. Like Wedgwood, a nonconformist, he was a benefactor and trustee of the Warrington Academy, the prominent educational establishment for nonconformists which ran from 1756 until 1782. Mr Whitehurst was John Whitehurst of Derby and London, clock and instrument maker and like Wedgwood a fellow member of the Lunar and the Royal Society. His wider interests included geology and his Section of the Strata at Matlock Tor was published in 1778 in *Inquiry into the Formation of the Earth*. It was Whitehurst who drew Matthew Boulton's attention to the Blue John from Derbyshire which he used in vase bodies. Wedgwood's daughter Susannah (Sukey) later married Robert Waring Darwin, (1766-1848) Erasmus Darwin's son; the Darwins were close family friends. Sukey and Robert's children included Charles, (1809-1882), the author of *'The Origin of Species'* in which he developed the theory of evolution propounded by his grandfather Erasmus in his poem *The Temple of Nature*. Sukey's younger brother John's interest in botany led to the formation of the Horticultural Society, now the Royal Horticultural Society, in association with Sir Joseph Banks. John chaired its first meeting in 1804. The Adam for whom Wedgwood shows such respect was the Adam Walker credited with constructing the paths on Lover's Walk. The Old man is a reference to lead miners and the engines mentioned were their devices for raising water from lead mines. An example is shown at Figure 35. Unpublished research by the Reverend John Drackley has demonstrated that the Matlocks at this time enjoyed a flourishing musical life and it is no surprise that Wedgwood found a competent band to entertain his family.

northern spas such as Matlock Bath, Buxton and Harrogate and that it reflected the greater need to socialise indoors in places where the climate was less agreeable for leisurely activities outdoors. The lack of formality was an attraction for some visitors though it did not suit John Byng[52] who, exhibiting the social reserve of his class, wrote of a 'desire I stubbornly opposed' when a small party of fellow guests embarrassed him by asking to join company and sup with him and his friend. Some guests chose to keep their own company when they 'retired to a private Room, chatted over the Pleasures of the Day, smoaked [sic] a Pipe, drank a Pint, discharged our Reckoning, and went to Bed.'[53] Camden[54] summed up Matlock Bath as 'much frequented by the neighbouring gentry…without the infection of Southern manners.'

For the BENEFIT of Mr. GREATOREX,
ORGANIST at *North-Wingfield*,
A GRAND
CONCERT of MUSICK
Will be perform'd at MATLOCK BATH,
On *Wedneſday*, the 9th of *Auguſt*, 1758.
PARTICULARLY,

A CONCERTO on the Harpſichord, by Mr. WISE, from *Nottingham*.
SOLO and CONCERTO on the Baſſoon, by Mr. SCAMARDINE, from *Grantham*.
SOLO and CONCERTO on the Hautboy, by Mr. F. SHARP, from *Stamford*.
CONCERTO for the German Flute, by Mr. MILLER from *Doncaſter*.
SOLO and CONCERTO on the Violoncello, by Mr. J. SHARP from *Nottingham*.
The Double Baſs to be perform'd by Mr. M. SHARP from *Grantham*.
To be accompany'd with ſeveral GENTLEMEN PERFORMERS.
The whole BAND to conſiſt of TWENTY PERFORMERS.
To begin preciſely at Four o'Clock in the Afternoon.
After the CONCERT will be a BALL.
TICKETS to be had at the Bath, *Royal-Oak* in *Cheſterfield*, Mr. TOPLIS's Shop, Mercer in *Wirkſworth*, and of Mr. FOX, Bookſeller in *Derby*, at 2 s. 6 d. each.

For the BENEFIT of
Mr. GREATOREX,
ORGANIST at NORTH-WINGFIELD,
The Annual Grand CONCERT
Of Vocal and Inſtrumental MUSIC;
Will be Perform'd
At MATLOCK-BATH,
On *Wedneſday* the 20th of *Auguſt*, 1760.
The Principal PARTS will be perform'd by
Mr. JONES, Firſt VIOLIN.
Mr. LAYLAND, Second VIOLIN.

A Solo Concerto, and Baſſoon Solo, Mr. *Scamardine*.
A Solo Concerto, and Hautboy Solo, Mr. *F. Sharp*.
A Concerto and Solo on the Violoncello, Mr. *J. Sharp*.
A Voluntary and Concerto on the Organ, Mr. *Wiſe*.
German Flute Concerto, Mr. *Millar*.
A favourite Duett, for two Baſſoons, Mr. *Scamardine*, and Mr. *Greatorex*.
French-Horn Concerto.

The Gentlemen of the Band of Muſic belonging to the Royal *Cheſhire Militia*, will aſſiſt in the Concert.

Miſs *Patty Greatorex* will perform ſeveral little Pieces on the ORGAN, and a Song in the Sacrifice of *Iphigenia*, between the Two Acts.

To begin preciſely at Four o'Clock in the Afternoon.

TICKETS to be had at the *Bath*, *Boat-Houſe*, *Angel*, and *Falcon*, in *Cheſterfield*, Mr. *Toplis*'s, Mercer in *Wirkſworth*, and of Mr. *Fox*, Bookſeller in *Derby*, at 2 s. 6 d. each.

FIGURE 16. **Advertisements from the *Derby Mercury*, editions dated July 14-21, 1758 and July 4-11,1760.**

Once or twice a year for several years in the 1750s and '60s the *Derby Mercury* carried advertisements for Grand Concerts to be held at Matlock Bath. Although the New Bath was open by this time the venue was clearly the Old Bath with its Long Room, suitable for concerts and balls, which the proprietors of the Bath had opened in 1751. The organist, Anthony Greatorex (1730-1814), may well have been known to the proprietors, who were Chesterfield men mainly, though he was a prominent local musician and some Matlock singers are known to have possessed music he composed. The concert programmes were not local affairs. They brought together musicians from a wide area suggesting that they were a bid to replicate the 'high' culture of the pedigree watering places. The events were a form of advertising for the Bath and some at least of the performers and audience would have sought accommodation there.

Private collection.

CHAPTER THREE

The Resort Grows

The New Inn, the third bath and the Hotel

Tyler and the Norths were not alone in recognising a shortage of accommodation in Matlock Bath. The first response to the increase in demand was the opening of a new inn, and in due course, the creation of a new bath. This extended the existing footprint of the resort along the valley to the north.

Unlike its Derbyshire rival, Buxton which enjoyed the wealth and creative passion of the 5th Duke of Devonshire, Matlock Bath had no such patronage and its growth depended on outside investment from individuals or groups of entrepreneurs who were prepared to risk their capital in new ventures within the young resort. The New Inn, (a modest building now known as Hodgkinson's), together with its 'stables and other offices' was the work of Thomas Brentnall, a wine merchant from Derby. He had bought Hascom Leys Farm from William Parsons in 1772[1] and the inn he built was still in his ownership in 1779 when he was declared bankrupt.[2] A year later his Matlock Bath estate was purchased from the Bankruptcy Commissioners by Dr Stephen Simpson from Wentworth in Yorkshire. Stephen Simpson and his brother Charles provided attractions for guests at the New Inn to rival those offered by the two older establishments, the Old and New Baths. Ultimately these included a new warm bath, a pleasure ground, bowling green and a landscaped walk up the hillside.[3]

Their 'very spacious, light and pleasant Hot-Bath' was erected near the turnpike on land belonging to the farm. Its water supply had not been successfully controlled by the time Stephen Simpson died in 1785 and it was his brother Charles, who inherited the estate, who announced in 1786 that the attempt to harness a 'powerful Hot Spring … by separating a Cold Spring from it' had been 'effected under the direction of John Mather'. Soon after, in August 1787, Robert Marsden was occupying the New Inn and as his announcement in the *Derby Mercury* makes clear, the whole complex was open for business. He introduced himself as 'late Agent to His Grace the Duke of Devonshire, for the Baths at Buxton' and promised his customers 'well air'd Beds, good Wines, Attendance and Accommodation, Coach Houses, private stables, good Hay and Corn'. He was 'happy to find that the new

FIGURE 17. View of Matlock, after Edward Dayes, engraved by Storer, published 1794.

This view[4] looks north towards High Tor from the top of the present Fishpond Hill. The prominent figures are standing on Temple Walk. In the centre of the picture, with the curve of the river behind, are the Old Bath's new stables. In front of them, partly obscured by the figures, is the Horse Pond. This survives as the ornamental fishpond in the Pavilion car park. The New Inn is the three-storey building among those on the left.[5] Beyond the New Inn, the furthest building with its gable end to the road is the bath-house which was run in conjunction with the Inn. Soon after 1813 the baths became known as the Fountain Baths, a name retained until recent times. In 1882 the site was extensively re-modelled, Figures 91 and 92. Nearer to the New Inn, the building facing the road, probably the bath keeper's house, is now Rose Cottage. Simpson's landscaping on Masson Hill is visible above the line of trees as a zig-zag path, a feature which survives in the upper reaches of the present day Waterloo Road and within the grounds of the Heights of Abraham.

Private collection.

Bath, Bowling-Green, walks to the Heights of Abraham and Pleasure Ground meet with general Approbation.' Advertising the following year Marsden gives details of the bath as 42 feet long, 15 wide and 14 and a half feet to the crown of the arch. By July 1791, George Bluett 'late Manager of the Rooms at Buxton, and Master of the Castle Inn in Chesterfield' claimed the addition of an 'elegant Fountain Room for drinking the Waters'. This is the first mention of a designated place for drinking mineral water in the resort other than the glass tumbler placed near the spring at the New Bath. No further reference to the facility has been found until attention is drawn to the fountain and alcove which Samuel Richardson added after his purchase of the bath in 1813.

The use the Simpsons made of their land was inspired. They landscaped it, planting trees about a zig-zag walk up the hillside to vantage points high on the west bank of the river, Figures 17 and 18. They named it the Heights of Abraham from its supposed similarity to the hills above Quebec made famous when James Wolfe stormed the town in 1759. Approached across the Hascom Leys Farm meadows, the narrow enclosure plot was skilfully used so that the loops of the path gradually led visitors to enjoy wider views, south and west over the length of the valley and its eastern rim and finally to the north, to overlook High Tor, a worthy reward for the climb. John Nash, in his diary in August 1796 drew attention to it when with his family party he 'took a walk before breakfast... up a Hill behind the Temple called the Heights of Abraham, the steepness of which was taken off by the Pathway up it being made zig zag.'

By 1789 Charles Simpson had purchased a further three plots of enclosure land adjoining his allotment on Masson, including 26 acres from Sir Richard Arkwright.[6] This purchase was significant in that it secured a footprint of more than 30 acres of hillside which both incorporated the zig-zag walk and offered later owners the opportunity for further development. They were able to sell the lower slopes for building while retaining the core which included the Heights of Abraham pleasure ground, an outcome which remains critically important to the quality of the landscape of modern Matlock Bath.[7]

The additional accommodation provided by the new Inn did little to resolve the resort's increasing shortage of beds and while Simpson had extended the range of outdoor facilities he did not provide the all important ingredients, a pump room and an assembly room and visitors continued to rely on the room used for dancing and large gatherings at the Old Bath. It was left to his successor to deliver both the new accommodation and the assembly room.

In 1797 the Simpson estate was sold to George Vernon, a solicitor, of Hilderstone Hall, Stone, Staffordshire. He was to have a profound effect on the character and future of Matlock Bath. It is probable that Vernon knew the resort and was aware of its increasing popularity and of the need for more accommodation. As the owner of a brass foundry, he may also have been interested in the prospects for calamine extraction.[8]

In 1798, Vernon began to construct a row of individual but interconnected buildings attached to Simpson's inn. Constrained by the steepness of the valley, the terrace reflected the gentle curve of the river and though the buildings were not uniform in size or detail, as part of a single plan, they formed an impressive and harmonious façade. The form of buildings reflected the way in which they were to be used, offering separate lodgings to accommodate guests and their servants; or individual rooms for guests who chose to share the communal facilities.[9] The terrace offered an Assembly Room, Card Room and Billiardroom. Opposite the new buildings on the other side of the road, flanked by two 'pavilions', was a short riverside promenade, see cover illustration, where guests might stroll to take the air and meet friends and acquaintances. In the 1780s Buxton's Crescent had been built for the 5th Duke of Devonshire by the architect John Carr at a cost of more than £60,000. Vernon's ambitious development, the Hotel[10], could not match such grandeur and sophistication but it was appropriate and attractive in its rural setting beside the river. It offered the accommodation and facilities contemporaries expected of a fashionable watering place though no Pump Room. His achievement is celebrated in Benjamin Roger's print published in 1801 Figure 18. George Vernon created the Georgian heart of Matlock Bath which is still its hallmark. His development was transformational, providing an elegant link between the two social centres of the resort, the Old Bath, and the Brentnall – Simpson development to the north.

In practical terms the Hotel could accommodate 'near 100 persons'.[11] This was a significant contribution to the resort's lodgings. Pilkington had estimated the visitor capacity in 1789 as 'about one hundred and fifty persons'.[12] Only thirteen years later George Lipscombe commented that 'nearly three times that number might be entertained'.[13] In 1810 Thomas Potts[14] put the number at 'upwards of 400' and Ward expanded the figure to 500 in 1827.[15] It is clear that Vernon had resolved the resort's accommodation problem. The warnings to travellers of scarce and inadequate lodgings were replaced by reassurances; 'there are good accommodations for the numerous company who resort to the baths.'[16] Food and drink for this seasonal population was supplied by the neighbouring markets where 'provisions of all kinds [were] plentifully supplied'. These were in Wirksworth on a Tuesday and, after 1790, in Cromford on Saturdays. And as was the custom at other spas some visitors would have brought their own food supplies. Such details as are known of the development of the settlement include little information about shops though the 'baker, pastry cook and confectioner' John Boden claimed his establishment at Matlock Bath[17] had been founded in 1792; and according to the lettering on the shop façade when, more than a hundred years later, it was sited at the corner of the Pitchings. Reeds's Grocery and Provision Stores began trading in 1798.

More often mentioned were the spar shops 'with which Matlock abounds' as the Duke of Rutland reported in 1796.[18] There is evidence of fierce competition. When one of the riverside pavilions was to let it was described as 'an elegant new erected shop facing the Hotel, Matlock Bath, 15 feet square, 9 feet high with excellent boarded floorings suitable for a Milliner, Jeweller etc with 6 sash windows' but with the caveat 'None needing to apply in the spar or petrifaction business. The person letting the shop is in that way himself.'[19] Today the Hotel survives as the shops and residences of South Parade with the original New Inn still called Hodgkinson's. The upper and lower stable yards up the Pitchings continue to give hints of their original use Figures 68 and 133.

Any assessment of George Vernon's influence on the appearance of Matlock Bath must include his contribution to its hillside setting. Like his predecessor he planted trees on the Heights of Abraham estate to enhance the picturesque landscape in which his hotel stood and sometime before 1808, his choice of design for the Round House, which was built close to the zig-zag walk, confirms that his commitment to the romantic effect was deliberate. The house, now much extended and known as the Lower Tower(s), was built in the then fashionable neo-gothic style. It is tempting to see the hand of the architect Benjamin Wyatt (1755-1813) of Sutton Coldfield[20] in its design though there is no firm evidence to support this view, only the coincidence that Wyatt purchased the Heights of Abraham from Vernon in 1808. Wyatt's obituary in the *Gentleman's Magazine* in 1813 described him as an 'eminent architect' though, when he worked on behalf of his relatives, the more famous

London based Wyatts, it was as a builder. In this role he built the new parish church at Weeford in Staffordshire, the family home of the Wyatts, designed by James Wyatt (1746-1813) and the Soho Foundry for Matthew Robinson Boulton and James Watt junior.[21]

FIGURE 18. **'View of the Hotel at Matlock Bath' dedicated 'To her Royal Highness the Duchess of York', print, Benjamin Rogers, published August 1801.**

Over the coach houses at the south end of Vernon's new building, on the left here, 'very lofty and handsome Assembly Room and Card-rooms' were created; the steps which gave access to these facilities are still in use. At the north end of the terrace, the Pitchings, led up from the original New Inn building, later Hodgkinson's, to the lower and upper stable yards with stalls for fifty horses. A 'Billiard-room' was added over coach houses (just visible here) at the foot of the Pitchings. The bath keeper's house and the bath appear on the right as on the earlier view. The first lodge marking the entrance to the Heights of Abraham is in Hascom Leys Farm meadows above and to the right of the bath. It stands at the bend of the path which later became the private road leading out of Vernon's upper stable yard, now known as Waterloo Road. Rosebank stands on the site now. The effect of the Simpson tree planting is shown in striking contrast to the 'naked downs' of Masson. High on the zig-zag path within the trees is Vernon's tufa alcove which still provides a resting place on the climb up the hill. Immediately above the present day Hodgkinson's, is the building held to have been the oldest substantial farmhouse in Matlock Bath, the Hascom Leys Farm. George Wragg bought it in 1680 and later it became known as the Old Bath House, (not to be confused with the Old Bath), then The Villa and at the time of its demolition in 1908, Ashfield House. It provided lodging for visitors to the first bath until 1728 when Marmaduke Pennell's accommodation on the bath site was ready for use. The prominent tall tree, shown more or less in the middle of the picture, stood in the front of the house and was feted as the 'remarkable lofty and handsome ash tree of great dimensions, justly esteemed a great curiosity and an ornament to the country.' Above the coach house block on the left is the Temple.

Private collection.

FIGURE 19. **Matlock Bath from a drawing by J, Farington Esq. R. A., engraved by I. Angus.**

FIGURE 20. **View of Matlock Bath from a drawing by J. Farington Esq. R. A., engraved by F. R. Hay**

These two views by Joseph Farington, both published in 1817 by T. Cadell & W. Davies, Strand, London illustrate the upgrading of the Old Bath's stabling and coachmen's accommodation which was completed before 1803. The left hand, earlier view across the river to Fishpond Hill shows the building which still stands on the slope of the hill (though now with the addition of a large twentieth century bay window) and below it, thatched stabling at the roadside. Above them the two storey building at the north end of the Old Bath was 'Mason's Inn, the Miner's Arms'. In the view above, no doubt from Farington's visit in 1801, in place of the thatched stable buildings, the shape of today's The Fishpond is recognisable. This view, with the curve of Waterloo Road in the right foreground, also shows the alcove across the river on the Lover's Walk see Figure 22 Joseph Farington RA (1747-1821), a topographical draughtsman of high repute, had made earlier visits in 1776 and 1791.

Private collection.

A local spat, The Hotel v the Old Bath

The turn of the century had brought an increase in the number of lodgings available to Matlock Bath's visitors and a marked improvement in quality and value for money. Joseph Farington's diary entry in August 1801 reports on this progress 'very good accommodation better indeed than I have ever seen at Matlock before'. He paid 6 shillings for 'a very good room' and remarks that 'others were available according to size from 3/6d per week to 6-7s, 8s and 12/6d.'

Farington attributed the improvements to the opening of Vernon's Hotel though his explanation of the circumstances might seem unlikely. He writes 'the cause of the great improvements at Matlock as having risen from a trifling circumstance. A Mr Vernon having purchased certain property at Matlock, on which Mason, who kept the Old Bath, remarked that Mr Vernon seemed to be a Dasher.[22] Vernon hearing of it said He wd prove to Mason that he was so and immediately began building the Hotel, with accommodations so surpassing what were to be found at the Old Bath that Mason was obliged to follow his example and to make proportionate alterations in his own House. To this circumstance the public owe much for the accommodations are now excellent.'

The Old Bath's proprietors did make significant alterations at about this time. In October 1797, Robert Mason had given them notice of his intention to retire after 28 years in their service and when his successor John Leedham, 'late head waiter at the great Hotel, Buxton' took over from Mr and Mrs Mason in April 1798, he announced plans for a major investment. The proprietors had agreed 'to lay out from one to two thousand pounds in the improvement of the premises'. In the same year Vernon had begun his new building. The date 1798 which commemorates the event survives on the hopper head of the drainpipe at 168 South Parade.

Vernon's tenant was Thomas Froggott, who had been employed for 18 years by Robert Mason at the Old Bath. By the middle of 1799 work on both buildings had finished and at the end of June Leedham advertised that the Old Bath improvements were complete.[23] Within a few weeks Froggott,[24] with rather more flourish declared that 'the extensive alterations and improvements to the Hotel are now complete... The New Assembly and Card Room, will open on Friday, August 16th... and a very elegant Billiard Room has been lately added'. *The Times* of July 3rd, 1800 gave its seal of approval reporting that 'Matlock Bath, Derbyshire is becoming a more fashionable bathing place than ever, the great additions and improvements made to the Hotel and other houses there, render the accommodations elegant and complete'. Leedham did not give details of the Old Bath improvements but it is likely that a building was added to fill the gap in the terrace and the old stabling and coachmen's accommodation at the foot of what is now Fishpond Hill was re-modelled. Adam later claimed that a large dining room and a billiard room was added at this time. An advertisement for the Old Bath in 1806[25] inflated Leedham's anticipated one to two thousand pounds expenditure on the premises claiming upwards of £3000 had been spent.

It seems that Froggott at the Hotel and Leedham at the Old Bath over-reached themselves; by 1806 both were bankrupt.[26] In July the following year the Froggotts were 'engaged to conduct the Business during the present Season' at the Old Bath. James Cumming followed and with his family provided a period of stability in the tenancy of the Old Bath. By May 1807 he announced that 'independent of the Natural Baths' he had erected 'one which may be heated to any temperature'[27] and in July advertised 'Musicians being resident in the House'[28] so that the Company had the privilege to 'command a ball on any night' independent of the regular Tuesday and Friday Assemblies. Cumming's reference to a heated bath is a significant step in keeping pace with the expectations of spa visitors. For a period in the following decade, Varley, the tenant at the former Hotel and bath, made a similar offer.[29]

The New Bath acknowledged the competition and soon added Hot Baths in its advertisements alongside its Natural Tepid Swimming Bath. The charges listed in 1838 in *The Matlock Tourist* were the same at all the sites:

Swimming or plunging bath 1s 0d	*Cold shower bath* 1s 0d
Hot bath 2s 6d	*Hot shower bath* 2s 6d

There are few specific references to drinking the waters in any accounts of Matlock Bath's spa culture and we are unable to assess the relative importance of bathing as compared with the consumption of water internally in the therapeutic services offered in the resort. Clearly Matlock Bath's water was renowned for both internal and external use but there are few details of how it was served. If there were specialised attendants supervising its use and poor women serving it as at Buxton, the equivalent of the so-called 'dipper' in Tunbridge Wells, we have not found them and we assume clients helped themselves from water spouts or cisterns at the baths. Not for the first time such information as we have comes from Thomas Short.[30] His advice to those who would drink Matlock Bath's mineral waters was as follows.

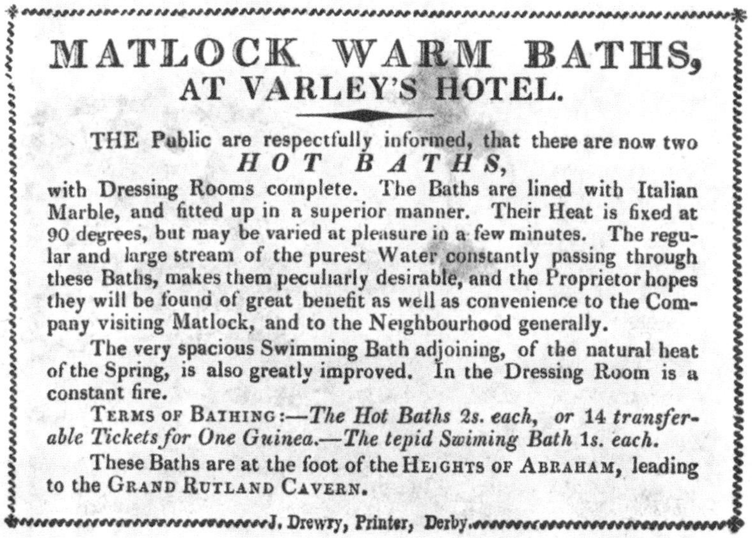

MATLOCK WARM BATHS, AT VARLEY'S HOTEL.

THE Public are respectfully informed, that there are now two *HOT BATHS,* with Dressing Rooms complete. The Baths are lined with Italian Marble, and fitted up in a superior manner. Their Heat is fixed at 90 degrees, but may be varied at pleasure in a few minutes. The regular and large stream of the purest Water constantly passing through these Baths, makes them peculiarly desirable, and the Proprietor hopes they will be found of great benefit as well as convenience to the Company visiting Matlock, and to the Neighbourhood generally.

The very spacious Swimming Bath adjoining, of the natural heat of the Spring, is also greatly improved. In the Dressing Room is a constant fire.

TERMS OF BATHING:—*The Hot Baths 2s. each, or 14 transferable Tickets for One Guinea.—The tepid Swiming Bath 1s. each.*

These Baths are at the foot of the HEIGHTS OF ABRAHAM, leading to the GRAND RUTLAND CAVERN.

J. Drewry, Printer, Derby.

FIGURE 21. **Printed advertisement card, about 1815.**

Private collection.

'*The waters should be drunk in the Morning, the sooner the better; three or four Pints here may be allowed each Forenoon, Breakfast about eight o'clock on Bohea Tea, Chocolate made small, or a thin Chocolate made of the weakest Bohea Tea, or on Milk; in some cases Green Tea or coffee may be allowed. Dine at 1 o'clock, and Sup between six and seven, or seven at farthest, on things of easy digestion, and going to bed, I should advise drinking half a Pint of Water. The Drinkers will find it necessary to remit some Days to prevent the Waters palling the Appetite. Inducing Faintness, Indigestion and Dispiritedness, and having once entered upon a Course of these Waters, nothing but great necessity should allow the Use of any evacuating Medicines, for they often prevent their good Effects, and always retard them, but as it is impossible to give particular Directions, suited to all cases and Constitutions at all times, so these general Directions will suffice, only these Waters may safely be used by all Ages and Sexes, even in the hottest Season, without danger. Both the kind of Exercises and their Degree must be suited to the Season, as gentle Riding, easy walking, bowling, Billiards etc and for Diversion, cards, Musick, Cheerfulness, Chess etc but all at proper Hours, innocently and moderately.*'

From his study of the effects of drinking Matlock Bath water he concludes

[The] 'primary Use, and chief Service of drinking [these] waters, is in all moderate spittings of Blood, whither from the Lungs, Wind-pipe, or Stomach; as also in
discharges of Blood from the Mouth, Palate, and Gumms, as in small scorbutic
Ulcers…in bloody Urine, bloody Stools and frequent Hemorrhages at the Nose; in
all inward Ulcers discharging purulent Matter, whether of the Kidneys, Bladder,
Ureters, Intestines, Stomach or other Bowels of the Breast or Belly; in a Diabetes, or
too plentiful discharge of pale, crude, sweet, Urine, vastly exceeding the proportion
of Drink taken into the Body, attended with violent Thirst.' [In] 'Diabetes there is no
need of… Caution with respect to the Quantity that may be drank… weak people,…
might boyle it away to one third or fourth part, and then drink it cold.''Drinking and bathing agree very well in Gleets, Fluor Albus, Cancer and Kings Evil.'
'Drinking is also useful in want of Appetite, Indigestion, and heat of the Stomach
and Bowels. In hectic Fevers, inward Ulcers, Atrophy and Blood-spitting, I should
advise the Water either to be Drank with Milk, or a Milk Diet.' [He forbids] 'the use
of all spirituous Liquors, as Wine, Ale, Punch, but especially Drams of any kind
of Spirits. Nor is it proper in these Cases to allow Meats of heavy Digestion;…as
Goose, Turkey, Duck, Salt Meats, Cheese, Beef or Mutton but above all not Pickles,
Aromaticks and Sauces.'

A century later Dr Granville,[31] seldom lost for an opinion, was cautiously appreciative
of the effects the water had on himself and the two or three patients for whom he had
prescribed it; 'drank freely as a common beverage through the day,' [it is] 'likely to prove
highly beneficial in dyspeptic and nephritic affections.'[32] Yet just four years earlier in
his local guide, Rhodes had noted 'for medicinal purposes' [the waters] 'are but rarely
taken internally.'[33] Whether through the lack of a pump room or the absence of its own
recognised medical men to promote the efficacy of its mineral waters, benefits enjoyed by
the larger spas, Matlock Bath was sliding towards the loss of one of the pillars on which
its reputation as a watering place had been established. The drift continued; and if there
was an attempt to revive the practice of taking the waters before the delivery of the pump
room in the Kursaal in 1910 we have not found it. By then Edwardian Matlock Bath was no
longer primarily a health resort and the water the pump room served was for the day trippers curious to experience a quaint custom. Had the pump room been provided a century
earlier how different Matlock Bath's history might have been.

CHAPTER FOUR

Landscaping the valley:
the arrival of the Arkwrights

1782 marked the arrival of the Arkwrights as significant landowners in Matlock Dale. Richard Arkwright purchased the Willersley Farm Estate on the east bank of the river Derwent which later provided a setting for the family's gothic mansion, Willersley Castle. Their contribution to the enhancement and maintenance of the resort's rocky, wooded eastern boundary was to extend over six generations and it is in no small part thanks to their consistent stewardship that Matlock Bath today still faces the same wooded backdrop at the foot and on the slopes of its rocky cliffs. The estate included Lover's Walk, which successive generations of the Arkwright family continued to lease out until the estate sale in 1927.

By 1785 the Walk had been extended northwards along the bank of the river and a new stepped and winding path up the valley side had been constructed. This was the Birdcage Walk of which the earliest record is from a sketch by Christopher Machell dated 1785. The Reverend Richard Ward's guide book of 1814[1] describes it as 'one that,

FIGURE 22. **Alcove on the Lover's Walk, Matlock Bath, watercolour, George Robertson about 1797.**

This small watercolour is another of George Robertson's views. This alcove[2] was a focal point in the Lover's Walk but faced away from the path from the ferry, offering a snatched moment of privacy and a vantage point for a vista of High Tor.

Derby Museum and Art Gallery 2010.

passing by that very lofty point called the *Bird-cage,* leads the visitor, with little difficulty, to the top of the rocks.' The walk and the rustic alcove at its foot have survived. It is not clear whether the new walk which can only have been constructed at considerable expense, was in place when Richard Arkwright purchased the estate or whether it was an initiative he encouraged or sanctioned.

By 1786-7 high on his new estate overlooking the River Derwent and Scarthin Rock, the site was being cleared for the recently knighted Richard Arkwright's new house. Plans were drawn up in 1787-8 by the London architect William Thomas.[3] In 1791 when the house was nearing completion it was damaged by fire Figure 24. The following year Sir Richard died and his son Richard (1755-1843) employed Thomas Gardner of Uttoxeter to complete the castle and the gardener John Webb (1754-1828) to landscape the estate around it. Webb who was a pupil of William Emes (1729 or 30-1803) and like Emes a disciple of Capability Brown, laid out the ground so that it was in harmony with the rest of the valley; his parkland meadows and woodland merging into the existing landscape. There was little formal garden except the walled kitchen garden which was well hidden behind the house. The wall which marked the estate's boundary with Lover's Walk, the public pleasure ground, was placed so that the Cascade could be seen from both the estate and from the Walk. Webb's influence extended into the wider Arkwright estate along the valley where overall he is said to have planted 350,000[4] trees over a period of 7 years. When Richard Arkwright junior opened his estate to the public in the late 1790s the gesture received widespread approval. Matlock Bath's visitors could make a circular tour via Cromford bridge to Willersley and there, as William Adam described,[5] on a prescribed route, take note of the 'grove' and the 'mural cliff' before being shown the Castle's walled kitchen garden and glasshouses, famed for their pineapples and winter grapes, and the spectacular view from the vantage point of Cat Tor. At the end of the tour, the Willersley gardener would escort them through a door in the wall which formed the boundary with the Lover's Walk and lock the gate behind them. They walked down to the river to cross back to their lodgings by the ferry. The privilege was granted daily at first but as early as 1802[6] George Lipscombe tells us 'some injury having been done to the shrubberies in consequence of this indiscriminate admission – visitors are now shewn the place by a guide, two days every week.'[7] By the late nineteenth century the grounds were open on Mondays only.

The sight of Willersley castle inspired one visitor to dash off a poem. He writes; 'the style of Sir Richard Arkwright's house, I confess, is singular; but, at the same time there is something in its relative proportions so well adapted to the situation, that charmed me with extacy [sic] and delight.' A lengthy poem followed from which we include these extracts.

Such, Architecture, are thy traits confest,
From times remote, invarious modes expresst;
That art renown'd, which elder ages taught,
And Rome, succeeding, to perfection brought,
Ere Europe's modern sons put in their claim,
In later ages, emulous of fame,
Hail, art sublime! preserv'd with constant care'

Offspring of Symmetry and Order fair,
O may we see thy votaries increase,

And in praise of the architect, William Thomas;

THOMAS, proceed, thy powers in full display,
Where Genius kindly points the destin'd way;
Boldly advance; the path before thee lies,[8]

FIGURE 23. **View of the Boathouse near Matlock, oil painting, Joseph Wright of Derby.**[9]

Benedict Nicolson attributes this painting to the mid 1780s. One of several scenes Wright painted of Matlock, the picture looks down the River Derwent within what is now the Willersley Castle estate and at bottom left shows a small boathouse. The foundation of such a building survives some 50 yards above the present Masson Mill weir. On the skyline is the lead smelting cupola, near the top of Cromford Hill.

Yale Centre for British Art, Paul Mellon Collection.

Objects of wonder and dismay: the Arkwright mills

Arkwright's earlier mills at Cromford had already provided interest for Matlock Bath's visitors, some with dismay at their intrusion into the rural scene, others with amazement. Some were fearful of the outcome. What if this new enterprise should fail and its many employees become a burden on the Poor Rate or, if it should succeed, how might this concentration of workers disturb the established social order? Neither fear was realised. Amateur and professional artists of the day, painted views of the new buildings; the Derby China Manufactory artists provided images of the mills for the decoration of fine porcelain ware.

Of a particular lasting and important practical significance was George Dempster's reaction to the sight of the mills.[10] He was MP for Perth and in 1783 on his journey from Scotland to attend Parliament in London stopped to take the waters at Matlock Bath for a week or more. He recalled his visit in a letter written in 1800.

'In the course of a forenoon's ride, I discovered in a romantic valley a palace of a most enormous size having at least a score of windows of a row and five or six stories in height. This was Sir Richard Arkwright's, then Mr Richard Arkwright's cotton mills. One of our mess-mates being known to the owner obtained his permission to see this stupendous work. After admiring everything I saw, I rode up to Mr Arkwright's house – knocked at the door. He opened it himself, and told me who he was. I said my curiosity could not be fully gratified, without seeing the head from which the mill had sprung.'

The incident led to Dempster involving Arkwright in short lived partnerships in Scotland in what became the great cotton mill sites at Stanley and New Lanark and to Arkwright training Scottish workers at Cromford in the factory system as he practised it.

FIGURE 24. **Near Cromford on the evening of 8th August 1791, Derbyshire (building on fire).**

The image is from Oldfield Bowles' sketch book. He was a visitor to Matlock Bath from North Aston, Oxfordshire carrying his sketch book with him on an evening stroll. His title does not name the building so the image has not been attributed until now.

Hampshire Record Office 36M93/1.

FIGURE 25. **Building proposed 'for an improvement on the estate of Richard Arkwright Esq.', sketch, about 1800.**

Around the year 1800, Richard Arkwright junior received a sketch and a written proposal from George Rawlinson (1734-1823) for a scheme to construct a bridge over the river in front of the Hotel which would then be linked by what he described as 'the shady walk' to the 'rock facing the Hotel Buildings'. Here there was to be a new building 'which was to be both ornamental and useful both to the Bath Company and others'. The sketch shows the north elevation of the pavilion which Rawlinson wished to site on the cliff top on Lover's Walk. Its flamboyant façade would have appeared as an eye-catching folly in the view from the Hotel and from Rawlinson's own new villa, Belle Vue. The pavilion would have provided a vantage point as well as shelter and temporary resting place for those who had struggled up the path to reach it or perhaps more sophisticated facilities for music and refreshment. Rawlinson's proposals are not explicit. The whole scheme, Rawlinson suggested could be paid for by a 'small tax' on those using the walk and by a lease on the building. The plan was never implemented and there is no evidence to suggest that the proposal was seriously considered but it was an interesting idea underpinned by what would have been a desirable feature in the resort at that time, a bridge across the river. It would be almost 50 years later when the station bridge was built and over 80 before Rawlinson's vision of a pedestrian bridge was realised.

Arkwright Society collection.

FIGURE 26. **Detail from Factory Children, coloured aquatint, *The Costume of Yorkshire*, George Waller, April 1814.**

Private collection.

Masson Mill the early years

In the last decades of the eighteenth century, as tourism continued to develop alongside the older lead mining industry, a startling new element had appeared in the local economy. In 1783-84 at the south end of Matlock Bath Richard Arkwright built a cotton spinning factory powered by the River Derwent. The enterprise would offer employment in the area for more than 200 years. It came to be known as Masson Mill and its construction aroused a chorus of adverse comments.

The Rawlinsons

An entry for George Rawlinson is included in Howard Colvin's *Dictionary of British Architects*.[11] He built his own villa Belle Vue, in Matlock Bath Figure 55 and is reputed to have built Walker's Hotel Figure 59. Maxwell Craven credits him with the design for Samuel Need's house, later called Glenorchy Figure 27 and potentially sees his hand in other local buildings but these attributions are conjectural.

George's son James (1769-1848) was a portrait and historical painter who worked in Derby and later in Matlock Bath. He was a pupil of George Romney and his portrait subjects included Erasmus Darwin and William Strutt. Both father and son had monumental inscriptions in All Saints' Church, Derby. James Rawlinson's daughter, Elizabeth or Eliza, was also an artist and in 1822, James published an album of lithographs of her Derbyshire Views.

The family's legacy to the Matlock Bath scene is the group of listed buildings which grace the hillside today – the first villa in the resort, Belle Vue, and in its former grounds, Montpellier House (later known as The Firs, then Hillside and now Montpellier) built sometime between 1833 and 1840 and Belmont Cottage which is dated 1847. James and Eliza were resident at Belmont Cottage when James died. Eliza continued to live there until 1853 when all three properties were put up for sale. She married the sculptor James Loft at Hassop Roman Catholic Chapel in 1856 and died in London in 1860.

Designs for a lodge for Willersley Castle in 1828-9 include an undated drawing signed Rawlinson. It is not known whether the drawing was made earlier by George Rawlinson and put forward by James or Eliza when a new lodge was proposed or was the output of a different Rawlinson. The design was not chosen for the building.

'Those who are pleased with viewing picturesque scenes will wish that [the mill buildings] could have been conveniently placed in any other situation.' And of this and other local mills. 'They are so placed, that they contaminate the most interesting views; and so tall that there is no escaping from them.' 'These vales have lost their beauty; the rural cot has given way to the lofty red mill.'[12] But despite the apparent incongruity between the Matlock gorge's sublime landscape and the red brick intruder, there were in fact many visitors who regarded this symbol of cutting edge industry[13] as an addition to their enjoyment of Matlock Bath even if they were unsuccessful in persuading the Arkwrights to let them inside the buildings.[14] Those who saw the mill as an intrusion seem to have overlooked its impact on the river and its rugged setting within the dale, the mill weir creating a large tranquil pond where once there had been rapids and fast flowing water. The level of the river was raised throughout the length of the Matlock village and in a later period the resort made good use of the opportunities this intervention had provided for boating, swimming and water based events.

The first industrial building on what is now the Masson Mill site was a paper mill Figures 28 and 29. In October 1768 the Lords of the Manor of Matlock gave George White, Gentleman, 'liberty to build Mills, erect Water Wheels upon a parcel of land adjoining to the River Derwent called the Masson at or near the Decoy.'[15] Soon after White entered into a partnership with Robert Shore and in March 1770 they purchased the land from William Milnes on which they built the paper mill.[16]

The development of this enterprise was known to Adam Wolley who explains that the paper mill at Matlock (near the New Bath) was built by Messrs Robert Shore of Snitterton and George White of Winster in 1771 with some additional buildings in 1772. In the same year the Manor Court granted them a 25 year lease to convey water to the mill. This was water from the river to power the mill.[17] It would appear that the first power supply proved inadequate because in 1773 or 1774, the partners agreed a 21 year lease at a £1-1-0 rent per annum with Edmund Hodgkinson for the privilege of erecting a weir for the use of the paper mill.[18] The partners made and sold paper until March 1777 at which point White ceased to be an active partner. He leased his half of the enterprise to Robert Shore.[19] The description of what is to be leased indicates the scale the undertaking had achieved by this date. It included half the mill along with 'all engines, wheels, presses, vats, drying houses, warehouses and all other materials utensils appurtenances and also the sole benefit of all apprentices bound to the sd George White and Robert Shore' and an adjoining close, here called Richardson's Pingle. All of this was leased to Shore for three years from January 1778 at a yearly rent of £200. It was agreed the large stock of paper should be sold to pay debts but while Shore sold the paper he did not pay White his share; nor did he pay him the rent. By March 1779 Shore owed White £650 and though he gave White a bond payable that September, White received nothing.

Shore was the manager of the Duke of Devonshire's copper mine at Ecton and in a position of authority and trust but in 1779 the Duke's auditor found that Shore was behind with the payment of wages, heavily in debt and in May he was forced to agree to the conveyance of all of his property to the Duke's trustees to meet the £3,600 he owed; a further debt of £1,400 was owed to other creditors. The following year in 1780 the creditors put Shore's half share of the property at Matlock Bath up for sale[20] and it was at this point that the paper mill and adjoining land came into Arkwright's hands.[21]

Meanwhile in 1778 Hodgkinson had purchased the Willersley Farm Estate from Edwin Lascelles for £6,800 and within a week sold it on to Thomas Hallett Hodges of Wirksworth for £12,050. Four years later in April 1782, Hodges sold it for £14,864 to Richard Arkwright who paid £6000 immediately and took a mortgage from Hodges for the remaining sum of £8,864 for a year. Arkwright took possession in 1783 when he had paid off the mortgage and interest. He now owned land on each bank of the river and in 1783-84 built his cotton mill beside the river just below the paper mill, the tailrace of the paper mill becoming the headrace of the cotton mill. The mill appears to have taken its name from the close on which it was built though it is not clear whether the name Masson was associated with the mill from the outset. Dr Stanley Chapman has suggested the mill was probably designed and built by Samuel Stretton of Nottingham (1750-1811) and that the water power engineering would probably have been in the hands of Thomas Lowe (1748-1823) also of Nottingham, two men known to Arkwright from other mill developments.[23]

Arkwright continued to work the paper mill. The Reverend Richard Warner writing in 1801 notes that the paper manufactory, added 'to the bustle in this part of the vale'. About thirty employees are 'making the blue, brown, and writing paper. Old ropes cut into small pieces, untwisted and g und, form the material of which the first article is made; coarse cotton and white rags are used for the second. Here it is manufactured, pressed, separated, sized, dried, and packed; and the process is so rapidly performed, that two men can make ten reams in a day.'[24] His description of the products and raw materials reminds us of the almost symbiotic relationship between paper making and cotton spinning; the one using waste cotton to produce paper; the other using paper to wrap bundles of spun yarn on their way to market.[25]

By 1838 when Richard Arkwright junior leased the paper mill to George Simons of Matlock for 21 years at a yearly rent of £90 it was making paper and paste board.[26] In 1868, 38 people were employed here.[27] George Simons retired from the partnership of George Simons, Henry Simons (his son) and John Pickard in 1874 and 5 years later the surviving partnership was dissolved. John Pickard carried on the business alone,[28] retaining the name Simons and Pickard until the lease reverted to the English Sewing Cotton Co. in March 1901. The paper mill was later demolished so providing space for the expansion of the cotton mill.

Samuel Need's House and Chapel

In 1771 soon after Shore and White had built their mill, Richard Arkwright had begun to build his first water powered cotton mill at Cromford. One of his partners and financial backers in this enterprise was Samuel Need, a wealthy Nottingham hosier and close associate of Jedediah Strutt. No doubt intent on keeping an eye on his investment at Cromford, and being a religious and philanthropic man Need built a chapel to serve the local community and an adjoining house. The house and chapel were beside the river, at the southern gateway to the Matlock gorge.[29] The chapel opened in August 1777; the event was recorded;[30] 'on Wednesday night the elegant new chapel, lately erected near Matlock Bath was opened for the first time to a numerous and very genteel audience. A most excellent sermon was preached upon the occasion by the Rev Mr Lester, who, we hear, is appointed by the founder as preacher in ordinary at that place.' In 1850 a new schoolroom was attached to the north end of the Chapel replacing 'a small and inconvenient' one which had been opened beneath the building in 1809.[31] Need died in 1781 and the house was empty when Richard Arkwright began to build at Masson, a short distance to the north of it, in 1783.

FIGURE 27. **Glenorchy Chapel and house, from the road, 1930s and a view of the house from the river with Woodbank (now Cromford Court) just visible in the background.**

The house and chapel were built by Samuel Need. The property was demolished for the 1960s A6 road widening scheme. The chapel headstone survives, thanks to the timely intervention of two generations of Lawrence Hodgkinson who bought the stone from the demolition contractors and built it into the wall beside the road to Masson House. It records the date 1777; the house was built at the same time.

The family of Harry Gill; private collection.

Glenorchy house and chapel[32]

Samuel Need's house and chapel are said to have fallen into disuse until they were discovered and purchased by Lady Glenorchy (1741-1786) in 1784, who thereby added Matlock Bath to the cluster of independent places of worship to which she had devoted her life.

Lady Glenorchy lived in the house from 1785 until her death a year later. She bequeathed the house and the chapel to her protégé the Rev Jonathan Scott together with a £5000 fund for the training of preachers and for evangelism in the area. The first minister was the Rev Joseph Whitehead, succeeded by Scott himself in 1793 until his death in 1807. Lady Glenorchy required that her heirs to the chapel and the congregation who met in it 'shall pay strict attention to this my will, concerning the Doctrines and Discipline to be observed therein' and only those 'who give

satisfactory evidence to the minister and to one another that they are the true followers and disciples of Christ by an explicit confession of their faith' shall be ministered to by the chapel.

The house achieved a certain fame in the nineteenth century with the birth there of George Newnes (1851-1910), regarded as the pioneer of modern journalism, who made a fortune from *Tit-Bits* and subsequently a clutch of other publications including *The Strand* magazine. He became a baronet in 1895. Newnes retained an interest in the locality, in 1893 investing heavily in the Matlock Steep Gradient Tramway. Until well into the 1960s there were older Matlock residents who regarded him with awe and affection, claiming him as Matlock's most famous son. The last sermon was preached at Glenorchy in 1946. The house and chapel were purchased for demolition in 1957 and became early casualties of the A6 road widening scheme.

The Cotton Mill

The cotton mill Richard Arkwright built at Masson was the project of a confident, experienced mill builder. Unlike his two earlier mills in Cromford which used the relatively easily controlled flow of water from a lead mine drainage sough and later the Bonsall Brook, this mill was powered by the River Derwent, a river with a reputation for being wild and

FIGURE 28. **Masson Mill and its surroundings, pen, ink and wash on paper, George Robertson, late 1790s.**

This early view of the mill at Masson shows the building as it was first constructed by Richard Arkwright in 1783 and before it was raised to incorporate an additional storey and a pitched roof. At the same time a second wheel was added. Warner's description[33] confirms that these changes had taken place by June 1801. In the foreground, the square building was later known as the manager's house and may always have had this function. By 1872 it had become two cottages.[34] Beyond Masson stands the paper mill built by George White of Winster and Robert Shore of Snitterton in 1771 which was driven by a single water wheel. The wooden vertical slats of the drying house where the paper would have been hung to dry are clearly shown. On the hillside, set back within a garden, what became known as Masson House (now Old Masson House) was built sometime between 1784 and 1792 probably by William Lovatt, who was the proprietor of the New Bath Hotel from 1766 to 1788. The stable block at the roadside was added on land purchased from Richard Arkwright in 1793 when Adam Wolley, (1758-1827), local solicitor and antiquarian, owned the house.[35] Masson Houses, the large block of housing which dwarfs the stables is traditionally believed to have been built as an apprentice house. The Arkwrights did not employ parish apprentices though they did take on some young people as indentured apprentices to learn the skills of cotton manufacture who could have lived there. Certainly this was the tradition understood by generations of local residents now deceased; but there is no formal evidence that this was the case. Alternatively the building could have served as a Barracks, the term used elsewhere (as for example in Milford and Cromford) to describe the building which provided lodgings for workers who were working away from home. Richard Arkwright sold Masson Houses in 1832. If Robertson's drawing is accurate then some time in its life, and certainly by the early 1900s, the block had lost its upper storey, Figure 139. In its final form the building was four cottages but with only two front entrances, each one serving two dwellings. All the roadside property was demolished for the A6 road widening.

Arkwright Society collection.

unpredictable.[36] Its temper is more restrained now; the Derwent dams, Howden, Derwent and Ladybower, which were built at the head of the valley in the twentieth century, hold back millions of tons of water in reservoirs supplying water to Sheffield, Derby, Nottingham and Leicester. In building a cotton mill on the Derwent Arkwright was following the example of the Strutts in Belper and Milford and the Evans' in Darley Abbey who by 1783 had both taken this step on sites lower down the river.

In the pages which follow we offer an account of the early years of Masson Mill interpreted through some of the illustrations which have survived from this period and beyond. The later development of the mill, from 1874 until its closure in 1991, is described in Chapter 11, see page 141.

FIGURE 29. **Arkwright's Mills at Matlock, albumen print with handwritten title, 1870s.**

The photograph shows the original mill now with the east-west extension which dates from the second quarter of the nineteenth century.[37] Note the hipped roof of the paper mill in the background

John Bradley collection.

FIGURE 30. **Masson House, watercolour, Mary Constance Clarke, 1836 and Masson House, family photograph 'Aunt Charles House, Matlock', before 1885.**

After Adam Wolley's death in 1827 Charles Clarke 1788-1863 occupied Masson House. He had married Wolley's youngest daughter Anne in 1821. He worked in Derbyshire as a barrister and subsequently as a judge and became a Deputy Lieutenant. He extended the house and gardens and raised the ground in front behind what, in 1838, Adam described as 'a lofty wall recently built up from the road' so creating the terrace seen here. In the 1970s Clarke's wall was set back and replaced by the present one to accommodate the road widening. Mary Constance Clarke was Charles Clarke's niece. The date of the photograph is not known. In 1885 Anne, Charles Clarke's widow, died and the house was sold.

Mr Miller.

FIGURE 31. **View of Masson Mill, Cromford, gouache on paper, George Robertson, late 1790s.**

It is probable that George Robertson, (1776-1833), painted this view for use by the decorators at the Derby China Manufactory where his work was reproduced in intricate detail. He is thought to have made sketches in the area from about 1797 and the surviving examples of his art suggest his scenes possess a high degree of topographical accuracy.

Derby Museums and Art Gallery.

FIGURE 32. **Detail from Drawing Frames, undated but probably 1830s.**

Private collection.

CHAPTER FIVE

Lead mining, Spar-turning and the Museums

The Lead Legacy,[1] a modern appraisal reminds us that Derbyshire supported 'one of the largest, richest and longest-worked orefields in Britain' and that this country was 'Europe's main supplier of lead for many centuries'. The industry was important in the Matlock area from at least the Roman period. It declined in the nineteenth century, but its imprint on the landscape remains in the irregular small hollows with associated hillocks of mine waste or lines of capped shafts in local fields which mark the course of lead veins worked under the surface. Finding the specialised plant communities characteristic of some lead mine spoil heaps needs closer observation. This account does not cover the history of the many mines in Matlock Bath nor how the industry in Derbyshire was of such economic importance that it was governed by its own laws and customs, but offers some examples of the local mining communi-ty's involvement with the development of Matlock Bath and its tourist indus-try and of the mineral products and the mining legacy which contributed to the visitor's interest and entertainment.

John Macky set the miner in the local scene.[2] 'Here are no Inhabitants except for a few Groovers, who dig for Lead Oar [sic] and whose Hutts [sic], I presume may be like the Houses in Wales; the biggest I saw was no bigger than a good Hogstye in my Country.' Defoe[3] travelling a few miles away at Brassington had been amazed to meet a miner's wife and family whose home was a cave and to discover that her five children were the third generation

FIGURE 33. **Half stereograph dated about 1860.**

Purports to show a miner's cottage at Buxton, perhaps the type of dwelling Macky had seen and described but it is probable that it shows one of the houses built by lime kiln workers and wrongly attributed by the photograph's printer.

John Bradley collection.

to be born there. These groovers, the lead miners, and their way of living and working, provided a source of amazed interest to the new explorers of the valley, explorers whose rambles often followed the worn paths which linked miners' homes to their mines.

FIGURE 34. **Matlock Baths from the Guilderoy Mine at the head of the Vale, Derbyshire, watercolour, pen and brown ink, William Day, probably 1789.**

Prominent in the centre foreground of the scene below is the gable end of the Hascom Leys farmhouse later known as The Villa. The largest single building to the right of it is the Temple and curving away into the distance is the terrace of buildings which formed the Old Bath situated on what is now the Temple Road car park. This busy scene, carefully drawn, shows men and women at work above the lead mine. William Hauptmann[4] called Day's picture 'a primer of contemporary mining activities'. A seated woman is shown breaking ore free from stone using a bucker, a flat hammer, while the man standing behind her wields a heavier hammer to break up larger lumps; near the edge of the terrace a woman washes or sieves ore in a tub. Against the bottom centre of the picture are three rectangular 'boxes' to one of which is attached a metal rod with a ring at the end. The small stooping figure in the background is holding a similar ring. It is supposed that the rod was used to lift the end of the 'box' to shake it and so separate ore from waste. Lying about are half a dozen shallow, oval, ridged trays or baskets, purpose unknown but their design suggests they could have been used for panning. The large wooden trough or tank was probably for water collection and storage. On this hillside level, in about 1810 Masson Cottage, and in 1839 Guilderoy, were built. For more than fifty years Guilderoy used one of the mine's shafts for its sewer.

Yale Centre for British Art, Paul Mellon Collection.

FIGURE 35. **A Scene in Derbyshire; Industrial Works spanning a River, watercolour, pen and black and grey ink, unconfirmed attribution to William Day, date unknown.**

The artist looks down the river; the pale grassy green patch in the break in the cliffs is wooded now but it is an identifiable feature in the grounds of Willersley Castle located more or less in line with the weir which directs water to the Masson mills. The apparatus shown here is part of a water engine for pumping water out of a lead mine. There were several such pumps along the valley in the second half of the eighteenth century where lead veins had become unworkable because of flooding.[6] They all worked in the same way. The miners built a small weir on the river to direct water to an undershot water wheel. In this view it is assumed that the wheel is hidden behind the tree on the right. A linked chain of rods or rails[7] attached to a crank on the axis of the wheel was moved backwards and forwards as the wheel turned. The earlier paper mill weir at Masson was constructed in 1773 and it is clear from several 1770s accounts that an engine or engines for unwatering lead mines such as this one worked with the paper mill weir in place. There is no clear evidence of the scale of the paper mill weir but it is likely that when the cotton mill was built ten years later, in 1783-84, a taller, more substantial weir was constructed in more or less the same place[8] to serve both the cotton and paper mills. Its effect was to form a pond upstream which drowned some of the mine draining sites putting the pumping equipment out of use.

Yale Centre for British Art, Paul Mellon Collection.

William Tyler's description of a Water Engine[5]

'In the mountain are several lead mines one of which was opened a few years ago, we went into it as it was a sight entirely new to us all, but what pleased us most was the contrivance for raising water from the lower part of the mine by a pump that is worked by a Water Engine on the river at a place that is near a quarter of a mile distant from where it is to raise the water. The extended line from the Wheel to this engine was at first sight thought to be only posts and rails to divide the meadow where they are set up, till we perceived the Railings in a regular motion advancing and then receeding [sic], which motion is performed

by a crank in the Axis of the Water wheel. These rails are strongly bound together with iron bars, and at equal distances are posts on which rollers are affixed to prevent the friction that would have been caused by sliding over an immovable surface, by this means the pump is more easily worked, which throws up a vast quantity of water at each stroke.

On the other side of the hill is another engine of the same kind, where a chain or railing does not move in a direct line but is made to turn round the hill and yet seems to work with the same ease as the other.'

There were many ways by which Matlock Bath's lead miners were able to exploit their skills and satisfy the visitors' curiosity. The mines themselves became assets of the tourist business when worked-out sections were formally opened as show caves and miners or ex-miners took on new roles as cavern guides. Geology was one of the new sciences. It captured the enquiring minds of the lunar men and the magpie minds of the fashionable who sought to fill their display cabinets with mineral specimens. These were sold as souvenirs, and as 'tempting additions to the visitor's cabinet of curiosities'.[9]

FIGURE 36. **Box of geological samples.**

This box was sold from Mawe's Museum, Matlock Bath and is dated to the 1840's. Such boxes came with a handwritten catologue of the contents.

Derbyshire County Council Buxton Museum and Art Gallery.

Serious mineral collectors are known to have transported boxes of geological samples from the area using the services of local guides and dealers. Josiah Wedgwood in his endless search for materials to improve the quality of his ware, came himself and on a visit with his father-in-law found a good source of 'carbonate of barium' in a mine near Matlock. On being told by James Brindley (1716-1772) that workmen at the lead mines near Matlock threw all their spar and rubbish into the brook to remove the dirt he exclaimed 'I long to be fossiling amongst them.'[10] Later Mawe's Museum advertised 'Mineral Cabinets, arranged and described, for the use of Learners, at from Two to Twenty Guineas each.'[11]

Matlock Bath's principal show caves

With the exception of the High Tor Grotto, the caves had all been lead mines. Cumberland Cavern was opened in the late 1700's, the Rutland Cavern in 1810 and the Fluor Spar Cavern by 1818. The High Tor Grotto, the Devonshire Cavern and the Speedwell Mine opened in the 1820s. When High Tor was developed as a visitor attraction, old mines worked from the surface there were introduced as the Fern and Roman Caves. Masson Cavern opened later and, along with the Rutland, is still shown on the Heights of Abraham. Mawe's Royal Museum opened the Gaskin Mine, with an entrance near the south end of Brunswood Terrace, but it was a short-lived venture, as was Victoria Mine in the Royal Pavilion grounds.

Johnson Grant's visit to William Smedley's cavern, (later known as 'Cumberland Cavern')[12]

'Saxton's Inn, at Matlock, though I believe not so fashionable as Mason's, [the Old Bath] we found excellent and cheap. After paying our bill for a night, and bathing in the pellucid cistern of the Matlock water, we walked next morning, July 5th, to Smedley's shop of spar and petrifactions, some in the natural state, and some ingeniously manufactured into vases, cups, seals and all varieties of furniture. In company with this virtuoso, [we] went to explore a subterraneous, deep recess and cavern, on the top of an adjacent hill. This is not only wonderful, on account of *the natural appearance it exhibits, but in having been the labour of one man, our ingenious and indefatigable guide, who, cleared away, with his own hands, in an Herculean toil of seventeen years, all obstructions from the bottom of the long passages, and caves and dungeons, that extend many hundreds of yards into the bottom of the earth. This place was discovered in a search for lead ore, which, with snow fossil, spar, and petrifaction specimens, as he proceeded, rewarded his assiduity, and soothed his labour.'*

We have emphasised the ways in which the lead miners and their families embraced the new opportunities which came their way but the relationship between lead mining and tourism, was not always harmonious. The miners took whatever opportunities their industry offered to interest visitors in the mines and their products and to profit by it. But the relationship worked both ways and miners found their long held rights under mining law threatened as the new entrepreneurs developed their land to offer the baths and pleasure grounds which served Matlock Bath's patrons. Jonathan's Gilbert's relationship with the miners is summarised in the panel which follows.

FIGURE 37. **The Heights of Jacob Fluor Spar Cavern, postcard, about 1910.**

The Heights of Jacob[13] was the name given to the area around the entrance to the Fluor Spar Cavern which was created when Jacob Raynes took over the cavern; when he died in 1904 it was reported to have been in his hands more than 40 years. There is a sign beside the figure on the lower level generously announcing SEATS FREE. It was no doubt a welcome sight for those who had just made the steep climb to reach the cavern.

Jonathan Gilbert and the miners[14]

The Heights of Abraham pleasure ground on Masson Hill proved to be a contentious issue during the period when Jonathan Gilbert was its owner. There was a long history of lead mining on the hill with records from as early as 1470 for the Nestus Mine from which Gilbert continued to obtain some ore. At the same time he discouraged other miners from exercising their rights on Masson, although Derbyshire's lead mining law allowing miners to establish a mine in a mining liberty except under dwelling houses, highways, orchards and gardens regardless of the ownership of the land.

He allowed access to the Heights for recreation, free to local people and at a charge to visitors and in 1823 the first case was to do with access. It led to prosecution for riot and assault when Gilbert claimed a group of men were 'determined to make it [his road] a public way' and his request for them to turn back was met with refusal and abuse, William Tommison 'tore his neckcloth and shook him violently' urged on by William Smedley. Perhaps the outcome in this case cemented an attitude of animosity to Gilbert personally because the two men were found guilty and sentenced to imprisonment in the House of Correction at Wirksworth. Their companions were bound over to keep the peace. Tommison offended again and was fined this time for digging in Gilbert's Fountain Gardens, and, unable to pay, was imprisoned for debt.

The following year the issue was less straight-forward. The case essentially turned on the definition of the term garden. On the face of it the defendants Edwin Bown and others were charged with damage, cutting down trees, and digging up the gravel road. The court heard Dr Johnson's definition of a garden and witnesses offered varied assessments of the site - a plantation; cows grazed there; a pleasure ground; a wood; gillyflowers and roses grew there; a highly ornamental ground; not a garden above thirty yards from the house – and they were probably all correct for some part of the hill at some time. The defendants were supported by the barmaster, Mr Anthony Alsop who considered the Heights to be mineral ground and by the deputy barmaster Francis Hursthouse but his position was compromised when he was forced to admit that he had proposed to Gilbert that if Gilbert gave up his share in a mine on Masson, Bown would give up mining in his ground. It transpired that Bown had been paid by John Vallance from Mawe's Museum who wished to open a show cavern in the mine in which Gilbert had a share. And though Gilbert's position was also weakened by the claim that he made only a token effort to work his own mines in his grounds, the judge, more familiar with Cornish mining law and misinterpreting

Derbyshire mining law found in Gilbert's favour.

He summarised the miners' view that if this ground was mineral ground it could not be appropriated for a garden but gave his own opinion that if mines were not worked for a length of time, the owner had a right to appropriate the land to a garden. His judgement was that 'there was no occasion to root up a tree; it was wanton trespass, but the plaintiff does not appear to have sustained any great damage, and a moderate satisfaction will suffice.' Bown was fined and Gilbert was awarded £10 damages. Subsequently Bown helped Vallance to develop the Devonshire Cavern as a show cave in old workings on the west side of Masson.

The judgement in Gilbert's prosecution of Thomas Kirkland and others which finally came to court in 1833, reversed the earlier decision. This time the defendants were accused of re-opening an old shaft near Gilbert's house in 1831 and doing more damage than was necessary. Aged miners, some whose memories stretched back before 1784 when the ground was common land, gave testimony on when and where mines had been worked and recalled oats, wheat and potatoes growing on the hillside before trees were planted. Joseph Paxton, the Duke of Devonshire's head gardener was called by Gilbert. He described the Heights as a pleasure ground. George Stafford, gardener to Richard Arkwright, called it rough wood with about 4 acres under good cultivation with new shrubs and flowers recently planted. The jury forestalled any summing up by the judge on this occasion and made its decision quickly; their verdict was for the defendants. They were entitled to mine lead there. The miners were awarded costs. Gilbert got a shilling in damages.

By the middle of the century little remained of the lead mining industry now evident through its principal legacy the show caves. The last serious attempt to mine lead in the area was many years later at Riber Mine, see photographs below.

FIGURE 38. **The Riber Mine, two photographs, about 1960.**

The Riber Mine was opened by the Johannesburg Consolidated Investment Company in 1952 on a site in Bath Fields approximately 200 metres up the path from the railway bridge arch near the cable car station. The mine proved uneconomic both for its original owners and for Derbyshire Stone Ltd who took it over in 1956. It closed in 1967. No further attempt has been made to revive Matlock Bath's oldest industry.

Reproduced with permission from the late Harry Higton.

By 1769, as this advertisement shows, shaping and polishing stone to create ornamental objects was already an established business in Matlock Bath and with a ready market among the well-to-do who could afford to drink tea and for whom vases were the new must-have. At this time Matthew Boulton of the Soho works in Birmingham and Josiah Wedgwood in his newly opened Etruria works near Newcastle-under-Line[15] [sic] were involved in what became known as vase mania, part of the rediscovery of classicism, largely among the fashionable, inspired by the Grand Tour. At first in 1768 Boulton bought vases from Wedgwood to mount in ormolu. Later finding

To be Sold,

At *Warmwalls Turnpike*, near *Matlock Bath*;

ALL Sorts of Marble Vases, Obelisks, Cups, Tea-Chests, Snuff-Boxes, Columns, Fineer'd Chimney-Pieces, &c. also Polish'd Petrefactions; being the Place where these Sort of Goods of all Kinds are made in the neatest Manner, by

Their humble Servant,

JOHN BOWN.

N. B. Wanted at the same Place a good Marble Sawyer, and a Polisher. They must turn well in the Lathe, and will meet with all proper Encouragement.

Derby Mercury, October 20th 1769.

these ceramics too fragile and difficult to handle he turned to fluorspar and marble from Derbyshire, in particular Blue John and these became a speciality which he sold to nobility and royalty at home and abroad.[16] [17]

Matlock Bath's trade grew and developed; in the range of products on offer; in the number of people it employed and in the sophistication of the sales pitches employed to tempt the visitor to buy.[18] The Museums of Matlock Bath were more shops than museums. They displayed some curiosities but they sold a range of goods from jewellery to fireplaces using marble, Blue John and other stones as well as specimens of minerals and crystals. Their products were fashioned in workshops in Matlock Bath and surrounding villages providing employment for cutters, turners, polishers and engravers.[19] For many years, the outstanding museum was that run by the Mawes. As a study by Hugh S. Torrens makes clear, though John Mawe (1766-1829)[20] had local roots having been born in Derby, he was in his early life a mariner and travelled widely. He acquired considerable knowledge as a collector of geological specimens and shells. In 1793 he became apprenticed to Richard Brown

(1736-1816) at his statuary and marble works in Derby and, in 1794 he married Brown's daughter Sarah and together with his father-in-law, Sarah and her brother Richard, he was involved in various enterprises including Museums in London, Scarborough, Cheltenham, Castleton as well as Matlock Bath. The latter, begun by Brown in a property near the New Bath in 1810 Figure 145 moved to the Parade in 1812 to occupy the former dining room of The Hotel.

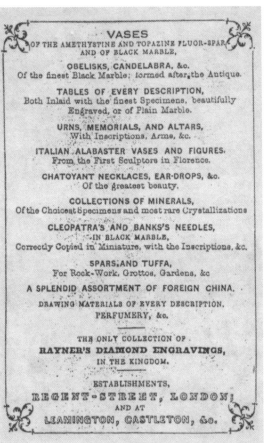

Part of an advertisement for Mawe's Museum from *The Matlock Companion*, 1832.

Mawe undertook collecting commissions for both Spanish and Portuguese royalty - hence his claim to be a 'Royal' Museum proprietor, and wrote books on mineralogy and collecting.[21] After John Mawe's death in 1829, his widow continued the business in Matlock Bath and soon after Queen Victoria's accession in 1837 was herself appointed 'Mineralogist to her Majesty'. She was assisted by William Adam from Cheltenham to whom we are indebted for the series of guide books, *The Gem of the Peak*, begun in 1838 and revised at intervals until 1857.[22]

The Matlock Bath museum trade was in the hands of a close knit circle of men who maintained a high level of expertise, their skills confined to a small coterie of craftsmen passed from one generation to another, they achieved a national reputation for the quality of their products. John Vallance who established the Central Museum in 1831 next door to Mawe's,

FIGURE 39. The objects shown here range in size from the gold broach and ear rings with a rose and forget me nots motif set in Ashford black marble to the 90cm high black marble ewer; the shallow spar tazza is 28cm high without its plinth. The miniature blue john milk pail, (7cm high) has a silver mount which is hall marked for Thomas Rodgers, cutler Sheffield, 1803. An inlay of daffodils, forget me nots and jasmine decorates the black marble platter (36cm diameter); for the pair of obelisks (46cm high) the motif is hawthorn and dog rose. All these items are located in Derbyshire County Council Buxton Museum and Art Gallery. The Blue John vase (about 45cm high without its plinth) is believed to be by John Vallance of Matlock Bath; it was viewed at the British Geological Survey, but was due to be returned to the Natural History Museum.

had been apprenticed to Richard Brown and later was agent for the Mawes.[23] John Buxton, a carpenter, worked for Vallance while he was managing Mawe's and after Mawe's death, set up his own successful museum at premises on the riverside at the south end of Museum Parade Figure 43. At some period of their history each of the three museums included Royal in its title. Vallance exhibited a wide range of black marble products at the Great Exhibition in 1851 including inlaid tables and vases along with urns, bowls and obelisks in fluor spar, a material to which he drew special attention and described as 'commonly called Blue John'. Samuel Rayner is credited with bringing diamond engraving on black marble 'to a high degree of excellence' while working for Vallance. Edward Bird, another specialist in black marble work whose workshop was on Fishpond Hill also exhibited in 1851.

There was intense rivalry between Vallance and Mawe, not a battle fought over professional skills in the mineral working trade, more to do with the lengths each was prepared to go to promote his business. Animosity was stoked by the guide books which championed the one and denigrated the other. Henry Moore was anti-Vallance and in *The Stranger's Guide,* 1837 described his portico see Figure 44 as a pair of huge obelisks supported on a pair of walking sticks or at most two slender bed posts. Fearing 'the bed-posts might be crushed to atoms by the vast load they are doomed to sustain' he exclaimed sarcastically 'What a wonderful architect!' Vallance's riverside Museum Gardens were 'Warts on the face of beauty' with artificial rocks and the 'humbug tale' of the 'celebrated royal rose-tree' which Vallance claimed had been planted where the Duke of York stepped into the garden from a trip on the river in 1815. 'His Royal Highness never set foot in the garden' was Moore's retort. Vallance's champion, *The Matlock Tourist,* published in 1838 by Henricus saved his contempt for Mawe's Royal Museum Library – 'a few commonplace books and supplied with two London newspapers and the Monthly Magazine…an apology for a library…an insult to royalty itself' where 'visitors pay sixpence per diem or two

FIGURE 40. **An obelisk.**

Probably from Mawe's portico, re-sited on the riverside land opposite the museum.

John Bradley collection.

shillings per week, each person.' He took issue with the name of Mawe 'being painted all over the Bath till it becomes wearisome to the sight' and with William Adam's practice of expecting visitors to buy something rather than 'indulging their curiosity in viewing these fine things'. They came to court over Adam's removal of a pavement sign which Vallance had fixed to Mawe's property, a case Vallance lost and for which he paid costs. Their feud aroused much local interest and even the 16 year old Augustus Arkwright, writing to his father Peter from HMS Barham in Malta Harbour in 1837[24] was keen to know how it was going. 'Does Matlock keep its gayety [sic] up. I expect there is more opposition than ever between the Museums. I suppose Mr Vallance's carries the day does it not.'

Spar and marble ornaments continued to be made and could still be bought in Matlock Bath well over a hundred years later but over time, cheaper trinkets replaced the products which had once found a ready market among the wealthy visitors of the earlier years and which now were no longer appropriate for the less well off who replaced them, Skills were lost. The cheaper Italian imports were blamed for the steady decline in the local industry.

Before the end of the eighteenth century, petrified objects produced in man-made petrifying wells, or 'encrusting wells' were added to the souvenir range Figure 41. It is not known when this practice began though Matlock Bath had been renowned for its fine examples of petrified vegetation at least since the early years of the century, see panel[25]. An associated trade developed making use of tufa the naturally occurring petrified stone for garden landscaping. Barker reported - 'many tons of tufa carried away for horticultural purposes' and claimed that he himself had ordered a few tons from the proprietor of Mawe's Museum 'to be sent to Earl of Mount-Norris's [sic] garden'.[26]

Petrifications in nature

Chambers drew attention to petrifactions occurring in nature. *'The beauty and elegance of the petrified ivy of Derbyshire with us has been long famous. In the mountains near Matlock-baths, in that county, there are many grottos which afford great quantities of this petrified ivy, as it is called, and of other incrustations of the same kind. The beauty of these caverns is scarce to be conceived; their roofs are hung with stalactitae and stalagmitae, in forms of clusters of grapes, and the incrusted plants are many of them as delicate and tender that they fall to pieces under the touch. It is very common in these places to see ivy creeping along the rock; in some parts the same branch will be found only incrusted in the common way; in other parts the strong matter will so penetrate its pores, that the wood and leaves shall appear wholly, petrified and in others the same branch shall be yet fresh and vegetating.'*

FIGURE 41. **Petrified objects, half stereograph, Alfred Seaman, about 1900.**

The production of petrified objects exploited the natural property of Matlock Bath's thermal spring water which formed a local curiosity, tufa rock. Miscellaneous objects, placed under a fine spray of the water gradually became encrusted by a layer of lime salts so that they appeared to be made of stone. Egg cups, birds' nests, hats and antlers were particularly popular subjects for petrifaction. Items had to be regularly turned to produce an even cover and to prevent them from sticking together but after about a year they acquired a reasonable coating and could be sold. The small grottoes and enclosed spaces in which this process took place, some of which were for production and some of which were for public display, came to be known as wells.

John Bradley collection.

FIGURE 42. **John Smith's Royal Museum Petrifying Well, photograph, about 1920.**

Sometime in the 1880s, the Smith family took over the Royal Museum business. The premises still included the riverside land opposite the Museum where boats could be hired and where this petrifying well stood. It was demolished during the road-widening of 1967-8 still in Smith family ownership. The first petrifying well, formed by the Boden family near the New Bath before 1800, Figure 143 was used as a production well by the Smiths.

Ken Askew collection.

There were at least seven petrifying well sites in use at various times in Matlock Bath's history. The Royal Museum Petrifying Well, shown above, survived in use until the road widening scheme of the 1960s. Its demolition marked the end of an era for one of the resort's stranger tourist industries.

CHAPTER SIX

The Hotel estate is broken up
and the resort expands

At the turn of the eighteenth century George Lipscombe,[1] who knew Matlock Bath intimately gave it a resounding endorsement. It had, he said, 'advantages superior to the majority of watering places'. There was 'gaiety without dissipation, activity without noise', it was 'tranquil without dulness, elegant without pomp, and splendid without extravagance. In it the man of fashion may at all times find amusement, the man of rank may find society by which he will not be disgraced, and the philosopher a source of infinite satisfaction.'

But in May 1803 its new, modern central showpiece, George Vernon's Hotel and its estate, was offered for sale by auction in London. Particulars of the property were distributed in Manchester, Liverpool and London as well as Derby, evidence of Matlock Bath's increasing fame as a resort. The advertisement indicates the scale of the Vernon investment. Despite the publicity no buyer was found. Ultimately the sale of the estate was both piecemeal and protracted. Some of the details are set out below.

In 1803 George Vernon's Matlock Bath estate stretched north westwards up from the river almost as far as Masson summit, a fine and ample canvas for his vision of hotel, pleasure grounds and bath. Step by step, the grand design was broken up. The sale of the property between the river and the upper slopes in parcels, many of which subsequently became building plots and the contraction of the bound-

Valuable FREEHOLD ESTATES,
MATLOCK BATHS, DERBYSHIRE.
———
TO BE SOLD BY AUCTION,
By Meffrs. SKINNER, DYKE, and CO.

On Thurfday the 12th of May, at twelve o'clock, at Garraway's Coffee-Houfe, 'Change-Alley, Cornbill, London, in one Lot ;

A Valuable and very Improveable FREEHOLD ESTATE, fituate on that beautiful Romantic and much Reforted Spot Matlock, on the River Derwent, in Derbyfhire, comprifing the fpacious Modern Structure

The HOTEL ;

With the moft capital Warm Baths, fuitable accommodations of Letting Rooms and Bed Chambers for near one hundred Perfons, Stabling for fifty Horfes, Coach Houfes, and every proper Building for carrying on the well eftablifhed Bufinefs of Tavern, Hotel, and Inn, erected within a few years at a confiderable expence, now in the occupation of Mr. Thomas Froggatt.

Alfo a Commodious DWELLING HOUSE and Offices in the poffeffion of William Barker, Efq. a neat convenient Houfe Let to Mr. Wild, a Dwelling Houfe and Shops to Mr. J. Bown, and about forty Acres of Arable and Grafs Land, all Let to Tenants at will, except a fmall part of the Eftate on Leafes which expire at Lady Day, 1808 ; the prefent clear Rents only amount to

Three Hundred and Ninety-two Pounds per Ann.

Alfo about Twenty Acres of WOOD LAND in hand, and feveral Valuable MINES of LEAD and LAPIS CALIMINARIS.

The Situation of Matlock is almoft univerfally known to be beyond all defcription for its beautiful Walks, Roads, Healthfulnefs of Country, and Celebrated Baths, which will ever render the Property of increafing value, and confequently well worth the attention of Gentlemen wifhing to realize

To be viewed by applying to Mr. Froggatt, at the Hotel, of whom Printed Particulars may be had ; at the Bell Inn, Derby ; of Mr. Drewry, Printer, Derby ; Mr. Wheeler, Printer, Manchefter ; Mr. Billinge, Printer, Liverpool ; Meffrs. Leigh, Braband, and Mafon, Solicitors, New Bridge-ftreet, London ; at the place of Sale ; and of Meffrs. Skinner, Dyke, and Co. Aldersgate-ftreet, London, where a plan and an Engraving of the Eftate may be feen.

N. B. Part of the Purchafe-Money may remain on Security of the Premifes.

Derby Mercury, 31 March, 1803.

aries of the pleasure ground, squeezing it higher up the hill, prepared the way for the next phase of the resort's development and the achievement of its modern footprint. Figures 43 and 45 describe some of the changes over the next 20 years. Significant for that next phase was the purchase of the Heights of Abraham by Jonathan Gilbert and of the Hotel's bath by his wife's uncle Samuel Richardson.

The sale of George Vernon's Matlock Bath estate[2]

The earliest known transaction was in 1799, when George Rawlinson bought a piece of the Hascom Leys Farm land on the Meadow Spot Close where he built his residence, Belle Vue. In July 1804, the year after the initial sale notice, a further attempt to sell the whole estate was also unsuccessful and when it was advertised again in November, it was divided into twelve lots. *The Times* offered the prospective buyer or buyers a range of inducements and hints for development. The Hotel itself might 'at very trifling expense be converted into 4 or 5 large and commodious lodging houses, which are much wanted in Matlock Bath'; the 'very heavy stream of water with a fall of near 40 feet' a feature of Lot 6, the Warm Bath, was seen as a potential source of power to drive a mill beside the Derwent; and for miners, great quantities of calamine might be expected to be got once the level was driven into the 'Nesto Pipe', one of the mines on the Heights of Abraham, 'about 5 fathoms of which only remain to be driven'. Later evidence suggests very few, if any, lots were sold although Lot 5, 'the small Piece or parcel of Land adjoining the turnpike-road and now used as a place for dung and for keeping fowls'[3] is not mentioned in later publicity. Perhaps somebody had seen a market opportunity.

In 1805 William Smedley, the same William Smedley who had developed the Cumberland Cavern, bought land to the south of Vernon's bath stretching up the hillside from the turnpike to Waterloo Road where Wellington House now stands. This purchase is of particular interest, because it is the first significant investment in development land in the heart of Matlock Bath by a local man with a background in the older economy of the valley. Smedley had been a lead miner and in his will of 1816 he is described as a petrifactioner. The family was upwardly mobile. His daughter Ann married James Pearson, a local man also from a mining background, who would describe himself as 'gentleman' in his will of 1838. Their family, sons William and James and son-in-law Edward Wheatcroft, all became property developers in Matlock Bath.

There was a new plan in 1808 when ten £500 shares were sold in a company formed to purchase the Hotel and Bath complex but 'The company's expectations were not met' and in 1809, 'The Hotel with the capital Warm Bath' was again offered for sale - no longer as a going concern and this time, in 19 Lots. From a newspaper notice of 1806 offering a letting, it is clear that by that date the Hotel terrace was already being occupied as separate houses. Mrs Meadows had been the tenant of Lot 3, (now The Princess Victoria, numbers 174-176 South Parade) in the advertisement of 1809. The detailed sale schedule (DRO, D161B/E55) now suggests Lot 19, the Hotel Bath, to be 'a most excellent situation for an Ale or Porter Brewery' with the arched bath if used as a cellar being 'capable of housing upwards of 500 barrels.' The 'lofty and truly elegant Assembly Room' over 'the large Coach House and Cellar, at the north [sic, south] end, though well calculated for the purpose for which it was intended, 'may be easily converted into one or two Houses'.

It is not clear how many lots were sold immediately. William Stone, a carpenter from Cromford, paid £105 for Lot 11, the Upper Stables in the upper yard which included 'the Post Horse Stables'. No potential bath keeper or brewer responded until three years later, in 1812, when Samuel Richardson, a banker from Derby bought the Bath. This was his second purchase from the Vernon estate; his first in 1810 was the first two bays of the Hotel (at the northern end) including the original New Inn. In the same year, Jonathan Gilbert, a surgeon from Derby, who was married to Richardson's niece, Martha, bought several lots including part of the Hotel, now no. 162-68 South Parade, adjacent to Richardson's purchase, and some Hascom Leys land. Meanwhile in 1808 Vernon had sold the Heights of Abraham to Benjamin Wyatt, architect and builder, from Sutton Coldfield for £3200. This sale included the lately erected Round House, today known as the Lower Tower(s), with its garden fenced out from the Heights of Abraham. This house is not mentioned in the 1803 sale particulars which might suggest that it was built by Vernon after 1803. Wyatt sold the Heights to Jonathan Gilbert and Richard Brown, in 1810 for £2600; a considerable loss on his investment. Gilbert later became the sole owner.

FIGURE 43. **Matlock Bath, from the Old Bath Terrace, drawn, engraved and published by H. Moore, Derby, about 1831.**

By 1831 'the Hotel' had come to be known as Museum Parade, its various buildings under different ownerships, as shops, museums and lodging houses. Prominent around the middle of the Parade is Mawe's Museum with its pretentious portico which was added in 1828 and the large projecting central window, a recent addition in 1831, which remains a conspicuous feature of the Parade today. The portico was a short-lived feature for it incited John Vallance to add an even larger portico when he created the neighbouring Central Museum in 1831. This part of the Parade may be seen in more detail in Henry Moore's drawing overleaf. In 1833 the authorities demanded the removal of both because they encroached on the pavement. The change of ownership of the land released by the Hotel estate sale encouraged developments along the riverside including the three storey building which became known as the Devonshire Hotel, Figure 44 and at the south end of the row the museum run by John Buxton, shown here in its original three-storey form and distinguished by MUSEUM written on the gable end. It was later rebuilt with only two storeys and was known as Fountain Cafe when it was demolished in 1967-68. On the hillside the luxuriant effect of Vernon's tree planting is striking. More building has taken place - highest on the hill to the left, is the Upper Tower(s), and in the trees lower down to the right, the earlier Lower Tower(s) which was in existence by 1808. The 'lofty' ash tree shown at Figure 29 is still prominent in the centre of the picture with Masson Cottage on the Upperwood Road level to the left. On Waterloo Road[4] Belle Vue and the two-storey 'Smedley Cottages' (later incorporated in the three-storey Wellington House) are shown and below them is the tall outline of Prospect Cottage believed to be built on land which Jonathan Gilbert purchased from the Vernon estate. In the foreground of this scene, to the left, is part of the Old Bath stables, now the Fishpond Hotel which remained in use in addition to the large block across the road on the present Pavilion site.

Private collection.

FIGURE 44. **Museum Parade viewed from the north. Henry Moore c. 1832.**

Except for the short lived porticoes seen here at Mawe's and Vallance's Museums, the Parade is easily recognisable. The three storey building on the left was a recent addition to the scene. It was known as the Devonshire when it was demolished in the 1960s.

The Heights of Abraham

In Jonathan Gilbert's ownership the Heights continued to be an important attraction for Matlock Bath's visitors supported in 1810 by the opening of a show cave called the Rutland Cavern. Earlier George Vernon had begun to drive an adit,[5] to the worked-out upper part of the Nestus Mine, perhaps intending to rework the mine for calamine. Gilbert completed the adit for use as a public entrance to the underground workings. Later when he built his residence, now known as the Upper Tower(s) close to the Cavern entrance, he enhanced the romantic style of the scene by using the same gothic style for the building as had been used for the The Tower now known as the Lower Tower(s) and added a castellated curtain wall to the cavern entrance.[6]

Jonathan Gilbert had tried to sell the Heights at auction in London in June 1825. The advertisement in *The Times*[7] described the property as 'the celebrated Heights of Abraham with the castellated Villa Residence called The Tower'. It did not sell and in 1833 he transferred the property to his son Samuel in exchange for assets elsewhere. Five years later in 1838 Samuel sold it to John Pechell and John Atkinson, who were described as merchants from Hull.[8] Their purchase now included 'two delightful Residences', one the principal residence the Lower Tower, where Samuel Gilbert had lived, and the other the Upper Tower, Jonathan Gilbert's house, with 'every convenience suitable for a small family' see plan, Figure 45; a four day sale of the contents of the two houses was advertised to follow.[9] The new owners also purchased land which included the site of the Guildereye mine on which, a year later, Pechell's residence, Guilderoy, was built.

The estate remained in the Pechell family for over twenty years[10], a period in which there were significant changes to life in Matlock Bath. The arrival of the railway as far as Ambergate in 1840 and nine years later to Matlock Bath, had brought a sudden transformation in the class and volume of visitors to the resort, a startling influx of day trippers. John Pechell's most conspicuous and lasting response to this new wave of customers was to add a new visitor attraction. In 1844, at a high point on the Heights of Abraham, a landmark prospect tower, the Victoria Tower, was built. It was said[11] to have offered 'one of the finest and most extensive panoramic views which nature anywhere presents.' And surely climbing up and down the tower's dark, tight spiral stair would have been a new exciting or alarming experience for the Victorian visitor. Pechell also built two new gothic style lodges as pay boxes for the Heights. 'A beautiful octogon'[12] was added on the original approach to the Heights above the original lodge, the other, West Lodge, at the top of West Bank, provided a new public entrance which is still in use today. The two marked a new lower boundary of the Heights; the final stage of the contraction of the estate to the area above Upperwood Road was completed by Robert Chadwick.[13] It has remained within this footprint to the present day but in 1984, in the long tradition of the resort offering new experiences for its visitors, a very modern entrance lodge was opened close to the railway station, the base station of the cable car, from which visitors are now transported high above the valley on their way to enjoy the attractions of the Heights.

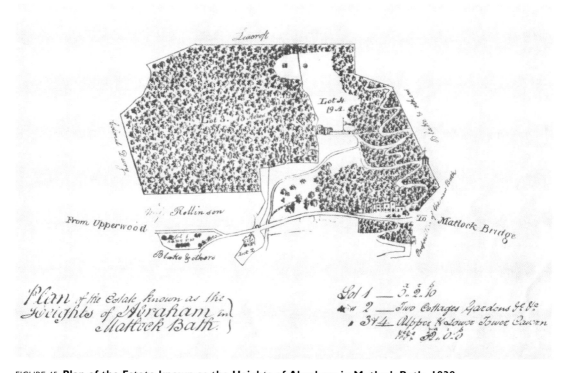

FIGURE 45. **Plan of the Estate known as the Heights of Abraham in Matlock Bath, 1838.**

This plan was used when Samuel Gilbert put the Heights of Abraham estate up for sale in 1838. It illustrates clearly the form of the original zig-zag walk created by Stephen Simpson within the narrow confines of his enclosure allotment and the short branch which was added to link the route to the Rutland Cavern and the Upper Tower. Lot 1 is the corner plot between Ember Lane, which ran to Bonsall, and Upperwood Road where later Devonshire Cottage was built. Lot 2 shown as two cottages, later to become three, was much modified subsequently to form the present castellated The Beeches on Upperwood Road. Lot 3 was the plantation on the Heights of Abraham. Lot 4 was the Heights of Abraham pleasure ground including the Upper Tower as well as the Lower Tower and the Rutland Cavern. Note that at this date the Heights of Abraham estate still extends below the Key Pasture bridleway, now known as Upperwood Road, with the sharp bend at the top of what is now Waterloo Road still forming part of the zig-zag walk.

Derbyshire Record Office D127 M/T 12.

FIGURE 46. **The Upper Tower Tea Gardens, postcard, about 1910.**

A closer view of the Upper Tower on the Heights of Abraham with a group of visitors at the Tea Gardens taking 'Teas and Refreshments at Moderate Prices'.

Tony Holmes collection.

FIGURE 47. **The cable cars lifting visitors across the valley.**

The cable car base station is visible in the trees at the foot of the slope to High Tor. Riber Castle can be seen on top of the hill in the background and below Starkholmes spreads across the hillside.

Photograph, 2004, Heights of Abraham.

More entertainment and better connections

The end of the Napoleonic War in Europe in 1815 brought a change in the pattern of tourism. Now wealthy and dedicated travellers could choose to tour on the continent again where the German spas had become the new fashionable destination. Granville described in 1841 that their place in Matlock Bath was taken 'principally…by people of the class of farmers and small landed proprietors.'[14] They came in larger numbers but for shorter stays. He classed Matlock Bath as holding 'an inferior grade' in the scale of watering places but as 'a summer retreat …superior to Buxton itself.' With the sale of Vernon's estate, the range of facilities offered to these new visitors altered. Until the early years of the nineteenth century most visitors to Matlock Bath had been accommodated in its principal establishments, the Old Bath, the New Bath and the Hotel. Now there were more lodging houses and more shops, some as a result of the division of the Hotel buildings into individual enterprises; others as new buildings added to the riverside frontage and on the hillside. In 1819 the resort's road system took on its present form.[15] The turnpike road which ran close to the front of the New and the Old Baths was diverted to the lower 'A6' level and short links of new road were built to connect the two. For the Old Bath the connection was Temple Road. The effect of the diversion at the south end is seen in Figure 60.

FIGURE 48.

View looking north with the Old Bath on the left, aquatint, Henry Moore, 1830.

A carriage and four passes the obelisk which stood at the junction of Temple Road with the turnpike after the turnpike had been diverted in 1819 to the level shown in the foreground here. It is believed that the obelisk was added at this time to alert travellers to the new access road.

Private collection.

The 'well frequented turnpike [was now] in the direct line from London to Manchester'[16] and the former New Inn (Hodgkinson's today) had become the principal coaching house. In the summer of 1835 'the following coaches ran through Matlock Bath:-

'A mail coach from London to Manchester, arriving at half-past eleven a.m., and returning from Manchester through Stockport, Buxton and Bakewell shortly after 2 p.m.; the "Royal Bruce," from London, through Nottingham and Derby to Manchester, between eleven and twelve a.m., returning at half past five; the "Peveril of the Peak," the like route and times; the "Peak Ranger," from the "Greyhound," Cromford, through Bakewell and Ashford, to Buxton, passing through the Bath at nine a.m. and five p.m.; the "Lord Nelson" from Nottingham at half past two p.m.; and from Manchester about three p.m. (evidently two coaches of the same name); the "Lady Nelson" at a quarter past ten a.m., and from Manchester twelve noon; the "Star" from Birmingham, through Tamworth, Ashby, Derby, and Belper, at nine in the morning, and from Sheffield, through Baslow and Bakewell, at a quarter

FIGURE 49. **The grand staircase in the Rutland Cavern, c1850.**

Private collection

to five in the evening; the "Quicksilver," the same route as the "Star," from Sheffield at ten a.m. and from Birmingham, by Lichfield and Burton, at four p.m.'[17]

Twenty years earlier more local services were already being advertised, to Buxton via Bakewell and, in competition, by Timothy Greenwood's 'new fast chariot' to Buxton via Newhaven.[18]

As we have shown Matlock Bath's clientele had over many years passed their time in pursuits such as bowls and billiards and, in the season, Assemblies at the Old Bath[19] where, 'when Matlock was a crowded watering place…danced the youth and beauty of the midland counties.' They walked by the river on Lover's Walk, took a turn round the New Bath Green to view the scenery and call at the spar shop, strolled along Temple Walk, perhaps stopping to choose a new bonnet ribbon at Miss Milns' repository or took their sketch books to capture a view. Some came regularly and met friends and acquaintances there, discoursed about the scenery and gossiped over tea or chocolate at the Temple or the Boat-House, arranging to meet later at a dance or a concert and, if tomorrow would be fine, planning to hire donkeys to carry them round the district. The more energetic climbed the steep hillsides or rowed on the river, wandered through Willersley's grounds or made excursions to local places of interest such as Haddon Hall and Chatsworth House. There was fishing and sometimes it seems game shooting.[20] On inclement days as Josiah Wedgwood described, parties of friends occupied themselves in their lodgings.

FIGURE 50. **The Romantic Rocks, Matlock, Derbyshire, 1848.**

Private collection

The scenery and many of these pursuits continued to beguile the visitors but in the early years of the nineteenth century new attractions were offered to relieve them of their sixpences and shillings. Sometime before 1818 the Dungeon Tors, (later called the Romantic Rocks) were adopted as a commercial venture and added to the visitor's list of things to see or sketch. As early as 1734, Dr Thomas Short of Sheffield[21], had drawn attention to the resort's natural features and particularly to these jumbled rocks behind the Old Bath which were for him 'like the Ruins of some frightful Mountains tumbled down'. In his day they could be reached only with difficulty scrambling over rocks and through brambles and that was still the case when Mr Rooke visited them in 1793.[22] After their adoption Moore[23] was impressed by their 'wild disorder' but disgusted by the 'wall and gate that checks the forcible effect of the first view'. Six years later Ebeneezer Rhodes, railing against being charged to move anywhere in Matlock Bath added 'There is something extremely ludicrous in the idea of locking up rocks…with a paling of six feet high, and exhibiting them for *"sixpence a-piece"*.'[24]

Some distinguished visitors

In the first half of the nineteenth century the scene was still enlivened from time to time by eminent visitors. On July 23rd, 1818 the Grand Duke Michael of Russia and his party stayed at the Old Bath

'and armed with Mr Moore's new publication of Picturesque Excursions in the Vicinity of Matlock proceeded to explore the romantic beauties of the place, and particularly of the Grand Rutland Cavern. For this purpose all the Ponies in the neighbourhood were put in requisition, on which the party ascended the Heights of Abraham...Their set out for this excursion formed a very singular and laughable spectacle, and appeared to afford much amusement to themselves; the Grand Duke mounted on a Donkey, which scarcely raised his feet from the ground, seemed to enjoy it much.... On leaving Matlock [Bath] about 3 o'clock in the afternoon...His Imperial Highness was greeted by the acclamations of the whole population of the place, who had assembled on Museum Row to witness his departure, and he acknowledged the compliment with the utmost affability and good humour.'

This is the occasion when other accounts suggest that the Grand Duke *'by one of those fine traits of high rank and high breeding reversed his position on the pony that his attention to the ladies [who were following behind him] might be marked by the highest possible compliment.'*

On August 25th 1825 the 6th Duke of Devonshire[25] recorded in his diary

'the finest day ever seen...set out for Matlock in my carriages – [Duke of] York & M in britchka and 4 with Forester on the box, next Mrs Fox & I in droschki and 3 next Kinnairds Louisa & ly Dorothy in Coach & six Bob Eden with Lindsey on the box. We went to the museum, and walked all over Mr Arkwright's grounds & went in the boat on the river. Coming home Mrs Fox and I were thrown out of the droschki! Such a tumble but not hurt.'

The Duke's carefree personal account makes no mention of the accompanying six out-riders, who with the coachman and postilions were in their dress liveries nor of the *'three remarkably fine horses abreast'* which drew the droschki, a recent acquisition from Russia. It is easy to imagine him showing it off at a slightly too fast pace, happily to no ill effect.

Preparations for the visit of Princess Victoria with her mother, the Duchess of Kent in October, 1832 produced *'festoons and garlands suspended between tall firs which lined the road, felled and brought on purpose from their native forests, - the Museum Parade was very striking; the Museums magnificent, being enriched with a profusion of flowers strung together in the form of crowns and wreaths, which hung gracefully from the windows and porticos, to form which, the county was scoured for ten miles around.'* In November 1839[26] the Duke and Duchess of Cambridge also passed through Matlock Bath making several purchases at the Museums and visiting the workshops connected with them. They were saluted by guns on the Heights of Abraham.

By 1818 Bown's public fruit garden was open on the hillside behind the Temple where 'company [might] gather delicious fruits at all times of the day' and where the proprietor 'gathers botanical plants of the neighbourhood'.[27] 'Tea and a variety of choice fruits' were on offer and the Devonshire Cavern in Upperwood, which was opened to the public in 1824, could be approached through the garden.

Opening former lead mine workings as show caverns proved to be the most widely exploited idea. The Rutland Cavern which Jonathan Gilbert opened on the Heights of Abraham in 1810, though not the first, emerged as the most popular and it remains an attraction to this day. Some of these ventures were short lived but several survived well into the twentieth century. Sir George Head[28] (1782-1855), an army man who in his retirement successfully turned his hand to travel writing, toured almost all of the caverns on his visit in the summer of 1835 and judged the Devonshire as adequate for demonstrating 'a good notion of subterranean scenery' and that the Rutland 'best repaid the pains of a visit'. He had a keen eye for detail and on his tour of the caves was stuck by the unfortunate lot of their custodians. There were so many 'cracks and gullies' open to visitors that competition forced the entry price down to one shilling out of which 'the poor people' acting as stewards found the cost of the ten or twelve candles needed to illuminate their cavern. At the Devonshire he was distressed by the actions of the guide's wife, who in her husband's absence, struggled up a steep ascent 'with a heavy infant in her arms'. It was, Head observed, poverty that drove her to these exertions.[29]

FIGURE 51. **The Cavern in the Alcove Walks, H. Moore.**

Private collection

In the early years of the new century Matlock Bath remained a flourishing watering place. The traditional clientele had become more difficult to attract as polite society resumed its affection for continental spas but there was increasingly a market to be developed among the professional and commercial classes. It is no surprise that in this climate investment continued to be made in the resorts bath facilities. When Samuel Richardson purchased the bath which had formed part of the Hotel estate he employed Joseph Wilson of Derby to landscape its grounds to include a grotto and small fountain where 'the water might be taken at all times of the day' and from which the Bath subsequently took its name.[30] A path winding up through the grounds offered visitors an attractive new approach to the Heights of Abraham's Lodge at the foot of the zig-zag walk. In the 1830s Jewitt[31] described Richardson's baths as a swimming bath and two hot baths each 'just adapted to contain one person', one for ladies and one for gentlemen. He complained of the poor design of the swimming bath, which fills the whole area except for a yard's breadth at the end communicating with the dressing rooms so that should a bather suffer cramp at the far end of the bath, help could only be given by somebody plunging into the water. He also regretted the absence of a Charity bath where 'the invalid, suffering under all the infirmities of nature, and bearing the additional weight of poverty and destitution, may resort to find solace from his woes, - an alleviation of his pains.' In Buxton the Buxton Charity provided such a service paid for by a levy of one shilling on each visitor on the first occasion of his dining in Buxton.[32] Later Benjamin Bryan adds some detail to the description of this bath house as with a 'low pitched arched roof in which were two circular openings, some two feet in diameter, for light and air, to which were fitted glazed dome-shaped movable frames, as covers.' A flight of narrow steps led down to the floor of the bath at the left hand side. He noted that this was the only bath in the resort which had at all times been open to the public.[33]

From village to residential community

The expansion of Matlock Bath in the early decades of the nineteenth century had included the shops and services needed by the tourists and the growing population of residents, but until 1842 the community lacked a church of its own. Matlock Bath's early family graves are in Matlock and Bonsall churchyards. Had Samuel Need's original intentions for the chapel he built at Masson Figure 27 developed as he had planned this might have played a more useful part in serving visitors and residents; but after its purchase by Lady Glenorchy[34] in 1784 it became home to a small and exclusive congregation of a severe Calvinist persuasion so that in the early nineteenth century it was neither large enough nor sufficiently mainstream in its mission to play more than a peripheral role in serving the demands of the Matlock Bath community. To attend a Church of England Sunday service it was necessary to take a coach or walk to the parish church at Matlock or go to Cromford or Bonsall. For those visitors who went on foot to Matlock, Barker explains 'the road is shortened by crossing the river at the boat-house'. At Cromford in 1838, the Chapel, which had been found to

FIGURE 52. Matlock Bath Church drawn by S Rayner, printed by W Kohler about 1842.

The church is shown here as it would have appeared soon after its completion and consecration in October 1842. The building was designed by Weightman and Hadfield of Sheffield in a style described at its consecration as 'early decorated'; 'chaste yet elegant.'. In the right foreground is one of Matlock Bath's small spar shops then run by Peter Smedley and with a petrifying well under the building on the left. The building on the right survives. In the background, the largest villa on the hillside is Guilderoy.

Private collection

be too small to accommodate its Cromford congregation and its Matlock Bath visitors, added balconies to provide more seating but within four years Matlock Bath had its own church and in 1858 the balconies were removed.

The church in Matlock Bath was built with funds raised by public subscription in a campaign in which George Withers Saxton, the proprietor of the New Bath had taken a leading part, acting as secretary of the committee.[35] It seems to have been a development that was widely appreciated with over 2,000 people, more than twice the estimated population of the settlement, joining the procession from the Old Bath to the site of the new church when the foundation stone was laid in June 1841. As the chairman of the Church committee, Mr Worsley reminded those assembled, 'the want of a temple wherein to worship God near their own homes, had long been felt by the inhabitants and more particularly by the visitors to Matlock Bath [of whom] many were induced to visit through sickness.'[36] In 1841 the estimated cost of the building was just over £2,000 but a further £1,100 was needed for an endowment and for a repair fund and when it was consecrated in October 1842, by which time the costs had risen to £2,250, there remained a shortfall of £350 still to be found. Nor were there funds to pay for a minister or for a parsonage and it was February 1844 before the Reverend William Gibbs Barker (c. 1814-1897), previously incumbent of St Paul's Walsall, was appointed to the living and a year later before the parsonage was available.[37]

About twenty years later the Victorian terrace which now forms North Parade, Matlock Bath Figure 54 was chosen as the site for the Wesleyan Chapel the construction of which was also strongly influenced by the desire to serve visitors and, consequently, was partly financed by grants from the Wesleyan's Watering-Places Committee. It was designed by Henry Fuller of London and Manchester and cost £1250 to build on land which had been purchased for £200 in 1864. 'The black Dissenting spire' which John Betjeman described was a late addition to the original design and delayed the opening until 1867.[38]

The self confidence which sustained the Matlock Bath Methodist congregation in its new chapel, and its contempt for the ritual of the established church, is evident in a poem published in the *Derbyshire Times* in March 1870. Its subject, the occasion of a marriage ceremony at the Methodist Chapel, Matlock Bath on Tuesday, March 15th. In the second stanza the climax of the ceremony approaches. The lovely bride and her plighted love are gathered round the sacred desk.

And in the enclosure; where the baptismal font
And the church table stands – the muniments
of faith,
The venerable minister of Christ appeared
Empanoplied with sanctity divine,
Who needeth not the coloured vestments poor
Of hireling priests; pretentious and absurd;
For as the Master great himself was there,
The shadow in the substance all was merged,
And hearts did burn with no unhallowed fire
But the pure flame from Heaven's great altar high.

The growing community was equipped with a church school in 1854 also funded by an appeal for public subscription. The Friends of Education had some difficulty finding a site for the project until they were able to report 'by the liberality and kindness of Peter Arkwright Esq., of Willersley, a sufficient site has been presented.'[39]

FIGURE 53. **The rear of the former Matlock Bath Holy Trinity School and Woodland Terrace seen from across the River Derwent, snapshot, 1972.**

This snapshot captures the surprising rear view of the school, on the left, and of Woodland Terrace compared with the view of the front of the buildings seen from the A6 road. It was taken not long before the conversion of the school building to residential use. The basement arches mark the position of the school playgrounds, boys to the left, girls to the right. The Master's residential accommodation lay immediately behind this playground area.[40]

A childhood recollection[41]

Ivy Lait's memories of her schooldays in the 1890s add a little detail of how the school was used. *'For a penny a week per child, the infants were taught in one room in the lower storey and learnt the alphabet forwards and backwards marching round the room. The aged 7s to 12s were taught altogether in one room above.'* She recalled celebrating Queen Victoria's Diamond Jubilee in 1897 with tea in the Pavilion [that would be the original Pavilion on the hillside behind the Royal Hotel] and sports afterwards. In addition to pocket money of a penny a week which was usually saved in a money box, and banked in the Post Office Savings Bank, there was an extra penny for the occasion. She spent it on the Switchback Railway and screamed in terror all the way round. Another penny bought a small china swan to float on the river where she recalled the wide weir with a rope fixed across it telling pleasure boats not to pass and the occasion, watched by large crowds, when 3 trippers did pass and one man jumped out and was drowned.

The land, part of a riverside enclosure allotment falls steeply from the roadside and its successful use involved greater costs than the Committee had anticipated. Nevertheless an interesting design was adopted which embraced the sloping site providing a single storey front elevation facing the road and a three storey rear elevation as shown in Figure 53.[42]

Expansion to the north and villas on the hillside

Matlock Bath now had facilities for residents as well as visitors. From the turn of the century there had been opportunities to build individual villas in the heart of the village

FIGURE 54. **The Promenade viewed from the north, photograph, late 1890s.**

This view is instantly recognisable despite the mutilation of the Promenade in the 1969 road-widening scheme when much of the garden was lost. The clear area in the foreground of this photograph was the site of the movable stage later re-located to 'a nicely sheltered Pierrot pitch on the riverward side of the Pavilion, where only artists of proven merit are engaged'.[43] Notice the telegraph pole; at this date carrying telephone lines.[44] In the background there are few buildings on Upperwood Road – and fewer trees compared with the view today.

Private collection.

as the Hotel estate was broken up. The architect George Rawlinson had moved from Derby to build his house, Belle Vue, on a close of Hascom Lees farmland in about 1800 and close by in the 1830s and 40s the family added Montpellier and Belmont, villas which had many tenants and uses. Investors in the commercial life of Matlock Bath, George Vernon and later Jonathan Gilbert, built the Lower Tower and the Upper Tower on the Heights of Abraham in the style of 'stuccoed Strawberry-Hill- Gothic castles' as

FIGURE 55. **View of Matlock Bath looking north from Temple Walk, c.1860.**

The picture shows the position of some of the villa properties. From *Derbyshire An Illustrated History*, 1979, DRO. 1. Upper Tower(s), 2. Lower Tower(s), 3. The Temple, 4. Guilderoy, 5. Masson Cottage, 6. Round House, 7. Montpellier, 8. Belmont, 9. Belle Vue, 10. Original Heights of Abraham lodge site, 11. Position of The Villa, 12. Old Bath Stables, now the Pavilion.

Nicolas Pevsner describes them.[45] For both men the choice of architectural style was surely deliberate, adding to the romance and drama of the Heights and encouraging their visitors to pay the pleasure ground's entrance fee. Close by John Mawe, whose widespread businesses included his Royal Museum in Matlock Bath, less ostentatiously, built Masson Cottage in an unadorned Georgian style. By 1839 the new owner of the Heights forsook painted stucco to build the imposing gritstone Guilderoy for his residence. Hascom Leys Farm caught the fashion and was rebranded as The Villa.

FIGURE 56. **The Villa, Matlock Bath**

Reproduced from *Gem of the Peak*, W. Adam, 1851 edition.

In the Dale, Ebeneezer Rhodes[46] waxed lyrical about the 'gem of the dale', referring to Mr Chinnery, the surgeon's Dale Cottage which had been built beside the turnpike in 1820; 'a building only two stories high – is profusely adorned with jessamine, passion-flowers, and Macartney roses, which are trailed amongst the trellis-work of the veranda, and spreading thence along the front of the cottage, cover the whole with beauty.' In the late 1820s Colonel Edward Payne[47], an incomer, built Torr Cottage, now the High Tor Hotel, and in the 1830s, higher on the hillside, Rock Villa, now The Rocks on what became known as St John's Road, both in the cottage ornee style. Thomas Robinson set Tor Hill amid landscaped grounds when he retired from business in Museum Parade.

When the arrival of the railway was awaited, land was offered for sale on the Holmes at the north end of village, see Chapter 7. Now, for some new or upwardly mobile residents, the railway offered the choice to live in Matlock Bath and commute to manage professions or businesses as far afield as Derby or Nottingham. The uptake was slow at first but in the 1860s, when Holme Road was in place to access building plots there, it attracted the middle class who could afford to build homes for themselves. It seems Masson Road was favoured first for this purpose. James Pearson built Brunswood House at the northern edge of the area and the road, now Brunswood Road, to reach his new villa.

In the same decade Victorian villas appeared in the Dale. Frederick Stevens built Heathbank, conveniently close to his business, the barytes works across the river at the foot of High Tor; Craven Villa and Riversdale followed. At the other end of Matlock Bath a good road (now known as Clifton Road) was constructed to access building plots, all with 'one or more views… Fences not to obscure views of adjoining plots.'

The New Bath's expansion across the years

During this period of growth and change in the resort, The New Bath's steady success was reflected in the expansion, illustrated by the images which follow.

FIGURE 57. **The New Bath Hotel, half stereograph, soon after 1857.**

The successors to George Saxton's family as lessees of the New Bath were Miss Ivatts (and later Mr Ivatts) and her niece Mrs Jordan. During their tenure 1856-1878 the original entrance court between the two wings was built over accommodating new sitting rooms and the main entrance was brought to face down the valley as shown here.[48] Their visitors included Dom Pedro II, Emperor of Brazil who stayed in August 1871, with the Empress and 'a numerous suite'.[49]

FIGURE 58. **Advertising brochure cover, c.1900.**

Thomas Tyack took over the Hotel in 1878. During his twenty year tenancy the hotel's rural setting was secured by the purchase of 14 acres of hillside land above it.[50] A substantial extension with a large dining room was added along the west side of the garden in 1888. The new wing appears on the right in the left hand picture. Ten years later the hotel responded to the developing trade from travellers in motor cars, building a road-house, the Roadside Bar or New Bath Restaurant, beside the main road below the hotel, Figure 60 and linked to it by an underground service tunnel.[51]

Ken Smith collection.

FIGURE 59. **Walker's Bath Terrace Hotel, photograph, 1880s.**

Ownership of the former Walker's Hotel passed to the New Bath Hotel in 1898 and by 1930 Trust Houses Ltd owned the whole complex. The company's significant addition was the fine outdoor swimming pool, the first outdoor pool to be fed by mineral spring water. It was opened to the public with stylish ceremony in June 1934. The building shown here provided changing rooms for the pool's public day visitors and some accommodation for hotel staff. A private house now stands on this site.

Derbyshire County Council Record Office.

FIGURE 60. **Matlock Bath overview from the south, late 1890s.**

The picture shows the area around the New Bath Hotel at the end of the 19th century in its most complete form when Bryan[52] describes the original indoor bath as *'very old-fashioned … built of heavy masonry … and not much used by visitors.'* The Hotel stands in the centre of the picture with the bulk of the Royal Hotel visible in the background and in front to its left buildings assumed to be carriage houses, later used as garages and a plot of open land where Rock Weir would shortly be built. Woodland House stands below to the right see Figure 141 and moving north from there along the main road is the hotel's Roadside Bar and Win Tor. In the bottom left corner is a cluster of houses at the bottom of the Wapping, see also Figure 140 which were demolished with the roadside properties in the 1974 phase of the A6 road widening.[53]

Tony Holmes collection.

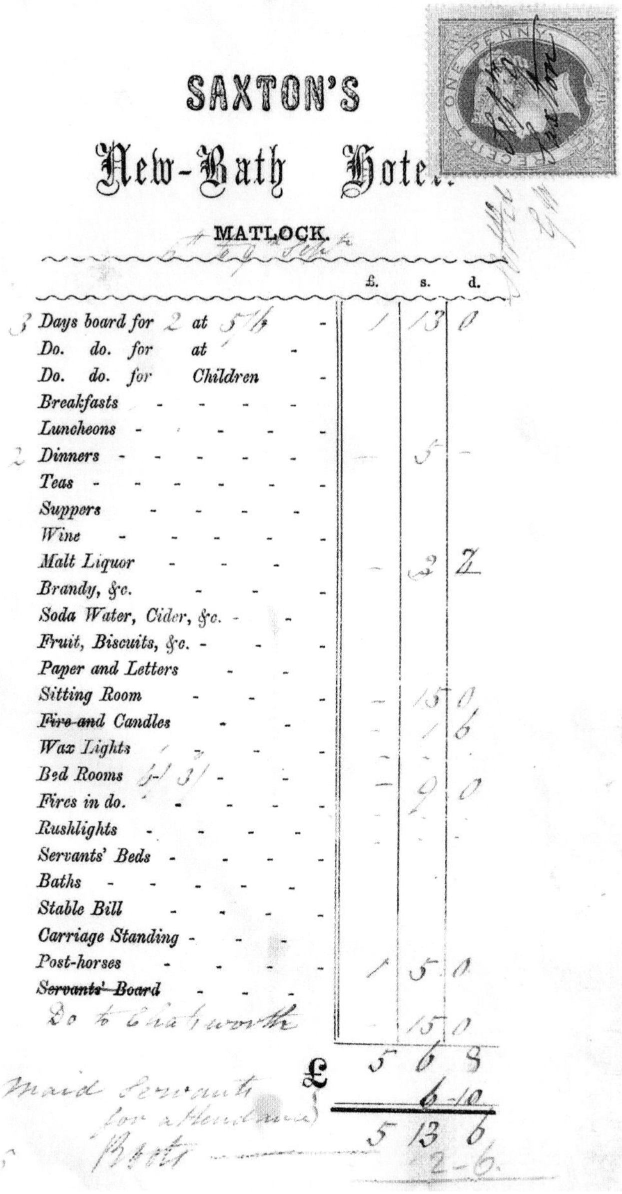

SAXTON'S
New-Bath Hotel
MATLOCK.

	£.	s.	d.
3 Days board for 2 at 5/4 -	1	13	0
Do. do. for at -			
Do. do. for Children -			
Breakfasts - - -			
Luncheons - -			
2 Dinners - - - -		5	-
Teas - - -			
Suppers - -			
Wine - - -			
Malt Liquor - - -		2	2
Brandy, &c. - - -			
Soda Water, Cider, &c. -			
Fruit, Biscuits, &c. -			
Paper and Letters -			
Sitting Room - -		15	0
Fire and Candles - -		1	6
Wax Lights -			
Bed Rooms -		9	0
Fires in do. - - -			
Rushlights - -			
Servants' Beds - -			
Baths - - -			
Stable Bill - - -			
Carriage Standing -			
Post-horses - -	1	5	0
Servants' Board - -			
Do to Chatworth		15	0
	5	6	8
£ maid servants for attendance		6-10	
Boots	5	13	6
		2-6	

FIGURE 61. **Bill for accommodation at the New Bath Hotel, c.1850.**

Private collection.

CHAPTER SEVEN

Matlock Bath and the Railway

In 1840 the tenor of life in Matlock Bath was shaken by a pivotal event in its history, the arrival of the North Midland Railway at Ambergate. Mary Cumming, the proprietor of the Old Bath, where the Cumming family had been tenants for more than 30 years quickly recognised the potential source of custom and until her death in 1842, she regularly advertised an omnibus service to meet the trains arriving there. She promised to attend punctually to orders for the private hire of carriages and offered to provide lunches and teas for some of the large excursion parties.

The report in both the Leicester and Derby papers of a day trip from Leicester on Wednesday June 22nd 1842 gives some idea of how such visits were organised. First and Second Class carriages were provided for fares of 12 shillings and 8 shillings respectively. The party, 500 passengers who left Leicester at 7.30am and 200 more who joined at Derby reached Ambergate at about half past ten. Some were carried onward by 'omnibus', some took to the Cromford canal in 5 or 6 large boats supplied with seats and awnings, and were accompanied by a regimental band, while a 'goodly land expedition jogged along the towpath.' By 12.45 the canal contingent had walked to Matlock Bath from Cromford Wharf some to take refreshment at the Old Bath, first class inside, second class in a marquee in the grounds, others to make their own arrangements elsewhere. Then they were free to explore the Heights of Abraham, High Tor, visit a cavern, navigate the river or stroll beside it and buy their souvenirs of the day at the museums and trinket shops. At 7pm the band struck up outside the hotel, the signal for the return journey to begin.[1] But dealing with a large number of trippers on a tight timetable required new skills and in the early days of the resort's encounter with this new form of tourism there were sometimes problems. One excursionist from Leicester seems to have returned home hungry and had the temerity to complain to the *Derbyshire Courier*. He was put firmly in his place. The 'second class visitors had anticipated dining on the green under a marquee. If they did not so dine in it must have been the fault of none other but themselves as a marquee was provided for the occasion capable of containing hundreds of occupants.' Nor was there a scarcity of food; the 'worthy and liberal landlord' gave his assurance that enough food was left over to 'furnish dinners to 250 or 300 persons' which might seem to explain why some had returned to Leicester unfed.[2]

In July 1844 a newspaper report with remarkable foresight reminded readers that now, 'in addition to the usual influx of aristocratic, wealthy and fashionable visitors at this time of year (the season being now commencing), means are afforded by the railways to the more humble class of passing some hours in the picturesque vicinage of Matlock, at a very trifling expense.'[3] But these early numbers were as nothing compared with the regular seasonal trade which developed and grew after 1849 when passengers came directly to Matlock Bath. Good Fridays, the traditional opening day of the trip season, brought excursion trains, extra trains, specials and service trains carrying crowds estimated to number twenty thousand or more.

FIGURE 62. **High Tor Tunnel, Matlock Bath, print engraved by Newman & Co published by Bemrose & Son, Matlock Bath, 1850s, but before 1858.**

The train shown here has emerged from the tunnel through the base of High Tor and is approaching the original station building at Matlock Bath. This was replaced in more decorative style in the late 1850s as shown on the facing page. The first vicarage stands in isolation on the left of the picture

Private collection

The huge impact the railway made in increasing the number visiting the resort and in creating the market for day visits was not accompanied by any obvious disfigurement of its natural beauty; the environmental damage was minimal. From the south the line pierced the gorge via the Willersley tunnel and soon after Matlock Bath station entered a series of tunnels taking it beneath High Tor to Matlock Bridge station. Cutting the tunnels, in June 1847 brought residents the thrill of reading in their local paper of danger narrowly avoided. There was, it was reported, a stringent rule forbidding pipe smoking in any part of the work where gunpowder is employed – the other day, [the] contractor saw [a] miner 'coolly in the act of pouring a heavy charge into a hole, at the same time solacing himself by puffing smoke and sparks about from a short pipe, an open can of about a stone weight of blasting powder standing nearby.'[4] Despite such incidents the Manchester, Matlock and Midland Junction Railway had opened for use in Matlock Bath on June 4th 1849. Within weeks the Railway Company was promoting day trips from neighbouring cities. The railway brought Matlock Bath within the range of day visitors from most of the Midlands and much of the north of England. The resort responded to the new opportunities vigorously and with enterprise, soon adapting its existing visitor attractions to the new market.

FIGURE 63. **Matlock Bath Station Buildings, stereograph, late 1850s.**

The style of the station building fitted Matlock Bath's image as the Switzerland of England, the branding which the rail company later promoted.

Ken Smith collection.

The Tripper's Paradise

Benjamin Bryan who styled himself the principal Matlock guide, was the proprietor of the Devonshire Cavern from 1832 to 1847 and then became the tenant of the Heights of Abraham. He sometimes chartered excursion trains with entrance charges to attractions in the resort included in the rail fare or as in this advertisement, offered free. He met the 700 strong party from Birmingham visiting in July 1844 at Cromford and conducted them through the Devonshire Cavern, 'illuminated throughout its entire length by upwards of 500 candles and displays of crimson fire...and arriving on the summit of the heights, a noble marquee and a fine band of music were found provided for their accommodation.'

It may have been on one of these occasions when Benjamin Bryan found himself 'leading the head of a party out of the end of a cavern when the tail end

SPECIAL TRAIN TO MATLOCK.

ON TUESDAY, JULY 19, 1853, on which day the HEIGHTS OF ABRAHAM, ROYAL RUTLAND CAVERN, lighted with blue and crimson fires, VICTORIA PROSPECT TOWER, the FERRY over the DERWENT, the LOVERS' WALKS, the HAG ROCKS, and a PETRIFYING WELL, will be thrown open to Visitors, entirely free of all charge.

FARES TO MATLOCK AND BACK.

From Nottingham, Beeston, and Sawley, First Class, 4s.; Covered Carriages, 3s. From Burton, First Class, 4s.; Covered Carriages, 3s. From Derby, First Class, 3s.; Covered Carriages, 2s. From Duffield and Belper, First Class, 3s.; Covered Carriages, 2s.

Children under Twelve years of age, Half-price.

The Train will leave NOTTINGHAM, at 8 15 a.m.; BEESTON, 8.30; SAWLEY, 8.40; RURTON, 8.30; DERBY, 9.30; DUFFIELD, 9.45; and BELPER, 9.52 a.m.; and return from MATLOCK, at 6.0 p.m.

Manager—B. BRYAN, 25 years principal Matlock Guide, who will accompany the Train, and conduct the party at Matlock. The Heights of Abraham will be open during the entire day, and the Rutland Cavern, from 12 till 2.

Refreshments at Moderate Charges.

Tickets at the MIDLAND RAILWAY STATIONS; of Mr. BRADSHAW, ": Journal Office," Nottingham; and Messrs. BEMROSE and SON, Iron-gate, Derby.

Derby Mercury 13, July, 1853.

95

of his group had not yet entered it.'[5] Rail travel offered Victorian philanthropists new opportunities to recruit and reward the deserving poor bringing the resort contact with people who would have been seen as among the lowest in the social order, a juxtaposition not without risk; though as this newspaper account of a visit by a Birmingham Sunday School in 1858 reports, it was possible to entertain such an audience and emerge unscathed. 'A special train of about ten carriages brought about three hundred persons to Matlock Bath on Monday. The trip was for the benefit of the Moseley Street Sunday School, Birmingham and the excursionists consisted of the scholars, teachers and friends. The price of admission to the Heights of Abraham, Rutland Cavern and Prospect Tower was included in the excursion ticket, and the weather being fine throughout, the party passed a pleasant day. The Birmingham shoe-black brigade sent a rather numerous detachment of its members, and the whole of the boys conducted themselves with strict propriety and decorum, and fully proved that the kindness of a rev. gentleman who paid for their tickets had not been misplaced.'[6]

FIGURE 64. **Matlock Bath from the Station, about 1869, print engraved and published by Newman & Co.**

This view illustrates the large number of people brought to Matlock Bath by the railway. Such streams of rail travellers remained a familiar sight until the 1950s when coaches and cars began to supersede the trains. At the beginning of the 1874 season the railway company had reported 'ample convenience has been provided at Matlock Bath Railway Station by the erection of a new platform.'[7] It was reputed to be one of the longest in the country.

Private collection

These large parties of the 'humbler class', intent upon a good day out sometimes had special attractions arranged to entertain them. In 1863 the *Wirksworth Advertiser* described a day when excursions brought 3000 from Derby, Nottingham and Sheffield with 3000 more from neighbouring villages. The Nottingham Ventil Horn Band played to launch a fete on the Heights of Abraham where there was hatchet throwing, 'more alarming than pleasing', the Corellis on double ropes and a high rope performance by A. Corelli, winner of two gold medals and a silver one 'for his performances before great personages'. On another day there were donkey races with ladies as the jockeys and a boat race for a silver cup.[8]

Well dressings also attracted an 'immense throng'. The first was held in May 1865 with

A busy day in Matlock Bath.[9]

'To assert that Matlock Bath is crowded on Good Friday is really to extenuate circumstances. To say that it is lively is to convey but an elementary idea of the hilarious jollity which prevailed. Rudely aroused on that buniferous day, Matlock receives visitors from half-a-dozen counties. There is a crowded train from remote Bradford and Leeds. Sheffield and Chesterfield call for two *specials*. Manchester and Stockport send ten excursion trains to Matlock and three extra trains of sensational length hardly satisfy the demands of Derby. Birmingham by special train sends her button-makers, Nottingham her *"bleating lambs"*, and Leicester her mill-hands; while dog-carts and traps contribute a large auxiliary traffic. Matlock is ready for the invaders, and resists their demands with boiled ham and mounds of beef, sufficient to victual an army corps. She lays in oceans of explosive beer, and makes barriers of buns. The supply of eggs for tea speaks libraries for the industry of the Derbyshire hens; while the professional commissariat is strengthened by half the private houses boiling *hot water for twopence a head*. The main thoroughfare is one sweeping, swaying crowd...The scene at Matlock [Bath] Station at night is the spectacle of the day. The Midland Company leave no precaution unadopted to ensure public safety. The station staff is trebly strengthened, policemen are employed to assist the porters, officials from Derby superintend the arrangements...Loaded train after train rolls out of the station, with mixed cargoes given to singing songs of a spiritual or spirituous character, the strains of *Sweeping through the gates of the New Jerusalem* in one carriage alternating with *Old John Barleycorn* from the companion compartment. The third train for Derby - a procession of thirty carriages - is the last special to leave ... the weary are speeding away to rest.'

three wells and a torchlight procession through the Heights enticing railway travellers from Sheffield, Nottingham, Derby, Chesterfield and Belper.[10] Some of the railway excursions involved so many hours in the train they seem scarcely worth the effort and expense. Nearly five hours travel each way from Cambridge at a cost of 8 shillings first class or 4 shillings 'covered' leaving Cambridge at 5.20 am offered just under 7 hours in Matlock Bath. Though visits to the Rutland and Devonshire Caverns, the Heights of Abraham and the Prospect Tower were included in the price, was it really worth ten hours sitting on the hard wooden seats provided for those who could not afford the first class fare?[11]

Not all visits from Birmingham ran smoothly as was the case when between three and four thousand persons overwhelmed the resort 'a great number of them being characters

The Last Train
Matlock

FIGURE 65. **The Last Train - Matlock, postcard, about 1910.**

One of a series of postcard cartoons sold to Matlock Bath visitors in the twentieth century. The *High Peak News* reported 80 trains in total including 26 excursion trains, calling at Matlock Bath on Whit Monday, 1911.

Ken Smith collection.

of the lowest grade, many robberies and a great deal of damage to the grass, walls, fences and other property in the surrounding neighbourhood' was done by them. On this occasion Benjamin Bryan, was quick to point out that his offer to show 'the principal attractions of the place' for £10, which was 'less than three farthings for each passenger', had been turned down by Chas Johnson of the Temperance Hall, Birmingham. Bryan concluded that this 'mistaken parsimony' and failure of the organisers to plan any diversion for the party 'soured the tempers of the pleasure seekers and… to some degree originated a spirit of wilfulness and mischief.'[12]

FIGURE 66. **A train on the down line at Matlock Bath Station.**

The picture is dated to about 1873-75. An interesting feature is the presence of lamplighters on the roofs of the carriages. The train, on its way to Matlock, would pass through the tunnel under High Tor. The carriage oil lamps are being lit for passenger security in the tunnel. This was a routine sight at one time. The lamps were thrown up to the man on the roof who inserted them. He was followed by a second man who lit them.[14]

The Midland Railway Study Centre collection, unidentified 900 class 2-4-0 on DOWN train; George Dow collection.

Over time the railway altered Matlock Bath in ways that were not universally welcomed. In 1903 Firth described the effects of the railway traffic as a blight, upbraiding the people of Matlock Bath. 'They have deliberately degraded Matlock Bath into a tripper's Paradise, and encouraged the railway companies to let loose daily in the summer-time among its sylvan beauties a horde of callous rowdies, who envy Attila his destructive secret, whereby the grass never grew again where once his foot had been planted. The debasing influence of the day tripper is everywhere visible in Matlock.' He complained of the shops which decked themselves with 'vulgarities and banalities to please their patron', the gaudy colours, the tawdriness of their wares, of the desecration caused by the cheap eating - house, the tea-room, the common toy and spar shop, the bars of the frequent hotels which dominate the street and the catchpenny or catch-threepenny touting boards which 'at last get upon the nerves'. He concluded that 'It is a wanton outrage to one of the fairest scenes in England.'[13]

CHAPTER EIGHT

The Response to the Railway's arrival

The railway revolution was complete. It had transformed Matlock Bath from a modest rural watering place into a growing resort catering predominantly for day trippers and short stay residents. Its pleasure grounds, caverns and scenery continued to be enjoyed by visitors though they were now shared with a growing number of well to do residents who found their living outside the valley commuting by train to one of the nearby towns. The wider railway network may also have contributed to the decline of the spa by enabling those seeking water treatments to travel longer distances to one of the many other spas with better accommodation and more sophisticated treatments and attractions. Whatever truth there may be in this analysis, as we have indicated above see page 80, we trace the origins of Matlock Bath's decline as a health resort to a pre-railway period, to the decades following the great European peace of 1815. These were the years in which[1] the new seaside resorts and those inland spas destined to flourish later in the century were energetically investing in new hotels, attractions and treatments. Harrogate which became the pre-eminent northern spa later in the century provides an interesting contrast with Matlock Bath. Here, in the 1830s, new initiatives provided public baths where treatments included vapour, fumigating and medicated baths, pump rooms and public buildings, one of them incorporating a large promenade room with an organ at one end of it.[2] All of this for a clientele which early in the season was 'full of clothiers from Leeds and cutlers from Sheffield – not a livery hat to be seen'; only later at the end of July giving way to 'coroneted chariots, britzchtas, and post chaises [with their] cargoes of aristocratic visitors.' Their season lasted until the Doncaster races in September.[3]

When the railway reached Matlock Bath in 1849 the resort had not entirely lost its own coroneted visitors[4] nor those from trade and business possibly including Sheffield cutlers, but it was trading on a reputation built up over many years and it was not investing in its future. There were of course improvements at the Old Bath and in the other hotels and there were new shops but between 1815 and 1849 the church was the only building that might be said to have enhanced the resort's facilities for the visiting public. It is surely significant that of all the English spas Granville visited, only Matlock Bath was unable to provide a contemporary analysis of the chemical properties of its thermal water; nor does his account of the baths and the facilities for drinking the water suggest that a robust use was being made of them. He was nevertheless generous in his praise of Matlock Bath as a place to live or stay finding it 'desirable and tempting offering excellent accommodation upon particularly easy terms much below those of Buxton.'[5]

Granville's visit was made ten years before the railway reached the resort. The spa was not dead and attempts would be made to revive it but underlying his description of the resort something of the future is already apparent. The primary focus would no longer be visitors staying long enough to take the cure;[6] increasingly it would be day trippers and short stay visitors of modest means who would marvel at the scenery and enjoy the pleasure grounds; and purchase cheap trinkets in the shops which had once sold elegant and costly locally turned vases, obelisks and candelabra.[7] This was a transformation the railway would accelerate feeding the resort its lifeblood in its new role as a scenic playground providing an enlarged hinterland and bringing visitors from across northern and central England.

Matlock Bath's development to the north

In 1844 when plans for extending the railway line north from Ambergate to Rowsley were in the air, the most northerly building in Matlock Bath was the bath house which had been built in association with the New Inn. The undeveloped land beyond was the Upper Holme a gorse-covered hillside with a quarry beside the turnpike at its foot and the Nether Holme, the strip of land between the turnpike and the river. The owner of the Holmes, Francis Blake, a Middlesex resident, advertised the land for sale in plots in July 1844.

At first only two plots were sold, one adjacent to the Fountain Baths subsequently the site of Fountain Villas, the other at the northern edge of the Upper Holme where in 1845 the vicarage was built. Then in 1852 Edward Greenhough developed the first block of Derwent Parade. It included his draper's shop 'fitted out in a style of great elegance' notwithstanding that a quarry was being worked close by.[8] Blake's directions for Greenhough's buildings were strict and it was his concern for their quality that provided the template which guaranteed Matlock Bath would have a Victorian terrace to match George Vernon's Georgian Parade. There were to be no more than two houses on the plot and no shops except as 'of such an elevation' as was shown on the drawing provided. Details of height and style, three storeys with a first floor balcony, were illustrated and Blake required to see evidence that not less than £700 would be spent on the build. The property was to be set seven feet back from the Turnpike; a line of studs still marks this boundary with the public pavement. Greenhough worked within similar constraints in 1864 when he built a second property next door to his shop on land which Blake had sold to Robert Chadwick and similar terms were applied to the adjoining plot where the Wesleyan Chapel was completed in 1867. It is difficult to believe that today even with the benefit of modern planning legislation a series of new developments spread over 15 years would achieve the overall effect accomplished by the foresight of this one Victorian landowner.[9]

But Matlock Bath's Victorian and Edwardian legacy was not solely the creation of private individuals of good taste. The settlement was fortunate also in the commitment shown by the Local Board and the Urban District Council in their approach to planning matters.

With limited powers derived from a responsibility for health and drainage issues, they were on occasion prepared to intervene decisively as Herbert Briddon the proprietor of the livery stables in the centre of the town discovered to his cost in 1893. He had erected a lock-up shop to sell toys and fancy goods to the trippers but did not adhere to the plans he had submitted to the Board. His shop was too large; too near the highway and at the front had acquired an 'objectionable verandah'. He was fined and given notice to pull it down but took no action evidently hoping the Board would not take matters further; perhaps they were bluffing. They were not. One morning at 6am 'a posse of men and police', 5 men and 6 police, surrounded his building and began to take it apart. With the roof gone and his stock unprotected, Briddon relented, agreed to remove the offending features and pay the costs and a fine. What a lesson this must have been for those intending to do business with the Board.[10]

Not all the developments in this part of the settlement were residential or commercial. In 1857, Thomas Wakley, Francis Blake's father-in-law, bought most of Blake's undeveloped hillside land from his mortgagors[11] but with a very different purpose in mind. In September that year Messrs Wakley and Weston, advertised[12] *To Ironmasters. Derbyshire Limestone from the Matlock Bath quarries lately worked by Mr Blake. Stone can now be supplied regularly. A sample may be seen at the Great Bridge Railway Station.* The firm was advertising locally the following year *To Quarriers and Miners'*[13] *seeking tenders for getting 600 tons of limestone a week from their quarries at Matlock Bath and delivering it to wagons at the Railway Station.*

Subsequently Wakley became a developer, in 1861 making a significant investment in the expansion of the resort by constructing a new road across the Upper Holme, today called Holme Road, so providing access to the building plots there.[14] With this new road in place development of the slopes of the Upper Holme behind North Parade began, the first being the spread of villas on Masson Road. Lower down the Albert Heights complex was a short-lived addition

Thomas Wakley

Thomas Wakley senior (1795-1862)[15] a medical reformer, doctor and radical independent member of Parliament, is remembered now primarily for his campaign to expose the adulteration of food stuffs. As the MP for Finsbury from 1835 until 1852 he supported both the Tolpuddle Martyrs and the Chartists in their demands for an extension to the franchise and argued for the abolition of the corn laws, Irish union and slavery. He became a coroner in 1839 and was instrumental in persuading the authorities that coroners should be qualified medical men. At the time of his death he was still the coroner for west Middlesex and the medical editor of The Lancet which he had founded in 1823. He used the magazine to campaign for reforms in the way medicine was practised and managed. His last campaign exposed the adulteration of foodstuffs and the water supply leading to ground breaking legislation. Though he is sometimes described as of London and Matlock Bath, it is not known whether he ever lived in the village. He had bought Guilderoy and the Heights of Abraham in 1860 but for health reasons he left England the following year for Madeira where he died in 1862.

Figure 89 but gradually the hillside acquired the terraces and individual buildings which are there today Figure 70.

FIGURE 67. **Matlock Bath from the station meadows, watercolour, artist unknown, about 1867.**

This picture is not signed or dated. The figures in the foreground are in meadowland beside the bridge built to serve the railway, the first bridge to be built over the river in Matlock Bath. The present Midland Hotel, beside the bridge to the left, was built in the 1850s as Thomas Smedley's spar shop, with a large shop window facing the road. It obtained an inn licence in 1869. On the other side of the road, to the right in the picture, standing in isolation is the Palatine Dining Rooms, licensed in 1874 as The Station and later named the County and Station. Along the hill to the right, the large house low down on the slope was Matlock Bath's first vicarage built in 1845 - at the opposite end of the village from the church. Derwent Parade, now part of North Parade, is complete as far as Rockvale House, present number 24-28. Beyond, the Wesleyan Chapel spire is visible, the chapel had been opened in 1867. There is no promenade; the first section was not opened until 1874. Holme Road still climbs across an almost bare hillside. Crowning the hill is the Victoria Prospect Tower built in 1844. The upper row of residential villas on Masson Road here showing Danbury Lodge as the top-most house, was developed in the 1860s. The Birklands, built between 1858 and 1860, stand below, beside the old Key Pasture Road.

Reproduced by permission of Matlock Bath Holy Trinity Church.

FIGURE 68. **View looking to the north from the Temple, about 1868, half stereograph, photographer John Clarke, Matlock Bath.**

The bottom left corner of the picture shows Waterloo Square which began life as the upper stable yard of George Vernon's Hotel and now forms part of Waterloo Road. In the square to the right, the buildings, now dwellings, have names reflecting their origins – The Stables and The Coach House. The former stabling and associated accommodation which stood opposite to them later converted to shops and dwellings has been demolished. The shop in the far corner of the Square had uses as Coates' the butcher's, a greengrocer's, a fish and chip shop and a cobbler's. The land behind it was part of the grounds of The Villa. There is some development on Masson Road and probably at Lyndhust on Brunswood Road, otherwise the hinterland behind North Parade remains undeveloped. John Clarke had a photographic studio in Museum Parade for more than 20 years from about 1864.

John Bradley collection.

FIGURE 69. **A view looking south over the Upper Holme. from the station area, about 1868.**

On the right what is now 256 The Dale is being roofed; high above it Holme Bank is in place at the corner of Masson Road and between them the Upper Holme fields remain undisturbed apart from Lyndhurst, here seen just above no. 256. Note the dark square of the shop window at the Midland.[16]

FIGURE 70. **A similar view from about 1890.**

Seen much as it is today except for the Albert Heights development. Its rooflines (two light-coloured roofs with a darker longer roof behind, see also Figure 89) are visible in the left middle of the view. Above them, slanting uphill is Clarence Terrace, built in 1879.

Private collection.

An object of awe and wonder

Time and again in these pages we have recorded visitors' reactions to Matlock Bath's scenery. From the first written accounts of the resort visitors have struggled to find words in prose or in verse adequate to the task of evoking their response to its extraordinary natural features. But significant as it has always been there was a period in the later years of the eighteenth century when the valley's landscape enjoyed special importance, its particular characteristics so precisely fitting contemporary taste that for a generation it became one of those places wealthy cultured people should try to visit and discover for themselves.

In modern usage, terms such as sublime, picturesque or beautiful tend to be used with a degree of interchangeability, but in a society where so much was questioned, analysed and redefined these words came to acquire distinctly separate meanings. Just as the enlightenment had its pioneer scientists and medical men establishing new boundaries so also it had philosophers of taste forging a new aesthetic and it was as part of this process that a more focused understanding of the sublime, the picturesque and the beautiful emerged. Edmund Burke (1730-1797) began the process in an essay published in 1756 in which he sought to identify the sublime and the beautiful in terms of the feelings they induce in the mind of the beholder, the sublime evoking the delight experienced whenever there is the idea of pain and danger without actual risk; in Roy Porter's words, the experience of 'terror enjoyed in security'. In contrast beauty stirs feelings of affection and tenderness.

The thrill, the frisson of terror, the sublime experience Matlock Bath offered was most

FIGURE 71. **High Tor from St John's Road, photograph, about 1900.**

High Tor was always an object of awe and wonder for visitors to Matlock Bath but the grounds were not formally adopted as a pleasure ground until about 1860 when Peter Arkwright enclosed the area and constructed pedestrian paths to the summit. In the foreground, in this view, the land beside the river is occupied by a wheelwright's yard. Raised above road level on the right are Torr Cottage and Ivy Cottage, now the High Tor Hotel, built for Edward Payne between 1827 and 1829 when John Buxton was paid the last £50 on his construction contract, see Colin Goodwyn's *History of Torr Cottage*.

obviously the towering presence of High Tor. Stukely had described it as 'a monstrous parcel of gigantick [sic] rocks seemingly piled one a top the other as in the wars of the gods, call'd the Torr ; there were a few inhabitants at [the] bottom in little cottages who durst trust themselves to so ruinous a shelter.' But this was not all. Matlock Bath also possessed natural scenery which was truly picturesque. This was a term used by the Reverend William Gilpin (1724-1804) when he visited the resort in 1772 and one that was particularly associated with him but it was left to Sir Uvedale Price (1747-1829) in 1794 to distinguish the three concepts, the sublime, the picturesque and the beautiful one from another. The essential quality of the sublime was for him 'greatness of dimension; it is founded on 'awe and terror' and 'never descends to anything light or playful'. He placed the picturesque 'between beauty and sublimity but distinct from either'.[17] So Matlock Bath with scenery both sublime and picturesque enjoyed decades of respect from visitors whose outlook had been shaped by the new enlightened taste. Gilpin was not unusual in drawing attention to the quality of the gorge, the river and the woodland; 'this is scenery of a different kind. Every object here is sublime and wonderful. Not only is the eye pleased; but the imagination is filled.' From the eighteenth century onwards many visitors and guide books expressed these sensations.[18]

Although the Tor lacked formal footpaths until the nineteenth century it is clear from

FIGURE 72 **Matlock Dale. photograph, George Washington Wilson, period 1870-81.**

The view looking north towards Matlock shows a curve in the Dale and on the right the works which were developed on the site of the Side Mine at the foot of High Tor. In 1838 Adam describes the mine as Mr Boothman's with miners' coes and an engine house with an 80 horsepower water wheel. Two years later, although the mine was 'out of work', he was impressed by the iron rod, about 301 yards in length, connecting the pumps in the mine to the wheel and raising water 'at such a distance from the real base of the power, at about 1000 gallons per minute when in full play'. The weir across the river which directed water to the mill goit serving the water wheel is marked by the abrupt change of colour of the river in this view; it was removed in the flood alleviation scheme of the 1970s. A water wheel remained in use there until damaged by fire in 1896 when it was replaced by a turbine. Sometime before 1851, the Dutch Lead Works was built on the Side Mine's waste hillocks; its business was grinding barytes. Later known as the Messrs Stevens Bros Dale Paint Works it was bought by Henry Wheatcroft of Cromford in 1898 and converted to a colour mill producing colour pigments. It became the head office for his company and for many years was known as the High Tor Colour Works The site remained in an industrial use until closure in 2013. A bridge crossed the goit to the High Tor Grotto. The bridge shown across the river was washed away in floods in 1881. In 1847 the land between the road and the river was built up with spoil dug from the High Tor Tunnel and dumped there by the Railway Company with permission from Peter Arkwright.[19]

John Bradley collection

earlier accounts that some visitors reached the summit. In 1724 William Stukely[20] for example describes taking 'the Pains to clamber on Hands and Knees almost to the top.' The summit could have been been approached more easily across the fields from the east from Side Lane at Starkholmes, from the south up the slope from Matlock Bath or from one of the miners' paths, but to use these easier routes was to deny oneself the 'dreadful pleasure' of scrambling to the summit.

As we have shown in an earlier chapter the lead mines and miners were also objects of wonder to strangers. Alexander Cozens view of 1756 (not reproduced here) shows miners' coes associated with the High Tor Mine and Thomas Smith's view published as a print in 1751 shows a mine adit. The early worked lead rakes, later known as the Fern and Roman Caves, which appeared as deep fissures cut into the top of the Tor, were exciting features for the early explorers and at river level, for a period from about 1830, visitors were shown into a lead mine known as Side Mine. Nearby, by 1827, a natural cavern, the High Tor Grotto was opened to the public.[21]

Taming High Tor

Taming the Dale's natural assets to make them available to a wider public less intrepid than the eighteenth century pioneers who had first discovered the gorge and had relished clambering up miners' paths and impossible slopes, did not take place until the second half of the nineteenth century. The investment seems to have emerged as a natural consequence of the growth which had taken place in both the Matlocks leading to a new perception of the Dale's potential as a place for recreation. As the Bath had colonised its northern extremity so Matlock had expanded to the south.

HIGH TOR
Natural Crystallized Cavern,
MATLOCK-DALE,
The Greatest Work of Nature's Crystallization in Derbyshire.

THE way to this Cavern is on the Turnpike-road northward, past Matlock-Bath Station Bridge, or southward from Matlock Bank. The approach is by a wooden bridge across the river Derwent, near the Paint works, and the entrance to the Cavern is at the foot of the High Tor,—no climbing of the hills to get to it, renders the walk to it pleasant, and being also dry and easy of access, Visitors will not have the remotest cause to be afraid. The High Tor Cavern was visited in 1856, by the Ex-Queen of the French, and suite, who expressed themselves highly gratified.

Visitors are cautioned against other guides, who would mislead them, and prevent their seeing this Cavern, which is the greatest curiosity in Matlock Bath. There is also an extensive collection of Derbyshire Minerals, at reasonable prices.

THOMAS CARDIN, Guide,
Proprietor and Practical Geologist.

Advertisement for the High Tor Grotto, 1862.

Matlock's development owed much to the extraordinary and obsessive genius of John Smedley. In 1853, four years after the arrival of the railway in the valley, a successful local hosier and mill owner, he began to practise a form of hydrotherapy derived from techniques developed in central Europe, which unlike Matlock Bath's therapies did not rely on the mineral qualities of the water it used.[22] While Matlock Bath had become widely known as a resort often referred to and understood simply as Matlock, the Matlock recognised as such today had remained a group of four separate small settlements around the Church, the Green, close to the Bridge and along the spring line on the Bank. The success of John

Smedley's hydro and his encouragement to others to invest in similar ventures resulted in further developments along Matlock Bank and subsequently in the other Matlock settlements which gradually coalesced into a single entity; the Matlocks as they had been known became Matlock. Smedley believed passionately in his hydropathic treatments and his generosity in making his methods known to others and his proselytism of what he regarded as a new science was largely responsible for Matlock's rapid growth. As it had done for Matlock Bath, so also, the railway brought to Matlock's hydros a clientele from all over the country. Shops and services grew up around the Bridge and gradually the Bank development crept down the hill to meet them.

As numbers grew in both resorts, the Tor lying between the two centres of population offered an exciting alpine route between them and demand grew for something to be done. It may have been this which prompted Peter Arkwright (1784-1866) to take the initiative and to develop what became known as the High Tor pleasure ground. Around 1860 Peter Arkwright enclosed the ground on the High Tor and laid out walks 'at considerable labour and expense'. An entrance some way up the path to Starkholmes from Matlock Bath was approached from close to the Matlock Bath railway station. It led to 'zig-zag walks…where seats [were] placed.' A carriage drive to the summit was created from Side Lane, now Starkholmes Road, along the route of a footpath which had been in use from at least the 1840s. This facility enabled the bird's eye view experience from the Tor to be enjoyed by more people, even invalids and the infirm though carriages were recommended not to go too near the edge as horses were 'easily frightened by blasting which is constantly being done.'[23] He also contrived the cliff ledge path, later called Giddy Edge and opened Fern Cave.[24]

In 1879 the Matlock and High Tor Recreation Ground Company leased the High Tor pleasure ground from Peter's grandson, Frederic Charles Arkwright. At Easter 1880 when the company re-opened the grounds for the new season, the visitors found that the entrance from Matlock Bath had been moved to its present position at the foot of the path to Starkholmes. From there led 'walks of easy ascent through an adjoining wood of forest trees of stately growth [which afforded] an agreeable shade in the summer months for pedestrians.' At the summit a 'spacious refreshment building' had been erected and it was the Company's declared intention to make a further 'spacious walk' as far as the footbridge near the Boat House Inn and provide tennis courts with seats for spectators. The work was in the hands of Mr Milner of London whose instruction was to 'render this spot, so sublime in itself from its natural features, one of the most attractive to visitors who frequent this neighbourhood in search either of health or recreation.'[25]

Sometime before 1899 the promised walk had been opened. It was used by pedestrians and also by carriages and had been given the name Grand Walk; it utilised a new entrance on Pigtree Lane, later called Pic Tor Lane. This offered a more exciting approach to the summit giving visitors a first glimpse of the dramatic scenery of the gorge from the Little Switzerland viewpoint. Tennis and quoit or skittle grounds were laid out near the Matlock Bath entrance and visits to both the Roman and Fern Caves were available. In 1897 a cricket ground is recorded on the flatter meadow to the east of the summit perhaps on the additional land which had been absorbed into the park along its eastern boundary during this period of development.[26]

In 1903 a new pedestrian entrance was made from Matlock Dale to the High Tor grounds crossing the river on a suspension bridge opposite Tor Cottage, later the High Tor Hotel. Messrs David Rowell & Co were commissioned to construct the bridge. Its entrance gate pillars still stand in the riverside wall but the bridge has not survived.

The High Tor Company's stewardship of the High Tor Grounds ended in 1975. Its last positive gesture in the spirit of public service for which it was established, had been many years earlier in 1921 when it placed 'a splendid café at the summit'.[27] The building was destroyed by fire in 1995 though by then the café had been closed for some years. This sad end was consistent with a long period of gradual decline and neglect in the promotion and upkeep of the grounds which had been in council ownership since 1924. The Tor has bene-fited recently from the Matlock Parks Project, a five year scheme completed in 2008, which has coordinated restoration of the chain of parks along the valley.[28]

FIGURE 73. **St John's Chapel, postcard, 1900.**

The Chapel of St John the Baptist on St John's Road was built in 1897 for Louisa Sophia Harris who lived at The Rocks, (formerly Rock Villa). It was designed by Edward Guy Dawber (1862-1938) later Sir Guy Dawber, an eminent architect who was president of the Royal Institution of British Architects from 1925 to 1927 and one of the progenitors of the Council for the Protection of Rural England. It is considered to be among his finest buildings. Internally the chapel is richly decorated by prominent artists of the Arts and Crafts movement, superb and unusual plasterwork mouldings on the ceiling by George Bankart (1866-1929) depicting fruit, flowers and birds, a notable east window by Louis Davis (1861-1941) and intricate wood carvings. It was built as a private chapel for Mrs Harris who sought the High Church practices she preferred which no other local churches offered at the time. The building was never consecrated so allowing Mrs Harris to erect a memorial in the chapel to her dog, Vida. St John's was adopted by the Friends of Friendless Churches in 1994. In 2012, in partnership with English Heritage and the Pilgrim Trust, the Friends undertook a comprehensive scheme of repairs using a range of skilled craftsmen and specialists to secure the building for the future. In 1904 at Harveydale at the bottom of St John's Road, Mrs Harris built St John's Terrace, three cottages in which Guy Dawber's design influence is readily apparent.

Ken Smith collection

FIGURE 74. **Bridge, Matlock Dale, carte de visite photograph, 1870s.**

In 1872 this attractive footbridge from the Dale to Pigtree Lane, now Pic Tor Lane, replaced the ferry service across the river near this point. Guide books refer to a ferry service 'to Matlock village' being run from somewhere near the Boat House by Mrs Brinsley, 'the Matlock carrier to Sheffield and Derby'. In the period 1840s to 1860s the service had been run by Mr Smith though it seems likely that it began much earlier, run from the Boat House itself. The Matlock Tithe Award, 1848, lists Betty Brinsley as the occupier of the three storey roadside building near the bottom of St John's Road. The bridge shown here was washed away when the Derwent flooded in 1881.[29] It was replaced the following year by a more practical but less beautiful box girder bridge.

John Bradley collection.

FIGURE 75. **The Boat House and associated buildings, photograph, c. 1870.**

The Matlock Tithe map shows property associated with the Boathouse Inn stretching some distance along the roadside and the Award describes it as Boathouse Inn, Cottage, outbuilding, yard, garden and part of quarry. The building furthest right was the inn where the sign reads T Rawson Boat House.[30] No longer a public house, it was redeveloped as a veterinary surgery in 2016. None of the other visible buildings survive. The six bay building shown was a coach house with harness room above. In 1893 the upper floor housed the Matlock Science and Art night school where the photographer W N Statham was the Art master. In the 1920s the ground floor housed Herbert Bowler's Garage; eventually the building was taken over by Derbyshire Stone. The smaller two storey roadside building to the south of it appears in Figure 11 and in an early print by Joseph Farington. Its use is not known. The OS map published in 1880 records a weighing machine sited near it. The building was demolished in the early years of the twentieth century. The small building at a higher level behind it is thought to have been the powder house for the quarry. At the extreme left of the photograph is the edge of the pair of semi-detached houses which still stand near the Boat today. Note the gardens beside the river and the boats

Tony Holmes collection.

Another development in the Dale

No trace remains now of a former industrial site in the Dale, the Matlock Bath Mineral Water Works, better known locally as Whittaker's or the Pop works which was squeezed into a narrow strip of land at the roadside to the north of Derwent House. It was begun by John Wheatcroft,[31] a cavern guide, in the early 1870s and carried on by his daughter Mary and her husband John Whittaker, using the trading name the Matlock Bath Soda Water, Lemonade and Aerated Water Company. In 1885 Mary took over the Pop works business and later advertised it as 'Whittaker Ltd est. 1886'.[32] By 1891 she was living at Derwent House. She advertised lodgings there and in 1893, purchased the disused Long Tor Quarry behind the works for £600. She showed the old Long Rake lead mine there as a show cave calling it with the brazen cheek for which Matlock Bath residents became famous, the Long Tor Roman Fluor Spar Cavern and offered 'Refreshments of a superior class' in the grounds. The Pop business used water from a spring in the hillside behind the buildings, as Mary was quick to make clear in a notice to the press to quash rumours that she used water from the river in her products. A lock-up shop was added to the south of the house in 1895 where visitors could buy spar and marble goods and mineral drinks; early in the 1900s she introduced a bottling plant at the works.[33] The 'pop' business used a number of brand names, Tordale being the best known, and also bottled for more widely known firms such as Bass, Offiler's and Guiness. John Gilroy's famous 'Guiness for Strength' and 'Guiness is Good for you' advertisements made a colourful display on the factory billboards.[34] Mary Whittaker was in her own way typical of many local business owners taking on any new venture that might turn a profit.

FIGURE 76. **Derwent House and the Mineral Water Works, Matlock Dale, photographed through a snow shower, 20th century.**

Three storey Derwent House stands to the south of the Pop works buildings and, above the furthest and original works building, the four gables of Hazel Bank are outlined by snow and at the roadside beyond is Tor Hill's coach house.
Harry Gill collection.

Picture right shows Tor Hill's intact coach house block with Tor Hill in the background, a half stereograph, photographer Alfred Seaman.
John Bradley collection.

FIGURE 77. **A Whittaker's Codd bottle.**

Like other pop makers Whittakers used the bottles patented by Hiram Codd in 1872. The gassy liquid was retained in the bottle by the pressure of the gas forcing a glass marble against a collar in the neck of the bottle. The drinker's tongue on the marble released the liquid. The collar on the bottle illustrated has fallen into the body of the bottle and appears as a brown ring.

Photograph Dianne Charlton.

CHAPTER NINE

The Old Bath closes

As the resort was being extended and modernised to the north, the original heart of the settlement, the Old Bath, was failing. Despite Mary Cumming's initiative to bring rail passengers from Ambergate in 1840 and no doubt other schemes to keep it afloat, the Old Bath was showing its age. Arthur Jewitt[1] in 1837 wrote warmly enough of 'this large establishment, composed of a series of white middle sized houses' which had a 'neat, cheerful and pleasing appearance', but Sir George Head, who had stayed there two years earlier[2] cannot have been the only one who noticed how old fashioned and run down it had become. 'The public room,' he wrote 'a large rambling apartment, of which the floor was so rickety, that at one part especially there appeared serious chance of tumbling into the cellar.' The furniture [in that room] looked 'ancient and uncomfortable'. His bedroom 'of which there were a score similar, in the same corridor, was no bigger than the state-room in a ship.' He commented on the scratchings on every window pane in the public room expressing sentiments like 'Now you are gone my dearest Miss B., Matlock has no charms for me' and under reference to 'Charming Miss A. Black-eyed Miss B. Grey eyed Miss F' another hand had written 'Are gone, thank Heaven.' He was surprised by the unannounced arrival in the dining room of 'the delegate of a trumpery band of music' who hoped 'his honour would remember the music' followed by 'fruit-women, offering fruit to sell.' Head likened them to a 'flock, attracted like condors of the desert, to pounce upon the first solitary stranger who, at the beginning of a season, arrives at the hotel.' Maybe this was the same band which two or three years later 'enlivened' the Bath during the season and was described as perhaps 'the single drawback to the felicity of Matlock Bath.' Despite his criticisms Head was still generous enough to conclude that 'with the enjoyment of so lovely a rural prospect as appeared without, it was over-fastidious to complain in fine weather of matters within.'

William Adam[3] challenged Head's view, claiming that he was not able to appreciate that the Old Bath was 'fitted up somewhat in the olden style but not *the less* comfortable and pleasing on that account.' In 1855 despite changes of proprietor, the *Manchester Weekly* returned to the topic, drawing attention to its 'spirit of hoar antiquity...large drawing room filled with furniture of long ago...old-fashioned orchestra.'

It is clear that the pattern of visiting and of visitors' expectations had changed and only a few years later Adam himself acknowledged this[4] referring back to the period when 'Matlock as a sweet and quiet retreat, was resorted to by numbers who annually resided in it from three weeks to as many months, and at such times upwards of eighty usually sat down to the "table d'hote" at the Old Bath. Now, although the visitors to Matlock are far more numerous, that practice is generally given up.' He described the present company as occupying private rooms and sometimes leaving 'for a few days or a week to visit the beautiful scenery or objects of interest in the neighbourhood. So great is the influx of visitors in this way, during the summer months, that Matlock often exhibits as much bustle and activity, with the passing and re-passing of carriages and coaches, as in some of the fashionable thoroughfares of London.'

A new era had begun and indications that it was a market in which the Old Bath might not flourish were soon apparent. On the death of Mary Cumming in 1841 Robert Watson 'late of the firm of Cooke and Watson, Victoria House, York' became the lessee and by 1843 had given the establishment a new name, Old Bath Royal Hotel claiming 'Every Modern Improvement has been adopted.' But by September, despite his efforts, the hotel was being offered to let again. The Old Bath survived this setback and a 'most sumptuous dinner' was served to announce its reopening in May 1844,[5] this time with Mr Greaves of the Rutland Arms, Bakewell as tenant. He was more successful but when his lease expired in 1858 the hotel finally closed although its Assembly Rooms continued to be used for some local functions.

In 1863 the several shareholders of the Old Bath estate took the decision to divide the

FIGURE 78. **Matlock Bath from Upperwood Road looking south, about 1870.**

In the centre background of this view, the Royal Hotel appears like some gothic ruin, with beside it to the right, the rubble from the Old Bath. In fact the Royal is being built though its owners were not able to complete it. In 1869 it was offered for sale 'in course of erection ready to receive the roof' and remained in that state for several years. Among the inducements to prospective buyers was the notion that its grounds might offer a suitable site for a railway station. At that time the Midland Railway was proposing to extend its railway line from Wirksworth to Rowsley.

The line would have crossed the Greyhound pond at Cromford on a viaduct and come through the hillside to emerge in Matlock Bath on the west side of the valley before disappearing again under the Heights of Abraham. The standing property to the right of the Royal survived until 1904, when, described as the old taproom, (a reference to its earlier life as the Miner's Arms) it was demolished to make way for a power house, garage and laundry for the Royal Hotel.

John Bradley collection.

property amongst themselves.[6] Edmund Gillings Maynard became the owner of the main building and offered it for sale in 1864.[7] It was evident from the name selected by the entrepreneurs who stepped forward to buy it that they had noted the spectacular success of the resort's near neighbour, Matlock Bank, following John Smedley's exploitation of hydropathy there. Their company was to be the Matlock "Old Bath" Hydropathic and General Hotel Co. Ltd and subscriptions were invited for 2500 shares of £10 each. The aim was to purchase the property and build new premises and, in 1865, the Old Bath was demolished. The construction of its replacement was begun at the southern end of the site to a design in the gothic style by A. Wyatt of Manchester but by 1869 the new company was bankrupt. The roofless building was offered for sale without success and the tools and unused building materials were sold to raise money for the creditors.[8]

The Royal Hotel plans

It was not until September 1878 that the Old Bath site was back in business, now the 'New Great Hotel'.[9] Major Wieland had completed the rebuilding and opened it as a first-class hotel offering accommodation for 150 guests. It had been restored and furnished by Warings;[10] it offered a new 40 feet by 20 feet modern swimming bath in the grounds fed by the mineral water spring and with six large dressing rooms.[11] It became known as the Royal Hotel; its facilities included baths but it was not an hydro and Bradbury's assessment that it was 'almost a hydro' did not satisfy those who continued to be heard expressing concern at the resort's failure to adopt modern practice and follow in Matlock Bank's footsteps.

Hydropathic baths were advertised at the Royal in 1888 and in 1891 London journalists were invited to the opening of Turkish and vapour baths;[12] but these were clearly not regarded as competitive with the baths advertised at Matlock and elsewhere. It was observed that the 'establishment of hydropathy in Matlock Bath would mean a considerable amount of additional patronage, and if Smedley's and 32 minor establishments could thrive at the Bridge and Bank it was certain they at the Bath would have a share.'[13] A journalist who covered the inauguration of the baths in 1891 managed to convey just how much the survival of the resort's traditional functions rested on the success of this venture. The once flourishing town famous for its waters and baths had, he said, suffered over the last decade 'from the apathy and neglect of the tourist and the invalid' who had preferred to turn 'their faces towards Hamburg, Spa, Baden and other continental health resorts.' He dutifully admired the new baths and the riverside setting and then turned his attention to the Pavilion Figures 93 and 94 noting its accommodation for 1,500 people; but with an honesty that cannot have endeared him to his hosts illustrated how far Matlock Bath 'had fallen from its high estate, recording a recent visit by two London celebrities that had produced takings at the door of only 14 shillings'; it seemed, he reflected, 'well-nigh incredible that a grand place like Matlock Bath with splendid facilities for reaching it (the Midland runs three trains a day from St Pancras in under four hours) should be overlooked by the gentry and dyspeptic while the continental bads are crowded with Englishmen.'[14]

Matlock Bath must have its hydros sooner or later argued the *Derbyshire Times*; and given that it is known that the Royal is available for purchase why can't a syndicate be formed to develop it as an hydro? That was in April 1902.[15] Two years later its wish had been fulfilled; the Royal was now in the hands of a syndicate of London and international businessmen. At a conference held at the Royal, the Urban District Council and the syndicate exchanged views on how they might bring Matlock Bath up to date as a resort. Their prescription included further exploitation of the mineral waters, thirty million gallons of which were allowed to run to waste each day, the provision of a pump room and new baths, and, they agreed, steps should be taken to reduce 'the excursionist traffic' which had 'grown to be a nuisance to the staying visitor.' There soon emerged plans for a new building on the site of Briddon's stables and a park on the adjoining land which, if built by the council, would be leased by the syndicate for ten years at a rent equal to 6% interest on the investment up to a maximum of £600 per year. There were to be baths, a pump room and a large hall for concerts, meetings and balls.[16]

In February 1905 plans drawn by Alfred Wiget of Zurich,[17] an architect and one of the Royal Hotel's directors, were made public together with the estimated cost thought to be about £37,000. This drawing detailed baths for ladies and gentlemen, treatment rooms, doctors' accommodation and all the facilities for electric and magnetic remedies together with the promised pump room and hall. The scheme was well received. The members of the Matlock Bath Improvement Association gave it their support. They appealed to the rate-payers to approve the UDC proposal to bring forward an Improvement Bill to Parliament which would authorise the loan they would need to cover the land purchase and building costs. On 6th February[18] a poll of the ratepayers was held. This was a requirement for the council if it was to obtain the statutory powers to raise a loan for the proposed investment. The result was decisive with 186 votes in favour and 91 against.[19] There was jubilation. 'Matlock Bath has awoke as one man to its own interests' in one local paper;[20] in another, this will place Matlock Bath 'on a level with the best inland watering places on the conti-nent'.[21] But quite apart from the huge cost was there really a need for new baths when the syndicate had already inherited a suite of them at the Royal? The plan survived the progress through Parliament of the Matlock Bath Improvement Bill, the legislation that would enable the Council to deliver its part in the project. The proposals were examined by the Police and Sanitary Committee of the House of Commons, J.E. Lawton as Chairman speaking for the UDC and for the developers, Dr Sharpe and Mr Harvey, Chairman of the hydro hotel syndicate. The Bill allowed the UDC to acquire land for the new building and surrounding grounds and to borrow £15,000 for the capital expenditure.[22] This was an extraordinarily ambitious proposal for one of the smallest urban districts[23] already carry-ing substantial debt. Nevertheless in August the Act received Royal Assent.[24] It cannot have been long after that the grand scheme began to unravel; the syndicate confining their hydropathic developments to the Royal and the Council, now acting alone, proceeding[25] with the purchase of the land for the large building which was to become the Kursaal,[26] and later came to be known as the Grand Pavilion.

A hint of what may have brought the partnership down was provided by Charlie White soon after he became Chairman of the Council in 1908; 'the Council,' he said, 'had failed to satisfy the demands of the Directors of the Royal Hotel'[27] and while we have no record of how he might have elaborated on this observation it seems probable it was the scale of the capital investment required to deliver Wiget's scheme that put an end to the original strategy. Once the baths and treatment rooms had been stripped out what remained was effectively an entertainment venue though one with a nostalgic nod towards Matlock Bath's past by the inclusion of a pump room; and even in its reduced form still a major undertaking for a small council burdened already with loan debt from its earlier water and gas interventions and beneath the long shadow cast by the knowledge that it must resolve the sewerage problem whatever that might cost.[28]

The case for this massive new investment was set out by J. H. Cardin, Lawton's vice-chairman in May 1906. He made three points; the council knew what it was about. 'Their stupendous Improvement Bill was not formed without careful foresight from the members and officials.' There might be some who doubted but look how wrong they had been over the gas undertaking in which 'last year's profits were equal to a relief [in the rates] of 3/4d in the £. And there really was no alternative; Matlock Bath's success depended on the amount of comfort they could give its patrons, so that when they went away they would long for another visit. That [had been] the basis upon which the Improvement Act was formed.'

The scheme lost momentum with Lawton's defeat in the 1907 council election but it was a temporary setback. Charlie White though he had campaigned on the issue of council expenditure found himself in 1908 Chairman of a council committed to 'the erection of [a] large pavilion'. This might have been the time to pause and reconsider the scheme in the light of the new realities but it was too late for second thoughts. Significant progress had been made in purchasing the land required for the building and its adjacent park and it would have been difficult to call a halt; and in any case there was no appetite among the ratepayers for such a decision. The panacea that had been set before them three years earlier had captured their imagination. This was to be the investment that would enable Matlock Bath 'to keep pace with other watering places'.

By the end of 1908 it was a Kursaal[29] that was to be built. It would include a ballroom, restaurant and council offices and by March the following year photographs[30] of the proposed design appeared in the press. 'The Kursaal is to be on the most up to date continental lines and will include a restaurant to hold one thousand persons, a theatre and concert hall, a roller skating rink and town offices. The grounds are to be laid out tastefully and a suspension bridge thrown across the river Derwent to Lovers Walks.' There was also to be a pump room.[31] The costs had now reached £35,000 and in March the Local Government Board approved the additional borrowing the Council needed and architects were appointed. These were John Nuttall of Matlock and F. W. Ackland Hodge of London,[32] a decision it was to regret and that would cost it needless expense see page 118. In due course each presented plans; Nuttall's were chosen ostensibly because his scheme was cheaper and the building occupied less area. Hodge was dismissed.

Final authorisation for the Kursaal was received from the Local Government Board in October, tenders were secured and by early December the successful bid was announced

Ackland Hodge versus Matlock Bath UDC

How Charlie White expected to handle the muddle arising from the Council's appointment of two architects to design the Kursaal and a willingness to pay only one set of fees is unclear. In the event he wrote to Hodge dismissing him on the grounds that his dishonourable conduct made it impossible for the council to 'have further connections with him'. Hodge on winning the contract to refurbish the Royal in 1904 as an employee of Waring and Gillow, had immediately resigned, undertaking the work on his own account. He was sued and lost and it was this that provided White with the pretext he needed to part company with him.

In the case that followed it transpired that Hodge wasn't actually an architect. He was, he said 'to all intents and purposes an architect and fully entitled to call himself such.' But challenged as to whether he had ever actually produced architectural plans his best answer was 'only roughly; I could produce them but the draughtsmanship would not be very good.' He had an office in Gower Street and employed a draughtsman and a boy and, he said 'his office was as good as any which was in Gower Street.' But he was not a member of any architect's society. He had his supporters. They included Dr Sharpe of the Royal and Mr Bolton, chief of staff of the architectural department of the Great Northern Railway Company who said Hodge had supervised work at King's Cross.

The outcome initially was an outright victory for Hodge. The jury found he had not misrepresented his position; had been wrongfully dismissed and in its view was entitled to £230 for his work; £260 for work done with Nuttall (the successful architect) and £280 damages. The case was adjourned for further consideration and five months later, on appeal, Hodge was awarded just £230. It was argued he could not claim wrongful dismissal as he had not received a contract. A lucky escape for White and the council. Nevertheless an expensive error of judgement which surely would not have arisen in Lawton's time in the chair.

with a promise the work would be completed in time for Easter 1910.[33] At first the target seemed achievable. Before the end of January 1910 the *Derbyshire Advertiser* was able to report 'the walls of the Kursaal are rising apace, and there is little doubt of its being completed in the specified time if not before.' It noted with approval that many of the workmen had been selected from the unemployed.[34] The optimism was misplaced. When the Kursaal was opened it was for the August Bank holiday and even then it was incomplete and its surroundings 'in a chaotic state'. When it opened officially at Easter 1911, it offered an elegant ballroom, a popular roller skating rink, spacious luncheon, billiard and reading rooms and, significantly for those worthies of Matlock Bath who had continued to regard themselves as guardians of a watering place – a handsome Pump Room; the grounds were completed in June. The *Derby Daily Telegraph* hailed a new era for Matlock Bath Urban District Council as a purveyor of public amusements for visitors.

The Pavilion lost money; even before the season was out the auditor announced it would be a burden on the rates with very little prospect it would ever pay its way. Just 18 months earlier when the architects were appointed and it became clear the scheme would proceed the boast had been; 'such income will be derived from the Kursaal that the rates of the town will be materially reduced.'[35] The following year, 1912, would not have dispelled the gloom cast by the auditor's forecast. It was wet and the coal strike 'materially affected the number of excursionists'; for the first time in 60 years there were no trips to Matlock Bath on Good Friday or Easter Monday.[36] The Reverend Charles Baker, who had been the vicar of Matlock Bath since 1883, claimed that Matlock Bath was being punished. The council invited him to explain his view but he did not. This provoked a storm of discussion but little practical response.

White's address to the electorate in March 1912 contained elements of self-justification and of reproach. In 1907, when he was elected, the Council was carrying 'enormous loan debt'; yet the pavilion had to be built; it had been demanded by a large majority. Now, instead of helping to make it a success the Council was being criticised. He had offered the 'catering and the pump room to Matlock Bath people and all that was offered was a paltry £25.'

The Pavilion proved to be no yellow brick road for Matlock Bath UDC or for the ratepayers. The pump room was never going to be the catalyst that would trigger the regeneration of Matlock Bath as a watering place; that life was beyond recall. Nor did it become the income generator the ratepayers had been promised and it remained stubborn and unresponsive to all attempts to make it financially sustainable, a burden to successive councils and generations of councillors. But when the history of the Pavilion comes to be written and its social and cultural contributions to the Bath and the neighbourhood are weighed in the balance we do not doubt a more positive assessment will emerge. White's elephant it certainly was; but white elephant? Not for the four generations who have such happy memories of time spent at the Pav.

FIGURE 79. **The Grand Pavilion with the obelisk and a spar shop, postcard, about 1920.**

The postcard view shows the Pavilion 'in the unimaginative and none too costly spa architecture of 1910, rendered and painted, with a dome' as Nikolas Pevsner summarised it in his guide to Derbyshire buildings in 1956. In the foreground is a spar shop with the proprietor, the photographer, T. M. Henshall standing in the doorway. Earlier it had been run for many years by the Pearson family[37] and later by Ogdens. The shop was demolished when tennis courts were laid out behind it in 1921. The lantern was fixed on top of the obelisk[38] in January 1899 but today it appears in its original form. The Peak District Mining Museum was established in the Pavilion in 1978. It tells the story of Derbyshire's lead mining industry, which was important in the area for hundreds of years. And it holds a potent reminder of the other significant strand of the village's history: the drinking fountain still stands in the former Pump Room. Now in the hands of a local charity, the building is being restored and brought back into use.

Ken Smith collection.

The Royal Hotel

As Matlock Bath struggled to achieve its dream attraction the owners of the Royal Hotel poured money into a high quality refurbishment which earned lavish praise from the press and guests alike. The hotel was opened 'in the capable hands of E. Thoma-Badrutt formerly [of] St Moritz, Engadine'; the medical attendant was Dr Sharpe, 'one of the most eminent physicians and a gentleman who has a practically unique reputation in connection with the treatment of all diseases of the nervous system, rheumatism, etc., etc.,' and a 'medical department [that] offered everything on the latest and most approved principles.' It was linked by lift to all floors and boasted 'an excellent staff in every department - the bath attendants are specialists in their business - men and women of long training and experience – and the waiters and all the other attendants are most assiduous and attentive.' Special diets could be managed according to medical direction. A range of alarming sounding bath and electrical treatments were offered and more were added as competition with the Matlock hydros drove them all to keep up with the latest ideas; but the Royal claimed to be 'the chief establishment in England for the treatment by Fango di Battaglia' which used volcanic mud imported from Italy. The Royal also acknowledged the earlier reputation and use of Matlock Bath's mineral water supply and advertised a Pump Room forming part of the entrance to the hotel.[39] A first-class orchestra gave concerts twice daily. The

The Pavilion, Church and Royal Hotel   Matlock Bath

Stengel & Co., London E. C. 39 Redcross Street 16032

FIGURE 80. **The Royal Hotel Hydro, postcard, about 1900.**

When it finally opened in 1878, the Royal Hotel was Matlock Bath's most prominent hotel. On the hillside above is the Pavilion which opened in 1884 and which is described in Chapter 10 see also Figure 93. Note in the left foreground, the entrance to and start of the Switchback, a gravity-powered roller coaster in the Orchard Holme, now part of Derwent Gardens Figure 103. Neither the buildings nor the Switchback have survived.

Ken Smith collection.

extensive grounds offered croquet, tennis and bowls and the swimming bath which was free to residents; arrangements could be made for golf and fishing. Though clearly part of the original company's concept, it had taken more than a generation to bring to Matlock Bath the hydropathic facilities which since the 1850s had served neighbouring Matlock so well.

Once established in its new format, the Royal succeeded in sustaining a well-to-do clientele which was in marked contrast to the day visitors and boarding house guests who swarmed through other parts of the resort during the season. Lieut. Col. Newnham-Davies stayed at the Royal soon after it opened in 1906. His report in the *Pall Mall Gazette,* a London evening newspaper, included a passage designed to calm his metropolitan readers' fears that visiting Matlock Bath might mean mixing with visitors to the resort of a lower social class than their own – the day trippers.

'The trippers' he assured them *'disturb the sunny peace of Matlock but little. They arrive by train in the morning, and start off at once by char-a-banc to Haddon Hall or Chatsworth, or one of the other show places of the Peak district. They return in the afternoon, eat a big tea, feed the fishes in the pond, listen to the band and the Pierrots, dance a little, maybe, and go off again by early evening trains. They are quiet decent folk in the main, who have chosen a day amidst beautiful scenery in preference to the fiercer joys, and as they interfere in no way with the quiet of the Bath and the comfort of its visitors, it would be churlish to grudge them their pleasure in the beauties of Matlock's surroundings.'*

He also addressed another possible misconception. Though the Royal offered medical treatments it was, he believed, a comfortable and well managed hotel. Only the 'marble fountain in the hall' which spouts mineral water and 'the shrouded figures descending by the lift to the baths' and 'the sticks some of the guests use to help rheumatic limbs' are reminders that 'Matlock is a "cure" as well as a pleasure place.'

The hotel's continued growth gives some indication of its success; in 1908, a new £15,000 wing[41] was added in which, in 1922, a 'white and gold' ballroom was created as part of the restoration required for the reopening of the hotel after it had been requisitioned during the First World War. Late on Easter Monday, 1929, while a ball was in progress, the main hotel building was fatally damaged by fire. It was not re-built.[42]

FIGURE 83. **Briddon's stables, photograph c.1895.**

After the Old Bath estate was split up in 1863, the stables and horse pond shown here were leased to Herbert Briddon and continued in use as Briddon's livery stables. In 1895 Briddon had licences for six barouches, one landau, three charabancs and one brake. Daily excursions to Haddon and Chatsworth each cost 3/- and to Dovedale 4/-. The firm's effects sold in May 1908 included 37 horses and 41 carriages.[46]

Ken Askew collection.

FIGURE 84 (top left). **View looking south, half stereograph c. 1905.**

On the right is Briddon's waiting room; on the left Pearson's petrifying well. The Fishpond is still connected to the property to the north of it at first floor level.

John Bradley collection.

FIGURE 85 (bottom left). **Visitors in Matlock Bath, photograph, 1880.**

This photograph bears the hand-written date 1880. In 1932, a note written by Harry Gill, a local photographer, describes the scene as 'a party of visitors setting off to the Heights of Abraham'. Donkeys were widely used for excursions round Matlock Bath and this party could just as easily be returning from the Cumberland Cavern. The horse-drawn wagonette may have been on a trip to the Via Gellia, one of several popular outings from Matlock Bath in that direction.

Greatorex family collection.

FIGURE 86 (top right). **Customers outside the Old Bath Tap, photograph, 1880s.**

This rare photograph printed on metal and in a leather frame is believed to date from the 1880s. It shows a group of customers, including an army sergeant, outside the Old Bath Tap when Joseph Wadsworth was the licensee. This building was part of a complex which had provided stabling and coachmen's accommodation for the Old Bath Hotel. Later some knew it as the Horsepond Hotel and, by the early 1890s, when William Wyvill became the tenant, as the Fishpond Hotel. The Railway Office being advertised here is believed to have sold tickets and may have handled parcels. Later the office was housed in a kiosk in the corner beside Fishpond Hill; it was removed between the wars

Ken Askew collection.

FIGURE 87 (bottom right). **View from Fishpond Hill, half stereograph, about 1880.**

The large building on the right hand side, which later advertised itself as Boden's Dining Rooms and may have been built for that use, was a further development on the former Old Bath estate land. It was demolished after a fire when it was in use as the Spa Glove Factory in 1929. Beside it was a small building described in the Old Bath estate partition particulars as a hostelry. When both buildings were demolished in 1930 the area was landscaped by the Council around a path down to a new boat landing stage and waterfall by the river. Notice the horse pond is bounded by a low stone wall.

John Bradley collection.

The dispersal of the rest of the Old Bath estate

After the division of the Old Bath estate, the stabling site on the opposite side of the road to the Fishpond was leased to Herbert Briddon; he added a roadside waiting room and a ticket office and offered excursions to all the local attractions and scenic routes. This was the resort's transport hub. Croston describes it as the 'general rendezvous of the ostlers, stable helpers, donkey drivers, guides and gentlemen of varied yet undefined occupations, of which latter class Matlock seems to have rather an over-abundance' and where 'a picturesque group of singularly impassive looking donkeys, accompanied by some youthful members of the inhumane society, [who] are amusing themselves by constantly poking the sharp ends of their sticks between the ribs of unfortunate animals, all the while keeping up a running commentary on the personal appearance of the passers-by.' [44]

Another important site offered in the 1864 sale of the Old Bath estate was what is now Fishpond Hill and the property either side of it. A local man William Pearson bought it; the Old Bath's stable complex beside the Hill; became known as the Old Bath Tap and continued to offer stabling; Pearson created shops on the north side of it and a petrifying well on the land to the south of the Hill.[45]

FIGURE 88. **Visitors on South Parade in their 'Sunday best', 1890s. Enlarged half stereograph, photographer Alfred Seaman.**

John Bradley collection.

This is one of several images we have used from the photographer Alfred Seaman. Seaman (1844-1910), opened his first studio in Chesterfield in 1881, was a founder member of the prestigious Photographic Convention of the United Kingdom in 1886, and as Seaman and Sons ran studios across the Midlands and the north of England and for some part of the time at Bank Road, Matlock and Temple Road, Matlock Bath.

CHAPTER TEN

Catering for the wet day, and other developments

'On these wet days the tripper seeks the shelter of the refreshment room, and there enjoys himself to the confusion of the proprietor. Dinner or tea is served close on each other, the room is occupied for hours, and the takings are small.'

As we have suggested elsewhere, the character of the resort changed dramatically as the railway brought day trippers in their startling numbers. Their agenda was more urgent, and their timetable more compressed than for the staying guests. They came only for the day, a special holiday day, in their Sunday best, expecting to have a good time. For them the scenery still held its sway but not as a subject for a study of geology or philosophy or to sketch. The climb to High Tor or on Lover's Walk brought a thrill of adventure to the outing, even a shiver of danger at the cliff edge, or climbing the dark stairs of the Prospect Tower and actual danger on the river as rowers tried to change places in a wobbling boat or misjudged the power of the river. There were sometimes tragic consequences when with the river in flood, boats out of control were swept past warning notices to founder on the weir.[1] There was the chance to pursue a courtship or be on the lookout for a new beau; there was the helter-skelter on the Ferry Grounds and the Switchback in the Orchard Holme; ginger beer and pop and corned beef teas. No mention of taking the waters now.

But what could these crowds do if their excursion day was wet and cold? As the second half of the nineteenth century progressed attention was drawn to this fundamental weakness, the lack of indoor amusements. Croston,[2] in 1868 saw it as a shortcoming for all visitors, as Jewitt had done 30 years earlier[3] observing that when the charms of the scenery began to pale, the lack of a promenade, a concert room or place of public assembly means that 'visitors remain isolated in their apartments with little social intercourse;' or in Jewitt's words 'the visitor can form no new connexions nor does he know how to pass his time.' Croston exhorted Matlock Bath to be more public spirited. The Local Board found itself unable to act but there were a number of attempts to meet these needs from commercial enterprises.

A local businessman, Frederick Edwin Leggoe, made the first gesture in 1879, some 30 years after the arrival of the railway, though perhaps not in the form Croston had had in mind. He built the Albert Heights complex Figure 89, which was approached from Holme Road or the Valley Steps. It offered gardens, swings, a skittle alley, a shooting gallery, quoit ground, a gymnasium, a dancing platform and covered roller skating rink 100ft by 50ft. There was a coffee room and temperance dining rooms where 'dinners, teas and hot water [might] be obtained on very reasonable terms'.[4] Leggoe's venture, offered a welcome escape from a rainy day, but the enterprise was short lived; by 1892 there were plans for demolition.[5] It had received little publicity and by this time there were other attractions nearer at hand. Derwent Parade, now North Parade was complete with hostelries, dining rooms and shops with stalls spilling out onto the pavement.

Another privately financed development with facilities for indoor public recreation followed in 1882 when William and Mary Howe took down the old Fountain Bath and replaced it with a public swimming bath. This was open in the summer from 6.30 am to 10pm. Bryan[6] gives its dimensions as 50 feet by 30 feet and, in comparison to the former 'small, close and

FIGURE 89. **The view across the Upper Holme from the station, 1879.**

The picture shows the Midland Hotel bottom right. The long building, middle right, on the hillside above it is Leggoe's Albert Heights development. Above it but on the other side of Holme Road is the Clarence Hydro, which in 1872 was advertising itself as Clarence House Hydropathic Hotel. This was Matlock Bath's earliest claim to offer hydropathy though with no detail of what treatment was available at that time. In *Abel Heywood & Sons Guide* of 1904 the Clarence, now with the title Matlock Bath Hydropathic Establishment, advertised its hydropathy as 'the "Mild System" as described in Mrs Smedley's Manual, and Dr Sharpe's (late Dr Hunter's) Bath list, and as given by proficient attendants.

FIGURE 90. **North Parade, photograph, about 1915.**

The view shows North Parade with stalls on the forecourts. The property on the right was built by the bookseller T. H. Holmes in about 1868 and called Portland House. Later this name was reused at Clifton Road, see map. It was built on land purchased from Edward Wheatcroft with a covenant that any building on the site would not at any time be used as an ale-house or beer house.[7] In 1899 Frederick Dalton had created the Central Restaurant in Holmes's property with a large dining room extension built at the back enabling him to legitimately advertise 'Seats for 500'. The single-storey building seen in the centre of the picture as Ratcliffe's Dining Rooms, was built by F. E. Leggoe in about 1890. He owned the neighbouring Rockvale House, now no. 24-28, and later built the narrow single storey addition to it, to provide an entrance to a bake-house which he built behind the house. It is believed that he also constructed the steeply climbing Valley Steps between the Central and Ratcliffes as a route to his Albert Heights development Figure 89. Today, 2019, the steps are still in use. The lock-up shop on the right was run by the Misses Frances and Grace Cardin at this date. Their father, John, mineralogist and proprietor of the High Tor Grotto, stands in the doorway of the shop.[8]

Ken Askew collection.

inconvenient' bath house, describes the new building as light and airy with an elegant iron and wood roof and a row of commodious dressing boxes down the east side each artificially heated[9] Figures 91 and 92. Unlike Leggoe's investment which was an entirely new venture, the Howes delivered a skilful adaptation of an existing business, addressing the opportunities presented by the Bath's new clientele, extending their focus from the health to the leisure market. Their plan included a new building with frontage to the road. housing their established stationery business at street level and an assembly room[10], 60 by 22 feet later used as a dining room, on the first floor. But the water cure was not entirely given up, the complex offering a pump room 40 by 22 feet and private hot baths. These were open from 8.00 am and were, Bryan claimed, 'calculated to meet the requirements of every variety of case and the needs of any applicant for their use.'[11] Later for a period, the building was advertised as the Matlock Bath Hydro with 'Full Board and Residence [in conveniently situated well-appointed guest houses close to the Hydro] with Spa and Hydro Treatment, from £4 4s weekly'. The efficacy of the Radio-active Curative Thermal Spring water was recommended.

FIGURE 91. **The Fountain Baths, photograph, between 1887 and early 1890s.**

The photograph shows, on the left, the façade of the Fountain Baths complex with Howe's stationery shop on the ground floor and the assembly room above. The next two pairs of houses forming Fountain Villas were part of the first phase of the development of this section of Matlock Bath when the hillside was offered for sale in lots in 1844. By 1847 the furthest pair had been built and the development was completed three years later.

Ken Askew collection.

FIGURE 92. **The interior of the Fountain Baths, photograph, late 1920s.**

Ken Askew collection.

The first Pavilion

The largest investment in the resort's amenities in the last quarter of the nineteenth century was made by the Matlock Pavilion and Gardens Company Limited. This was formed by local businessmen and incorporated in 1882; 10,000 £1 shares were offered. Like F. E. Leggoe, they recognised the need for a venue for indoor entertainment. Work began in 1883 and on 28th July 1884 they opened their Pavilion. The opening event was a lavish affair despite the disappointment of not securing the attendance of the Prince of Wales. They made do with Lord Edward Cavendish who was met at the railway station by the Matlock Volunteers under the command of Captain F. C. Arkwright and escorted in procession through the town to the Pavilion. The building was designed by John Nuttall of Matlock Bridge, in Paxtonesque style, with much cast iron and glass and built at a cost of £7-8,000 on the hillside behind the Royal Hotel Figures 93 and 94.[12] Approached by gas-lit carriage drives from Temple Walk and Clifton Road, the Pavilion had a frontage of 228 feet, and a central hall 95 feet by 60 feet 'with rich dark red curtains'. At the north end there was a large refreshment room; at the south end offices and in the central transept a concert

FIGURE 93. **Central hall and South end of Matlock Bath Pavilion, photograph, soon after its completion in 1884.**

Derbyshire County Council Local Studies Library.

hall seating a thousand people.[13] It was set above 'three terraces with trim shrubs and gay borders of geranium and calceolaria'. During the summer months a band performed daily and it was the venue for concerts, plays, pantomimes, poultry and flower shows, dances, political rallies and celebrations. A contemporary account records about 6000 passing the turnstiles to attend the flower show there in 1886.[14] The grounds in which it was set included terraces and paths leading to caverns, the Speedwell and the Victoria, alcoves, tennis courts, and greenhouses. The area enclosed the Romantic Rocks or Dungeon Tors, the natural rock formations which had long been an attraction to visitors. A few small cottages at the northern edge of the site were demolished.[15]

On that opening day in July 1884 it was not only the large financial commitment resting in the balance; what were rapidly seen to be wildly extravagant expectations had become associated with the project. It offered the facilities the resort had needed for decades; surely this was the development that would turn back the clock, once again attracting the long staying visitors the resort had lost.[16] The Pavilion was not a financial success failing to break even every year until 1888, by which time its debt had become unmanageable. A crisis meeting of shareholders, confronted by a demand for between £8 and £9000, recognised they could not continue and in February 1889 the company was wound up. Earlier the directors had been asked why not make it more popular? The reminder that 'these are the days of tobogganing slides and switchback railways' met with the response 'If you make a place more popular in the accepted sense of the word you destroy the aristocratic air that pervades it. To cater for the thousands means to exclude the select.'[17]

The Pavilion had no licence to sell alcohol. The refreshment caterer, John Boden, applied annually to the September Licensing Sessions but was persistently refused; and there were restrictions on the entertainments that could be offered during Lent. But such constraints were not the cause of the Pavilion's failure. More fundamental issues determined its fate; decades late and conceived for an audience that had long departed the resort and would never be persuaded to return, it proved ill-equipped to find a place in the real market. It was a business that from the outset was designed to fail. Mr Williams from Birkenhead bought the Pavilion but ran it for only a year selling it to a Mr Emerson from Hull.[18] In 1905 it was purchased by the Royal Hotel. It was closed to the public in 1911, its use reserved for the hotel's guests though it could be hired for special occasions.

FIGURE 94. **Two views of the interior of the Pavilion.**

John Bradley collection.

After being requisitioned during the First World War, it was re-opened with improvements including electric lighting and re-named the Palais Royal. There was no such re-birth after use by the army catering corps in World War II; it fell into dereliction and became a dangerous playground for children who were baffled by its garish paintings of sides of meat; their use as teaching aids in the training of would–be army cooks only becoming clear to them many years later. The building was demolished in the 1960s. A hint of its former grandeur is reflected in the wide sweeping carriage drive and the stonework of its battlemented terracing which since 1978 have been used by Gulliver's Kingdom.

The great days of the Royal Pavilion were recalled with affection by Reginald Finney in a series of newspaper articles published in 1951. The building was clearly etched in his memory as the home of the cultural, social and musical entertainments of the late Victorian and Edwardian eras. With obvious pleasure he records the 'do' in 1898 to celebrate the wedding of Miss May Lawton, the eldest daughter of J. E. Lawton, the cotton master and the resort's most prominant local resident, when all Matlock Bath's young people got a commemorative gift, the band concerts including performances by the Guards Band and other 'crack brass combinations', the 'cream of minstrel shows', the pantomimes and melodramas, the winter monthly Masson Mill parties 'when management and staff let themselves go to the music of the works band' and played Kiss in the Ring - and the carnivals Figure 95. He wrote 'One of the best carnivals I have ever seen ended there with a final ball attended by King Billy Daniels, his Consort and his Court'. Perhaps most difficult to imagine today is the vividness with which he recalled the political rallies and lectures held there. He himself doubted whether there would ever again be such political fervour as when, in celebration of Victor Cavendish, later the 9th Duke of Devon-

FIGURE 95. **Matlock Bath carnival float, photograph, date uncertain but 1920s.**

The seated figure wearing a crown is "King" Billy Daniels. He and his court were photographed near the New Bath Hotel.

Greotorex family collection.

shire, being first elected to parliament in 1891, the horses were released and manpower hauled his carriage up the long slope from Temple Walk to the Royal.

As the Pavilion stood derelict, Finney asked his readers: 'Does not the old place deserve a better fate?' There was no effective response.

Celebrating the Jubilee

March 1887 found the resort's most prominent ratepayers meeting[19] together to consider how the community might celebrate Queen Victoria's Golden Jubilee. They had in front of them an offer from F. C. Arkwright of land to lease on the east side of the river on which to create public walks providing they would take responsibility for erecting a bridge to reach it and the new fencing that would be required. This was the catalyst for the ambitious plan that emerged from the meeting. It included not only the bridge and the new walks but on the west side of the river the much needed promenade.[20] This was an idea with a long history. A generation earlier in 1852 James Clifford Newbold had proposed a scheme said to have 'originated with the late George Stephenson and for which the valuable aid of Sir Joseph Paxton might be gratuitously relied upon in due course.'[21]

As in 1874[22] when 300 yards of promenade had been created, the new section which would extend it southwards would also have to be funded by public subscription there being no prospect of the responsibility being taken up by a Local Board still bruised from its recent encounter with the Local Government Board. In 1882 the LGB had refused to sanction borrowing for the Local Board's own scheme for a promenade until the Bath's sanitation problems were addressed see page 169; an issue of such magnitude that would not be resolved in the foreseeable future and so with no capital funding within its gift, the Local

FIGURE 96. **North Parade, photograph, early 1880s.**

At this date 'the approach to the railway station along the Parade was seared by an ugly stone wall which hid away the beauties of the river.'[23] Part of Fountain Villas on the left of the picture, was in use by 1880 as a Ladies College and was run by the Misses Peall who offered 'Board and Instruction in Branches of a solid English Education at a price of 35 guineas a year.'

Reproduced by permission of W. W. Winter Ltd, Derby.

Board's contribution to the Jubilee plan was restricted to taking on the Arkwright lease and the maintenance of the completed scheme.

Much was expected of the jubilee proposals. They were perceived to be transformational. They would popularise Matlock Bath and bring more visitors, increasing 'permanently the population as a health resort and even as the plans were under discussion at the rate-payers' meeting, 20 tradesmen pledged £5 each.[24] It was in an atmosphere of euphoric self confidence that the Jubilee committee embarked on its task. It was not long before it became apparent it was chasing an elusive target. Costs of £400 rose to £500 and then rose further. The members of the committee, determined to hand over the development free of debt, put in their own money, only admitting defeat finally when they learned of legal bills not included in the plan. In January 1888 seeing there was no alternative, they appealed to the Board; after a fraught debate it reluctantly agreed to cover the £30 shortfall.[25]

By the middle of August 1887[26] the work was complete. A promenade 17 feet wide had been created alongside the Derwent as far south as Mr Howe's Public Baths; and by crossing the new bridge, supplied by the Butterley Company there was now access to a new river-side promenade with a gated entrance from Lover's Walk, and 'circuitous walks' up the slopes laid out on the land leased from F. C. Arkwright and now to be known as the Jubilee Grounds. It was a remarkable achievement from a small community; in today's money[27], in just a few months, the committee had raised at least £65,000 and delivered a complex scheme involving land purchase and lease, legal aspects, design, contracts and site works. This was a development rare in the history of the resort that did not disappoint its promoters; indeed it surely exceeded their expectations. It opened up an alternative attractive pathway to the streams of trippers coming from the station and offered them a first view of the river. The promenades also provided a venue for some of the entertainments expected in a Victorian resort, riverside spectacles, minstrel and pierrot shows, concerts. The venue was enhanced when public subscription raised the money to build the bandstand on the Jubilee Grounds in 1893. It did not offer much shelter until 1908 when the UDC added the public shelter and lavatories at the north end of the Promenade.[28]

FIGURE 97. **The Jubilee Promenade from the south, photograph, about 1890.**

Note the Jubilee Bridge in the background and the absence of riverside railings.

Reproduced by permission of W. W. Winter Ltd, Derby.

FIGURE 98. **A busy day along North Parade, after 1906.**

Compared with the last picture note that the promenade railings have been changed to unclimbable fencing securing the promenade so that a fee could be charged for entry. The blinds over the shop fronts are a prominent feature in this and many other views. Their purpose was often, as here, to protect the pavement stalls rather than to prevent goods fading in the shop window displays. The cab rank for horse-drawn carriages beside the railings and another one at the station attracted complaints about the sloppy and filthy condition under foot and the very offensive smell. There are new buildings on Upperwood Road which were added in the first few years of the twentieth century.

In 1906, the council began buying the promenade land which they had previously leased and decided a charge should be made to enter it. The proposal was met with a clamour of local opposition and scorn. 'Busy Bee' of the *High Peak News,* adopting the role of Matlock Bath's conscience regretted the unenviable notoriety Matlock Bath was gaining 'as the only health resort in the Kingdom without a sufficiency of free seats' ignoring the value of seeing visitors feeling 'comfortable, happy and welcome' rather than 'sour and grudging'. Matlock derided Matlock Bath for its high rates, for giving away its birthright, for its failures per square yard and ridiculed the idea, then under discussion, of a pump room with – who wants to pay for a glass of water? It boasted of its own recent progress going from strength to strength, and its recently opened Pic Tor Promenade, the only free promenade in the district.[29] Despite the outcry, unclimbable fencing' was installed along the Promenade with

FIGURE 99. **Kiosk and turnstile on the Promenade, postcard, about 1910.**

This view looks north along the Promenade towards the Midland Hotel. The folded down white canopy of a movable stage visible in the distance was the venue for pierrot performances. For Easter 1910 Mr W H May's Smart Society Cadets from Southport were hired to give three performances a day. Large audiences were expected. The war memorial stands on the site today.

Ken Smith collection.

turnstiles and wooden pay kiosks at the gates where visitors were charged twopence.[30] A policy it later regretted, changing its mind and reopening the promenade though by Whit Monday 1911 it was closed again except for the area round the Jolly Japs pierrot stand. Eventually the turnstiles were moved. One was placed at the entrance to the Jubilee Bridge and continued in use until the road-widening scheme of 1968-9 destroyed the Promenade, reducing it to a small area of garden so that access to the bridge was now from the pavement Figures 99 and 101.

Well into the twentieth century, guide books continued a dismal commentary on the threepenny and sixpenny charges demanded to go here or there in Matlock Bath. And there were many complaints of noisy touts seeking customers for their 'miraculous cavern' or petrifying well or boating station in competition with hawkers and stallholders shouting for the attention of the passers-by and all trying to make themselves heard above the bawling of brake and wagonette drivers. In the 1890s the Board and later the UDC intervened to curb this nuisance and evidently to some effect by 1898 winning praise from the *Derbyshire Times;* 'In days not long gone by Matlock Bath was an atmosphere impregnated with the torturing shouts of 'tea and hot water; 'hot dinner' or 'this way to the finest petrifying well

in Matlock.' All this is being suppressed by the authorities. There is no street hawking. 'Matlock rock' is not boomed as it used to be.'[31]

Early in the twentieth century on this stretch of the river - overlooked by the Promenade, the Venetian Fete was organised. This annual Fete, one of Matlock Bath's special attractions which still continues, had been inspired by the celebrations held to mark Queen Victoria's Diamond Jubilee in 1897. Each year the woodland is illuminated and the river made the setting for a procession of decorated boats. Originally the woodland decorations were whitewashed geometrical shapes and like the boats, had designs picked out by candles in coloured glass pots – 13,000 candles were recorded one year - lit with the help of local children earning precious pocket money. For some years the celebration was held twice, on a Saturday in May and again in September but later was restricted to September only and subsequently held over a longer period making use of the darker evenings to extend the visitor season. Over 8000

FIGURE 100 (top) **Pierrots performing in the bandstand, photograph, about 1905.**

Tony Holmes collection.

FIGURE 101. (bottom) **View of the entrance to the Jubilee Bridge.**

The sign board advertises 'Entrance to Lovers' Walks. Performances by the band 11-12 2-4 6-8.'

Ken Smith collection

paid for admission in September 1906[32] when Lover's Walk was 'resplendent with thousands of coloured lights' and a show of aquatic fireworks preceded the boat procession. The competition for the best illuminated tableau on land was an additional attraction. As late as the 1950s, on the opening night of the Fete, the A6 through Matlock Bath was closed to traffic and huge crowds thronged the thoroughfare. The event today is held further south on the river and electric lights have long since replaced the candle pots.[33]

FIGURE 102. **Boats dressed for the Venetian Fete, photographs, 1909 and 1926.**

The decorated boat moored at the landing stage in front of Fountain Villas in May 1909 is a model based on a proposed but unused plan for the Kursaal, the building now 2019, called the Pavilion. At this date, rowing boats could be hired from this and several other landing stages along the river. Behind the man holding the ladder, a circular wooden decoration for the Fete leans against the fence. Some at least of the interested onlookers should probably be engaged in suspending it. The decorated boat depicting the Switchback in Derwent Gardens, was the prize winning entry in the Venetian Fete in 1926.

Ken Smith collection.

The amusement park

The amusement park which was launched in 1889 on the Orchard Holme, (now part of Derwent Gardens), a strip of flat riverside land in Matlock Bath, was a latecomer to Matlock Bath's clutch of pleasure grounds and different. A small private venture targeting day trippers, it was in stark contrast to the Lover's Walk on the opposite bank of the river which, more than 150 years earlier, had been created to satisfy the tastes of the fashionable aesthetes and the gentlefolk.[34]

The entrepreneur behind the Orchard Holme development was Herbert Buxton, a local businessman for whom, in April 1889 Mr Bratby began to construct a gravity-powered switchback roller-coaster. This was a new form of popular entertainment which proved a great success in Matlock Bath.[35] The screams of terrified riders drew crowds of interested onlookers to watch from the roadway above despite complaints of the smells from

Mr Buxton's son's pigs and fish boxes during the many years the southern end of the pleasure ground was used as a tip for domestic rubbish and road scrapings. The Orchard Holme offered other, more traditional attractions, riverside walks and gardens, a thermal water fishpond, a petrifying grotto and a café which was opened there in 1907. In the entrance to the Switchback there were penny slot machines and local intelligence had it that on busy days Buxton had to carry his takings home in a wheelbarrow. In the early 1930s the gardens fell into disuse and when Mr Hackett from Southport took over the site the switchback was found to have no foundations and was dismantled.[36] In 1951 Matlock Urban District Council purchased the gardens and in 1968 the body that organised and promoted the annual fete, the Matlock Bath Venetian Fete and Illuminations Committee, became the lessee.[37] Developments instigated during the Illuminations Committee's tenure in 1969 included a new bridge linking the Derwent Gardens to the Lover's Walk; a band stand, replaced by one in the Victorian idiom in 1993-94, and water gardens.[38]

FIGURE 103. **The Switchback under repair or alteration, photograph, about 1913.**

The Switchback Railway in the Orchard Holme.[39] The cars were gravity powered which meant that travellers had to make up for some loss of height on each leg of the trip by walking up the last few yards at each end. The cars were manhandled back to the required height to be launched again Figure 104. The picture shows the proprietor's brother Edgar Buxton in the bowler hat with, from left to right, Bill? Frost, Tom Frost and Bill? Barber. Edgar Buxton was killed in France in May 1918.

Private collection.

FIGURE 104. **Passengers alighting from the Switchback, early 1900s.**

Two more of Percy Rowbottom's images.

Ken Smith collection.

FIGURE 105. **Brass band in the Orchard Holme, about 1910.**

This band posing in the Orchard Holme is reported to be the Masson Mills Band. To meet the demand for bands to play on the Promenade and at the Pavilion during the season, visiting bands were employed, some military, some commercial and some from other towns in the county. In the 1890s provision became more local with the formation of the Matlock Bath and District Military Band in 1891 and the Masson Mills Prize Band in 1893. Among other local bands, the Pavilion Band and the Lea Mills Prize Band were also regularly employed.

Ken Askew collection.

FIGURE 106. **Boating on the Derwent, after T. Allom, engraved by Lowry, published by Fisher, Son & Co, London, 1836.**

This view looking south towards Cromford from the level of the boat landing stage behind the Pavilion shows in Ebeneezer Rhodes' words 'a pleasant alcove for the loitering traveller to rest in and if further amusement is required it is here at hand: Walker's spar Museum and workshop adjoining will furnish a pleasant half hour's lounge.' The shelter is still in use, the shop is no longer open.[40]

Private collection.

FIGURE 107. **Boat landing stage on the River Derwent, photograph, about 1885.**

This later view of the opposite bank of the river shows the area from which rowing boats may still be hired in season. The area to the left, behind the ivy- covered boat-house, was the Orchard Holme, now Derwent Gardens. The shed on the extreme right has an upturned boat forming a picturesque roof. There were other similar shelters along Lover's Walk in living memory.

Reproduced by permission of W. W. Winter Ltd, Derby

The Ferry Grounds

The area beside the river to the north of the Orchard Holme was known as the Ferry Grounds. It had been at the heart of Matlock Bath life since the eighteenth century. The ferry plied from the landing stage there taking visitors to explore Lover's Walk and later there were rowing boats for hire. Enjoyment of the river scenery was always alluded to in descriptions of a tourist's day; boating by moonlight sometimes to musical accompaniment was an added delight. John James Audubon (1780-1851) visiting in 1826 made his own accompaniment 'I rode and I sung, up, down, and up the Derwent again.' He was relaxing on a trip to Europe which he had made for the more serious purpose of finding a publisher for his drawings, the images which famously survive in his book *The Birds of America*.[41]

FIGURE 108. **Half stereograph, enlarged, Alfred Seaman, early 1900s.**

The ferry landing stage, Lover's Walk.

John Bradley collection.

More landing stages opened in the nineteenth century as other landowners exploited the river bank but this site has remained in continuous use. Regattas were staged here in the late nineteenth and early twentieth centuries and not just as local events. In 1904 the regatta was advertised as far afield as London,

Liverpool, Manchester, Sheffield, Nottingham and Bradford and brought large numbers of visitors. Matlock Bath's Rowing Club which was based in the Derwent Gardens did not re-form after the 1914-18 war. Despite the river being heavily polluted[42] there were swimming events too and in 1907, the quarter mile swimming championship of the Derwent, previously confined to Derbyshire entrants, was opened to all England.

FIGURE 109. **Some attractions for visitors, stereographs, 1890's.**

Feeding the fish. Penny slot machines which dispensed fish food were introduced in summer 1898.

At leisure on the Promenade

John Bradley collection.

CHAPTER ELEVEN

Masson Mill 1874-1991

In 1872 Sir Richard Arkwright's great grandson, Frederic Arkwright (1806-1874) considered selling Masson Mill and those few parts of his Cromford Mills still in use.[1] Masson Mill was valued at £5,874. In May of that year I. P. Clarke and Co of King Street Mills, Leicester showed interest in leasing the mill. The Company's letter of enquiry read 'we quite understand in our interview with Mr Arkwright that the mills do not pay now, but still, at a moderate rent, we have every confidence that we could make them pay.' No agreement was reached and it would seem Frederic was at a loss to know how the mills might be brought up to date. It was left to his son Frederic Charles Arkwright who became squire at the age of 21 in 1874 to solve the problem.

When Masson Mill came into the hands of Frederic Charles Arkwright (1853-1923) the new young landlord is unlikely to have had any greater knowledge of the cotton industry than his father but whether by luck or good judgement it was he who secured a future for the mill, the outcome that had eluded his father. The solution came in the form of a 31 year old cotton spinner from Dukinfield, John Edward Lawton (1848-1915). He began his work at Masson in[2] 1879 first as manager then, after a year, stepping up into a partnership. This was formalised in March 1883 in a legal agreement with Frederic Charles Arkwright.[3] Their partnership was to undertake the business of cotton spinners and cotton manufacturers under the name of Arkwright and Company. Lawton was to 'devote a fair and reasonable amount of his time' to its management. The contract allowed him £200 per year for his hotel and travelling expenses although the money was to be retained within the partnership as capital. He did not move to Matlock Bath immediately, retaining his interests in Dukinfield, even serving as a member of the Local Board. By 1891 he had moved to Matlock, the census of that year shows the family in residence at Glenorchy Villa, Matlock Bath.[4] The agreement set Arkwright's contribution to the capital of the enterprise at £8,500, being the value of the stock and plant to which Lawton was to add £1000 immediately and a further £500 within three months. Losses were to be borne by the two partners in proportion to the sums they had contributed to the capital and net profits were to belong to the partners equally. The business was to pay £333 per year to rent the 103 cottages currently occupied by mill employees and owned by Arkwright.[5]

FIGURE 110. **Masson Mill.**

The modern postcard on the left shows the stylish façade of the mill which Richard Arkwright built in 1783-84. The venetian windows and the elegant bell cupola give the projecting central bays an architectural style which would not look amiss in a country house, though do not be misled, the design is intensely practical. The projection housed the stairs, lavatories and offices on each floor so that the working floors in the body of the mill were clear of obstruction and could house machinery with maximum efficiency. The mill appears to have 5 storeys here but the ground floor and the original entrance door with a Gibbs surround[6] and flanked by venetian windows is below the entrance shown here which is approached by a bridge across the yard in front of the mill. In 1900 working space was increased by building a single storey extension over the yard. Arkwright forsook local gritstone, to build this mill in red brick on a stone plinth as he did at Wirksworth when he built the mill now known as Haarlem Mill[7] The brasher red brick of the 1911 extension at the Masson site is just visible at the right hand side of the picture. The earlier black and white picture on the right shows the mill in 1956 before the restoration of window openings and the bell cupola. The cupola had been removed some time after the second world war but was restored and replaced by English Sewing Cotton and the Arkwright Society in 1975 as part of the European Architectural Heritage year programme. The bell was a feature of great importance in the early mills when few employees would have owned a clock. It rang to mark the beginning and end of the working day. In the morning those who had not passed through the gates before the bell stopped ringing were locked out for the day. The Masson bell was used until 1939.

Historic England.

From the description of the machinery that would remain in use and was included in the agreement, it is clear that the mill was still spinning cotton; there were carding engines, drawing frames, roving frames and ring throstles as well as the winding frames and doubling frames needed for making thread.[8] It is clear that successive generations of the Arkwright family had failed to re-equip the mill with up to date machinery. In August 1855 the *Manchester Weekly Advertiser,* recorded comments from a German visitor to Masson Mill who was himself familiar with his own country's Cromford Mills at Ratingen. He described 'the great inventor's machinery, mahoganied by age, still at work there after more than seventy years of toil and [turning] out…a much better product than the new machinery, though not producing with the same speed.' Ten years later when James Arkwright who had had some experience of running the business earlier in his career, came to live at Oak Hill at Cromford to help his father Peter, in the management of the mills,[9] the local press had reported the remodelling of Masson Mill with "new and beautiful machinery". But clearly that had not been enough and essentially, John Edward Lawton's role was to modernise the mill. Its machinery was archaic; its products uncompetitive and its power supply unreliable.

In 1884 Lawton's attempt to get rid of what he described as 'antique machinery...very suitable for Museums, Exhibitions and such like purposes' in a sale[10] at Cromford Mills met with little success and six years later, in 1890, the upper floors of the five storey mill/warehouse building at Cromford still contained 'many ancient and curious cotton machines, stranded relics of the early days of manufacture.'[11]

Masson's power supply was fine apart from when the river Derwent was in flood and the two wheels were drowned or in times of drought when there was insufficient water to run the machinery.[13] The result was short time working or a total shutdown and it was to this problem that Lawton turned his attention in 1888 when a steam engine was installed to supplement the water wheels Figure 111.[14] At the commissioning ceremony, Lawton reviewed the recent life of the cotton industry, reminding his audience

Calling in the Professionals: the Melville partnership.

The earliest evidence of the Arkwright family recognising the need to enlist professional expertise occurs in the 1830s in the partnership between William Melville (c. 1777-1847) and James Charles Arkwright (1813-1869) who had stepped in to help his father Peter (1784-1866) manage the Masson and Cromford textile enterprise. William and David Melville of Nottingham and London ran an established business dealing in hosiery, lace thread and cotton. But in May 1832 the partnership between these two brothers broke up and at some point after this and certainly by 1836, William had entered a new partnership, his new partner being J. C. Arkwright. Exactly what function Melville performed is not clear. Chapman suggests it was Melville's marketing connections and expertise that attracted the Arkwrights, and this may have been the case. He was in no haste to move house remaining resident in Nottingham until 1842 when he relocated to Oak Hill, the house Richard Arkwright (1755-1843) had recently built in Cromford. The partnership survived until 1846 when it was dissolved by mutual consent 'the business to be carried on by J. C. Arkwright'. Melville died the following year.[12]

that Masson Mill had started when the total consumption of cotton in this country was not more than 1000 bales weekly and Great Britain enjoyed nearly the entire textile trade of the world. The margin then was 9 shillings and two pence per pound compared with three and one eighth pence now and it was no secret that Mr Arkwright had continued to work these mills for many years past at a heavy loss. 'The sole influence which [had] operated in his mind has been a deep-rooted, inborn consideration for the people employed here; and an anxiety to promote the welfare of the district.' The costly machinery[15] being inaugurated [that day] was evidence of that concern and of the wish 'to avoid any further irregular working, and so secure continuous employment for all concerned.' His partner, confirming the many years of poor performance, added 'since he had the ownership of the concern, for a period of 14 years, he had not received sixpence out of it.'[16]

Lawton also installed new production machinery[17] and by 1883 had already begun his work. Mr Young who managed the Cromford Mill workforce, speaking on behalf of the work people of both Masson and Cromford at F. C. Arkwright's wedding celebration remarked on 'the introduction of modern machinery and the new systems of working which [had] already so materially improved [the work people's] position and prospects.' He paid tribute to the 'considerable sacrifice' made by Arkwright in keeping them in work so following the 'generosity of [his] ancestors, who had kept their work people employed during the cotton famine.'[18]

At about the same time the mill embraced steam power Lawton made the decision which ensured its survival and defined its future. Recognising the trade at home and abroad was increasingly precarious he switched the main focus of production towards sewing threads for the new and rapidly expanding retail market. With the benefit of hindsight this may seem a routine managerial decision; an obvious change in strategy. Closer examination reveals just how complex this operation was for those implementing its delivery and how easily it might have become a costly mistake. Our view of the process derives from a report in February 1891 from Richard Webster (c.1850-1922), the mill manager, and George Hough. The year 1890, as they catalogue its episodes, emerges as difficult for the mill's traditional trades and not

Advertisement, *The Sunday School Times*, February 1886.

helped by the breakdown of the power transmission system and repairs to the larger of the mill's two water wheels; events which brought the entire mill to a standstill for the entire month of July.[19] Later in the year the MacKinley Tariff, which imposed a sharp rise in the duty paid on imported goods, disrupted the American trade in gassed thread and led to further irregular working while the markets for skeins in Bulgaria, Romania and Egypt for a period of three months ceased altogether, putting about 100 of the workforce on half time. The report concludes 'the consequences of these setbacks would have been serious had it not been for the grey sewing cottons' i.e. the new sewing thread products.

It is not clear when Lawton began the reorientation of the mill but, by 1890, though the new spooling machinery[20] had been installed, the workforce was still learning how to operate it efficiently and there were still changes being made to existing machinery.[21] Even the mill's 'Sanitary arrangements and lavatories' were altered, provision being made for the 120 working in the new spooling department 'so as to secure the cleanliness and neatness which is all important amongst such expensive material.' These adjustments to the machinery and buildings were routine compared with the unrelenting grind of the staff training. For 'everyone engaged in the Spooling Department' it was 'a year of trouble and hard work'.

'The class of people required is much higher and superior to the average and their training has been a source of constant care, trouble and great expense. All the native labour employed has had to be taught and after weary months of teaching the proficiency attained by many has not been what is essential and the process has had to be gone over and over again with others.'

They still lacked a full complement of trained staff.

> 'The machinery of the Department requires 24 Hank Winders. Of this number
> we have successfully trained 17. 6 Ballers have been trained, 4 are women from
> Manchester – 60 Thread Spoolers; 37 can now do the work; 3 are from Manches-
> ter, 12 are learning and 8 have yet to be taught. We have now trained labour from
> the district working the three Self Act machines. In the Making Up branch the
> lack of securing efficient labour has been accomplished.'

Making thread of marketable quality was just part of the challenge; it then had to be sold
and this required a sales team. Their first task was to establish a brand and acquaint
the market with this new name in sewing machine thread. They seem to have achieved
immediate success.[22] Between July 1890 and February 1891 3000 ledger accounts were
opened and 1801 customers supplied of whom 721 had reordered. For the 1891 new year,
10,000 calendars and a large quantity of samples were distributed in and around Manchester, leading to the largest retailer offering a 5 year order. Abroad, openings for the new
thread were secured in Melbourne, Calcutta, Madras, Constantinople, France, Spain, City
of Mexico and Vera Cruz. The response was so positive that the authors of the report could
claim despite all the costs in promotion and manufacturing, the new venture had already
reached break even and they predicted by June 1891 there would be a clear nett profit.
For them this was the future of the mill. 'The gassed yarn trade was full of uncertainty...
and played out. The Nottingham portion [had] disappeared altogether.' Yet however the
MacKinley Tariff might turn out or whatever the changes in fashion they were confident
the retail trade would prosper.

> 'As a thread Manufactory Masson Mills in its building, accommodation, its
> machinery, and the class of work people, when trained, [afford] peculiar and
> important advantages for a permanent and expanding business of a substantial
> and very profitable type. Its location set between the large centres of population
> [gives] it a great advantage over almost every other competitor. On account of
> the enormous difficulties in its very nature and of the great expense and cost of
> its establishment at the beginning, there are very few thread makers. Whilst the
> consumption of thread is daily, if not hourly, expanding, because outside and
> beyond the necessities of an increasing and prospering people every household,
> however humble, indulges in the ambition of a Sewing Machine, and just as the
> competition of the score of Sewing Machine makers resides in the regular improve-
> ment of their machines involving a higher rate of speed, so those machines require
> cotton, and not merely an increased quantity but an increased quality, and as this
> problem of quality has been solved to the satisfaction of the public by 3 or 4 thread
> makers only, it follows that a limitless field is open.'

The years that followed would show that the new marketplace was neither limitless nor
without fierce competition, though the six cord sewing cotton[23] branded with an early
version of one of Sir Richard's spinning frames did establish the Arkwright name on the

nation's high streets. Successful as it was, Lawton's regeneration of the mill could not alter the fact that Masson remained a small producer and so, like its peers, vulnerable in competition with larger players, and the extent of its profitability in the 1890s is uncertain see page 161.

Though the Mackinley Tariff was modified in 1894, four years later, protectionism remained an issue for British producers. The way round this barrier was to establish manufacturing facilities within the United States but this was a remedy available only to large well-funded enterprises and not to single mill companies. Coats had addressed the problem with some success. They had begun manufacturing in the United States as early as 1869 and by 1896, when they took over Clarks, their greatest rivals, also based in Paisley, they controlled about 65 per cent of the American market, 80 per cent of the cotton sewing thread market in the UK and had become the largest company in British textiles and manufacturing. Their competitors in the home market, some twenty or so small producers, faced with the prospect of increased pressure on their existing markets from the Coats-Clark merger recognised they were facing an existential threat. Immediate action was required if they were to survive.

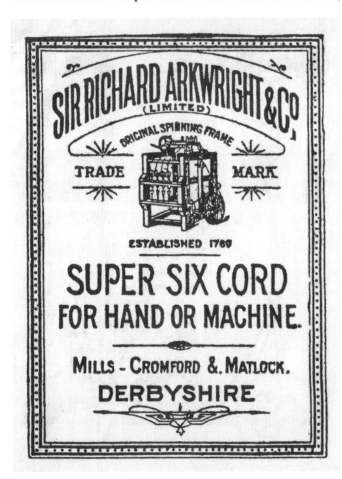

It would appear that among the first to recognise this threat and identify a solution was John Edward Lawton. His solution, the creation of an English combine to bring together the leading sewing thread manufacturers outside the Coats behemoth, was to have far reaching consequences for the mills in the Derwent Valley, in our judgement even to the extent that had Lawton not acted as he did the working lives of Masson Mills and those in Belper and Milford in sewing thread production, might not have extended much beyond the early years of the twentieth century. We include an account of Lawton's part in the creation of the English Sewing Cotton Company at pages 156 to 165.

Masson Mill was throughout its working life a major source of employment for the settlements surrounding Matlock Bath though not for the resort itself which well into the nineteenth century had a resident population too small to sustain a large enterprise. It offered continuous rather than seasonal employment though predominantly for women and children. Detailed records of the numbers of mill workers engaged by the Arkwrights have not survived and the best we can offer is a series of estimates from sources sometimes of uncertain reliability. In 1789 the figure was said to be 800; by c.1800 the Cromford Mills and Masson were considered to employ 1,150 but by 1833 the payroll for Masson was 350 (see the panel below); and by 1865 it had about halved to 156. The most reliable information which has come to hand relates to March, the following year, when George Tissington[24] provided his employer, Peter Arkwright, with the following information which we must assume included the workers still employed at Cromford where the severely reduced water supply had restricted operations mainly to preparatory and finishing processes such as winding and the making up of bundles for despatch.[25] This account is of particular value as it provides not only a comparison with nine months earlier when the effects of the cotton famine would still have been evident but offers an analysis of where the business had recruited its workforce. In March 1866 there were 210 full time and 31 half time, compared with the very much smaller numbers of 70 and 15, in June the previous year. Of the full timers, 123 lived in Cromford, 48 in Middleton, 27 in Bonsall, 8 in Matlock Bath and 4 in Bole Hill. There are also reliable figures for 1868 which records a workforce of 186 for Masson alone and in 1883 200 for Cromford and Masson together.[26] These are not the statistics of a vibrant healthy business. They reflect the exigencies of the cotton trade the Arkwright family's management of the mills and the effects of the cotton famine of 1861-5 which put half a million British millworkers out of work.[27]

Medical Examination of the Factory belonging to Messrs. ARKWRIGHT (Cotton Mill), at Matlock, on 4th June 1833.

Temperature — Highest, 74.

Ventilation — Indifferent.

Cleanliness — Moderate.

Work — Begins at six o'clock and ends at seven o'clock.

Relaxation for meals — Half an hour for breakfast, one hour for dinner, quarter or half an hour for tea.

Hot water afforded gratuitously or not — Gratis.

Holidays in the year — Christmas Day, Good Friday, Shrove Tuesday, half a day Whit Monday, 12th May half a day, half a day at Bonsale Wakes, four days at Cromford Wakes.

Medical assistance — Provided by the master gratuitously.

Total number of persons employed of all ages — About 350.

Total number of persons employed below 18 years of age — About 110.

General appearance and situation — Old.

Examination

Extract from *British Parliamentary Papers, Employment of Children in Factories,* 1833 D3, page 260.

There is some evidence that the Arkwrights, shielded from the competition experienced by other employers in the larger textile centres, with what in effect was a pool of captive labour, paid well below the going rate; according to one estimate perhaps 12 or 20 per cent lower than Preston or Blackburn. William Dodd who visited Masson in December 1841 records boys starting at 2 shillings a week advancing by 3 or 6 pence a year; men earning 10 shillings and women 6 shillings a week with the overlookers receiving 12 or 13 shillings; all worked 12 hour days and a 72 hour week. There was little mobility. *'They do not shift about from place to place as many of the factory people of large towns are in the habit of doing; but often spend their whole lives in these mills and bring families into the world with no better prospects than their own. Of course they see and know little beyond the beautiful and romantic hills by which they are surrounded.'*[28] Some more detail of the working of the Arkwright mills will be found in *Cromford Revisited*.

FIGURE 111. **Masson Mill, from the south, photograph taken between 1888 and 1897.**

The water wheels at Masson Mill were said to develop 325 horse power[29] but when the river was low or in flood they could not work effectively and production was interrupted. In 1888, to provide auxiliary power, a 100 horse-power high pressure steam engine from Messrs Marshall, Sons & Co. of Gainsborough was installed at the south western corner of the mill with a chimney, visible in this view, constructed inside the mill and a boiler house situated between the mill and the manager's house. In August the engine was christened with champagne by Frederic Charles Arkwright's wife, Rebecca, and was given her name. This is described in the Stott survey as a 90 H.P. compound condensing engine with belt drive to the 1st, 2nd and 3rd storeys and recorded as 'insufficient to supplement the wheels in a time of drought.' Earlier, in February, Masson Mill had acquired its own electricity supply and was partly lit by electricity,[30] a development which was 'judged to be a great success'

Ken Askew collection.

In October 1897 the celebrated firm of architects, engineers and valuers, Stott and Sons of Manchester was commissioned to survey and value the Masson Mills prior to the purchase of the Arkwright textile interests by the new sewing thread combine, the English Sewing Cotton Company. The survey described the business carried on at the mills as 'that of cotton doubling, gassing, spooling etc'. It provides a room by room description and includes a date for every significant machine or piece of equipment in the mill. Lawton's influence is clear; one or two winders had been in the mill since 1879 but they were the exception; the machinery for the most part had been renewed in the last ten years.

Stott's considered the power source particularly carefully. They found the wheels offered 325 horse power on average for eight months of the year and 130 horse power for four.

They estimated the cost of delivering this level of power with a steam plant would be £1500 compared with the cost of the existing system which they estimated to be £200 per annum, a very significant saving. Nevertheless they recommended spending £3000 on supplementary steam power to work an average of four months each year which they estimated would cost an additional £120 per annum and they noted that the proprietors were to pay for a new 170 H.P. replacement wheel and that a new engine house was in the course of preparation. Dr Chapman[31] states the older of the two wheels was replaced at this time and that a 500 H.P. compound steam engine was installed, both at the expense of the existing partners. We have not been able to confirm the purchase of a new wheel but have found evidence that casts doubt on the acquisition of such an engine. It is from an advertisement that appeared in the *Derbyshire Times* in January 1904. It suggests the purchase of this large engine was not made by the partners but some years later by the English Sewing Cotton Company. In 1904 there were three engines for sale at the mill; one a horizontal engine with a 5¾ inch cylinder, a second described as a new horizontal engine by Marshalls with a 4½ cylinder and with a rope drive and vertical boiler; and a third, a compound engine, 100 H.P. also by Marshalls. This had cost £800 and is described as having very little wear. We cannot account for the first of the three but believe the second was the one being prepared for in 1897. It has a vertical boiler which fits with the Stott description of a vertical boiler in the small engine and boiler house and the rope drive indicates its purpose, which again supports our suggested interpretation. The third engine, was, we believe, Rebecca, the engine installed in 1888, whose boiler smoke alienated the local residents and which from its occasional use might well have suffered very little wear.[32] On this basis the 500 H.P. compound steam engine Dr Chapman refers to was not installed until 1900 a major component of the improvements initiated by the new combine and which included the new chimney and engine house, all part of the £12,000 it is alleged to have spent at Masson in the first five years of ownership. This engine was supplied by Petrie of Rochdale.

The Stott survey also identifies a new sprinkler system, its water tank in its own tower, and they note there is a manager's house and a paper mill yielding an annual rent of £95. The overall valuation was as follows:

Land and water rights	£16,623
Buildings including sprinklers, lighting (partly (partly gas, partly electric) and heating	£12,451
Motive power	£4,430
Machinery and plant	£15,379
Total	£48,883

The amount Frederic Charles Arkwright received from the sale of his textile interests was very much larger than this. To the £48,883 was added further amounts for goodwill and for property and water rights at Mellor and two buildings on the Cromford Mills site bringing the total to £123,000, part of which was paid in cash and the remainder, through debenture stock in the new company.

There were immediate benefits for the mill. During the period 1900-1901, Masson Mill was altered substantially to plans provided by Stotts[33] Figure 112. A massive chimney of 150 feet and a new engine house were erected to the north of the mill. With a little difficulty a 36 ton boiler and economiser were delivered in May 1900. Robinson's traction engine from Sheffield was employed to move the boiler from Matlock station but found it could not take it up the rise by the fish pond in Matlock Bath in harness so it had to be used as a hauler from the top.[34]

By September 1900 the chimney 'an ornament to the mills' was reported to have reached its limit and to be 'high enough to take all the fumes far enough from humanity, a decided improvement on the stack erected some years ago'. This was a reference to the complaints of smoke nuisance from John Adams Wheatcroft who was living at Masson House in 1888 when 'Rebecca', had been installed. The expenditure of £12,000 at Masson Mill between 1897 and 1902, years in which it was barely profitable, see page 161, was surely the result of Lawton's high office within the new company and essential for its survival as a production unit within the English Sewing family.[35]

In July 1910 an account of a visit to Masson Mill was featured in the *Derbyshire Advertiser*. Steam was now the prime mover, the river a source of power only for the dynamos which generated electricity for the lighting. The raw material, spun cotton, mainly Egyptian but with some South Sea and some American, was received in skips delivered by Midland Railway drays, 'an hourly sight on the Derby road'. The cotton was wound, doubled, gassed as necessary and left Masson warped for weaving or as sewing thread on reels for further processing. The mill was now part of an integrated system within the English Sewing Company, the thread travelling to Belper if it was to be mercerised, or to Skipton to be bleached.[36]

The mill worked day and night pausing only for meal breaks. The night shift operated entirely by men, was more highly paid, though its main attraction was not the money, rather 'the holiday of three whole days at the end of the week.'[37] While much had changed there was much that was familiar from earlier periods of the mill's existence. The workforce 'laughing chattering girls' still drawn primarily from 'Cromford, Bonsall and the Matlocks' pass 'to and fro with their dinner baskets, morning and evening.' The company employed a woman at the mill who cooked the food they brought with them to eat in the dinner break. It was, we are assured, a popular place to work and 'in spite of the less flourishing condition of the cotton trade, very fair wages were still to be had.' 'Strikes' our visitor was told, 'are unknown here. We are equal to settling our little differences ourselves.'

Five months later, in January 1911, work began on a new mill to the south of the original. Workmen were employed to work round the clock over the first months and by May it was said to be nearly complete.[38] At the end of September the opening of the new mill was celebrated with a tea for 350 at the Kursaal followed by a concert and ball. It initially offered work for an additional 50 staff and, it was hoped, in due course, this would increase to about 150, bringing the total workforce to about 550.[39]

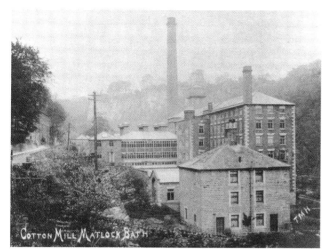

FIGURE 112. **Cotton Mill, Matlock Bath, postcard, 1900 – 1901.**

The picture shows some of the alterations commissioned by the English Sewing Cotton Co Ltd in 1900. The most striking are the 150 foot chimney and the remodelling of the east-west wing 'with new building on top of old from two storeys height' and with ventilators on the roof, to accommodate a new gassing department. At the same time the yard in front of the mill was covered to provide additional working space. Between the chimneys is the tower containing the water tank which supplied the sprinkler system, in place by 1897.

The signature TMH refers to the local photographer Thomas Meredith Henshall. Private collection.

FIGURE 113. **The construction of Masson Mill, 1911.**

Glynn Waite collection.

FIGURE 114. **The bowling green with the 1911 Masson Mill in the background, photograph, between 1921 and 1926.**

The new Masson Mill, shown in the background of this photograph, was erected on the site of the manager's house and part of the adjoining allotments shown at Figure 111. Plans included provision for a 70,000 gallon water tower. By March 1921 the rest of the allotment ground had become a bowling green. It survived in that use until the late 1920s when the works were again extended by the addition of Glen Mill. When completed in 1930 Glen Mill was expected to employ an additional 600 hands but trade was so poor it was some time before it was brought into use. The whole Masson Mill complex ceased production in 1991 when the business was moved to Scotland and the mill now houses a museum and shopping village with car parking in the former Glen Mill building.

Ken Askew collection.

FIGURE 115. **View to the south from the top of the tall chimney, snapshot, 1960s.**

This view looks south over the roof of the 1911 Masson Mill with the red brick water tower advertising its name and date; Glen Mill lies beyond it and to the south of that a steel-framed shed which housed the canteen. The roadside buildings at South End on the right include, nearest to the camera, the Rutland Arms with Boston House and Fairview Terrace to the south of it. They were demolished in 1974-76. The red brick Glenorchy Villa survives at the foot of the drive to Cromford Court. Lawton lived there some time after joining F. C. Arkwright in the mill. His new house Woodbank, now Cromford Court, is just visible through the trees on the hillside above the Villa. The houses shown built up the slope at South End are the survivors of formerly 8 back to back dwellings which were begun some time before 1784 by Thomas Pearson. This was speculative development offering cottages for rent for Matlock Bath's growing resident population. A development so close to Masson Mill yet not associated with the Arkwrights was surely a response to the economic opportunities created by the success of the mills.[40] After Pearson's death in 1820, his son-in-law Thomas Poundall added further cottages and converted and demolished others to make room to build the Rutland Arms in 1837.

Ken Askew collection.

Details of the Masson Mills' progress during the twentieth century have proved elusive. In September 1914 the enlistment of men joining the forces led the manager, Mr Webster, to wonder how they would keep going. At the same time he announced the company's generous decision to pay half wages to those taking this step and with the guarantee of re-employment at the end of the war.[41] When that time came the Masson men who returned each received a silver cigarette case inscribed with their name and the words 'welcome back to the Masson Mill 1919'; this presentation was made by Mrs Webster the wife of the long serving manager.[42]

There are hints of the pain suffered by the workforce during some difficult years between the wars. In September 1929 wages were reduced by one third in the pound with the result that even a man working from 5.15 am until 5 pm would earn less than £3 a week.[43] These events led to protest meetings in Belper and Milford but not in Matlock Bath; nor was there any talk of joining a union. It would seem the independence spoken of with some pride in 1910 lived on and may have continued to the end of the mill's life as a working unit.[44] One of Masson's last managers, asked how he dealt with the unions, explained it's not the union I contact; I speak to the heads of the several family groups we have always had here and in that way keep in touch and explain what is happening.[45] The impression that throughout its life the workforce always included these extended families is confirmed by the oral tradition, family histories, company publications and the names on the mill's long service board. Masson was a popular place to work and daughters followed mothers, sisters

FIGURE 116. **South End and Fairview Terrace, photograph, 1950s.**

The end of Fairview Terrace is shown on the right hand side in this view. Higher up the slope, South End cottages survived but from the 1880s one by one they were knocked through and took on their present form. The stepped path in front of the cottages follows the line of one of Matlock's ancient uphill routes, Carnell Lane.

Private collection.

followed sisters, boys followed fathers and so across the generations, a long and proud tradition of skill and commitment was established and sustained. There was a rueful satisfaction among those put out of work by the closure of the mills on hearing, from one of the few who moved with the work to the company's mill in Scotland, of the poor quality of the product that mill was turning out; the Scots it was said didn't know what they were doing. 'Of course they didn't' was the reply 'they were not bred to it like we were.'

Those who worked at the mill remember it as a happy place but though they felt part of a community and among friends it did not become a social hub for them. The long established practice of recruiting among the local villages meant they were too dispersed[46] to return to the mill to socialise there or nearby. Of course there were social events, dances[47] whist drives and in the 1920s evening classes.[48]

The second world war brought a heavy demand for crepe yarn to weave into bandages and some production of crepe continued after the war alongside other doubling of cotton and rayon mainly intended for weaving, knitting and braiding. Later, with the increasing populari-ty of tea bags, the cotton string on which they hung, became an important product.[49] The major post war development however was the introduction of core-spun thread for high speed commercial sewing machines, the synthet-ic internal strand providing strength and the cotton wound round it the ability to withstand the heat generated by the speed of the machine. And with the establishment of a new spinning unit in the west mill in Belper in

FIGURE 117. **Advertisement, about 1895.**

Private collection.

1977 the Derwent Valley Mills became an integrated production unit; cotton spun in Belper was wound and doubled at Masson and Belper and dyed in Milford.[50]

By 1947 only the ground floor of the original mill was in use for factory production,[51] the remaining floors being used for storage and for the canteen. It was in part of this under-uti-lised space in 1971 that the mill opened its doors to the public, hosting an exhibition of early Arkwright textile machinery. This was a major component of the Arkwright Festival programme marking the bicentenary of Richard Arkwright's arrival in Cromford.[52] The Festival was also the trigger for a long and fruitful association between the senior and local management of English Sewing (later Tootal) and the Arkwright Society (the char-ity established as a result of the Festival's success), Sir George Kenyon, Chairman of the Company 1976-1979 serving the Society in various capacities, President, Vice President and Chairman, over many years until his death in 2008.

From 1971 when tours began, until Masson Mill stopped work in 1991 and closed in 1992, the old mill was enjoyed by large numbers of visiting parties, a tradition re-established by its present owner, Mr Robert Aram, when he reopened the mills after extensive repairs and adaptation as a museum and shopping village, a fitting northern gateway to the Derwent Valley Mills World Heritage Site. The historic importance of Masson Mill, the best preserved of the Arkwright mills and certainly the most attractive, was recognised by English Heritage when the boundaries of the intended world heritage site were under consideration in 1999. There had been a proposal from ICOMOS UK which would have restricted such a site to Cromford and little more. A wider vision prevailed; Masson's significance was recognised and the boundary of the world heritage site inscribed by UNESCO[53] in 2001 was drawn to include Masson and the southern portion of Matlock Bath which surrounds it, Figure 118.

Masson Mill, seen at its birth by contemporary aesthetes as an anachronism among such picturesque scenery, today enjoys the accolade of international recognition. This is well deserved. But for its well-being in the long term it is the use that is made of the site rather than its status as a monument that will determine its survival. In its current use as a retail and heritage visitor attraction it continues to offer employment and makes a valuable contribution to the leisure economy of Matlock Bath. It would appear to be a formula for a sustainable future.

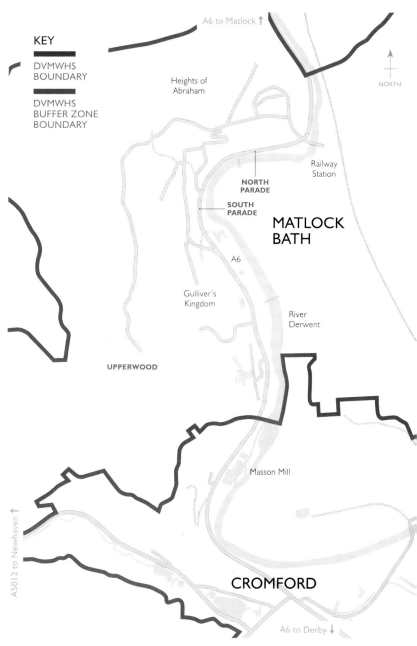

KEY

DVMWHS
BOUNDARY

DVMWHS
BUFFER ZONE
BOUNDARY

A6 to Matlock

Heights of
Abraham

NORTH

Railway
Station

NORTH
PARADE

SOUTH
PARADE

MATLOCK
BATH

A6

Gulliver's
Kingdom

River
Derwent

UPPERWOOD

A5012 to Newhaven

Masson Mill

CROMFORD

A6 to Derby

FIGURE 118. **The northern boundary of the Derwent Valley Mills World Heritage Site**

Lawton and the English Sewing Cotton Company, 1897-1905

Manufacturing sewing thread, the business into which Lawton had steered the Arkwright company, was dominated by a Scottish company, J. & P. Coats. This had grown up in Paisley but by the 1890s had become a huge concern owning mills in many different countries including a large enterprise in Pawtucket, Rhode Island through which the company was able to mitigate the effects of the American tariff legislation. In 1890 it had been taken public. Its evident success and generous dividends soon established it as a blue chip investment and in 1896 it had no difficulty in raising the money to buy Clarks, also a Paisley company and its longstanding competitor. Coats had become the largest company in British textiles and manufacturing.[54] The strength of J. & P. Coats in markets at home and abroad enhanced by their takeover of Clarks, presented the other UK sewing thread manufacturers, some twenty or so small producers, with a challenge they could not ignore. Faced with the prospect of increasing pressure from the enhanced production and manufacturing strength of this mammoth competitor, a number of them came to realise combination was the one solution open to them which might ensure their survival.

Lawton, it would seem, was among the first to identify and articulate such a strategy. It was an approach that seemed to mirror the format that had brought Coats such prosperity; but whereas Coats had developed a centralised management exercising rigid control, the new creation, the English Sewing Cotton Company was in its first incarnation little more than a federation of separate producers.

In July, 1897 when the company was registered, there were seven participating businesses but by November this had grown to fifteen.[55] How so much was achieved in so short a time is uncertain; the history of the English Sewing Cotton Company has yet to be written. But there is substantial evidence that J. E. Lawton was the prime mover both in bringing the companies together and, soon after, in delivering control of the American Thread Company to the new combine. As early as November 1897[56] he was described as 'one of the small handful of gentlemen who have been mainly instrumental in the formation of the [company]. And from Algernon Dewhurst, the company's first chairman, he received even greater credit, Dewhurst describing the company as having been 'brought into existence, very largely, if not entirely, by the skill and perseverance of his excellent friend, Mr Lawton'.[57]

The prospectus inviting investment in the enterprise reached the public in November 1897. The *Derbyshire Times* greeted it with rapturous applause.[58] The new company, it wrote, brought together the names of Arkwright, Strutt and Manlove and was a 'consolidation into a powerful and wealthy corporation of all the principal old established and well known English thread makers' not already included in the Coats combine.[59] The paper saw a great future for the new combine going so far as to say' we can cordially recommend it to our readers as a sound and paying investment'.

This optimism was widely shared. Investors flocked to buy shares. Before the end of December 1897 the shares were selling at nearly a 100 per cent premium[60] the ordinary shares being twenty five times oversubscribed. This was a remarkable outcome; the prospectus

FIGURE 119. **Woodbank viewed from the south, photograph, between 1901 and 1911.**

Lawton built his imposing new residence, Woodbank, on the hillside above Glenorchy Villa on land bought from F. C. Arkwright in 1899, laying the foundation stone in June 1900. The house, which was named after his house in Dukinfield, was completed in 1902[61] to plans prepared by Messrs Stott and Sons of Manchester. It was said to have cost £20,000. It was supplied with electricity generated at Masson Mill. Alice Taylor, famous in her later life as the author Alison Uttley, recalled watching from her childhood home Castletop Farm as the house was being built and admitted that on shopping trips to Cromford excuses were made to drive further than the village so that they could look up to the 'monster house towering above the road'. She was particularly amazed by the talk of the village, a rumour never confirmed, that the house had fourteen bathrooms. She confessed that at that time she had not seen a bathroom. It actually had 16 bathrooms and 13 lavatories or so Arthur Lawton advised the Council when he sought their agreement for a water supply in December 1890. It seems in his spare time Lawton played billiards. At Glenorchy Villa, he built an extension off the half landing to house a billiard table and his plans for Woodbank ensured that he had a billiard room appropriate to the scale and style of this 'palatial' house which, it is suggested, was among the last houses of its size to be built in Derbyshire. Both houses also had a photographic darkroom though which family member was interested in photography is not known. The Lawton family left Matlock Bath in 1910 and in May 1911 it was let to the Co-operative Holiday Association and was opened as a guest house the following year.[62] It failed to find a buyer when offered for sale in 1917 and later in that year, as part of the evacuation plans made during the First World War, housed 60 boys from Folkestone School. The *High Peak News* recorded its re-opening by the Friendship Holiday Association from Ilkley in 1932 and for about thirty years it remained in use as a guest house known as Cromford Court. In 1980 after lying empty for some years and several unsuccessful attempts to find a use for the building, it was rescued from further decline and became the headquarters of the missionary society, New Tribes Mission. It was offered for sale in 1998 and subsequently reverted to use as a private residence.

Ken Smith collection.

had offered no details of profits actually admitting recent profits had been comparatively small[63] and had not attempted to quantify the benefits of reduced production and distribution costs. But with Coats delivering a dividend of twenty per cent the expectation of similar success was compelling. And a year later when the new company secured its position in the American market through the bundling together of thirteen companies to form the American Thread Company, in which it then took a controlling interest, a prosperous future seemed secure.[64]

Leadership of the ESCC in the early years was in the hands of three managing directors, Algernon Dewhurst, also chairman, and two Derbyshire business men, Lawton, the vice-chairman and, W. M. Manlove whose business was at Holymoorside near Chesterfield with a dyeworks at Cathole and an outpost at Unity Mill in Belper. The Derbyshire network was further extended by board membership which included John Hunter representing Strutts and George Wigley from Wigleys of Derby.[65]

It was the American deal that secured Lawton's reputation within the company and amongst its shareholders and it is certain he worked tirelessly to complete it. The process began in August 1898 with an approach from two Americans one of whom, Mr J. R. Dos Passos,[66] a New York lawyer and speculator, held the options to purchase the bulk of the stock of the companies that were to form the American Thread Company.[67] By April Lawton was in the USA about to be joined by his chairman, Algernon Dewhurst to talk about the new company and its relationship with ESCC.[68]

This was followed by a series of visits to the United States which, Lawton claimed, led him to cross the Atlantic twenty times over three or four years.[69] All went reasonably well for the company in its early life and there are especially positive reports from two of the Derbyshire businesses. In December 1899 the *Derbyshire Advertiser* recorded buoyant trade in Belper both at Strutts and Manloves, the latter 'having worked overtime most of the year; while at Milford the development of mercerised cotton had seen 'the large works at this village more fully occupied than for many years past' with new cottages being erected for workmen.[70] The mood changed abruptly when the results for 1900-01 were announced. The trading profit was thirty eight per cent less than the preceding year and the interim dividend was covered only by transferring £50,000 from the reserve; all this in a year when the J. & P. Coats' dividend was[71] fifty per cent. The shareholders were outraged. They had been duped. The search for an explanation began; the architects of their misfortune were to be hunted down.

Lawton himself offered one of the first diagnoses of the company's poor performance.[72] It was the result of mismanagement at board level. It had been 'an awful mistake to put into control of the various businesses purchased by the company the men from whom the businesses were purchased, because these men had got into one groove and could not get out of it.' Many of the same men were also directors of the combine and could not operate effectively in both capacities. Holding these views, Lawton may have formed a favourable impression of Charles Diamond, the most articulate of the aggrieved shareholders, who seemed to share his opinion of the board's competence, or perhaps he realised what a dangerous

John Edward Lawton (1848-1915)

John Edward Lawton was born in Manchester, the son of William Lawton, cotton spinner. In May 1873 he married Ellen Garforth, a member of a wealthy and successful local family which had interests in engineering, iron founding, coal mining and textiles. He and Ellen raised a family of six girls and two boys and it was her maiden name that he gave to the house he built on Clifton Road at Matlock Bath in 1900. His first employment was with her uncle, J. B. Kynder, an accountant, auctioneer, valuer and estate agent, who had various business interests. By 1881 he had achieved the status of cotton spinner, employing 40 women, 60 men and 20 boys. Among his other early commercial interests he also set up a yarn agency with an office in Cannon Street, Manchester. It was this practical experience of the cotton business and of management that qualified him for the role he accepted at Masson mill.

His engagement in local politics seems to have begun at about the same time as his employment at Masson, while he was still living in Dukinfield. He stood for the Local Board, nominated by the Liberals, and served a single term.

Masson cannot have consumed more than a fraction of his working life. His energy was boundless, enabling him to engage in multiple business ventures too numerous to catalogue here; many of them at the same time as he was implementing his rescue of Masson mill. A man with a keen appreciation of the flamboyant gesture in his personal life, in politics and in business, he knew how to create his own limelight. In 1883 he became involved with the Astley Mill company which planned to erect a cotton mill designed by Stott and Sons of Oldham, that would employ 2-300 people working 84,000 spindles. By June 1885 he had become chairman, and with the mill built, presided over an opening ceremony that bore all the hallmarks of the Lawton brand. The new mill was thrown open to thousands of visitors with a tea for 1,600 people. Throughout his business life he continued to invest his time and capital in new ventures in the UK and abroad, many of them unsuccessful, but it was only in the years between 1897 and 1902, with the formation of the English Sewing Cotton Company and the American Thread Company, that briefly, he walked on the world stage.

Even while he was attending to the infancy of the new sewing thread enterprise he found time to both lead the Matlock Bath UDC and to accept a national role in the District Councils' Association. He was chairman of the executive Council when the Annual Meeting and Conference of the Association was held in Matlock Bath. A year later he stood as Liberal candidate for Salford and was unsuccessful in a tight contest despite hiring a huge elephant on polling day to carry sandwich boards advertising the Liberal cause. In the same year he gifted 8 bells to Matlock Bath church.

He was a man with the common touch. He organised fortnightly entertainments for the Masson Mill workforce and in 1893 formed the Masson Mill Band. When his daughter, May, married in 1898 he took 700 employees in two special trains to the pantomime matinee in Manchester and arranged a smoking party for 1000 men at the Pavilion behind the Royal Hotel. He and his family became larger than life figures dominating the local scene. He ran a small electric boat on the river and extended his boat house below the school for the use of the Rowing Club. For some years Lawton's second son, Bertie, was captain of the Derbyshire cricket team and the family entertained W. G. Grace, the famous Gloucestershire and England cricketer, at Woodbank when he was playing in the district. Grace sometimes took part in the family's cricket games and invited the young Bertie to play for him in London County games.

The family left Matlock Bath in 1910. Lawton died at his son's home in Buxton in 1915 and was buried in Dukinfield. Described in his obituaries as a man of great energy, he was active in many roles, a 'genius in commerce' and 'with a gift of personal influence which won him many a battle.'[73]

figure Diamond could become and thought it best to keep him under close observation. Whatever the motive in August 1901 Lawton invited Diamond to join the board so becoming the first member who was not a representative of one of the companies that had been sold into the English Sewing combine.[74] Diamond described himself as a newspaper proprietor[75] and journalist and he proved himself to be a skilled communicator and a formidable adversary.[76]

FIGURE 120. **Bobbin labels from *Through the Eye of The Needle*, English Sewing Cotton Company.**

It took Diamond about six months to acquaint himself with the facts, publish them in a circular and to realise his position as a board member did not provide him with the power base to effect the changes in the management of the company that were required, and that he must appeal to a wider constituency.[77] By January 1902 he was mobilising his fellow shareholders urging them to replace the three managing directors with an executive and by March shareholders' groups had formed in Glasgow, Durham, Manchester and London.[78] He was, said the *Leeds Mercury* 'resourceful and indefatigable and his efforts are being backed by a powerful body of shareholders' said to include Coats. The aim now was to achieve a 'clean sweep' of the existing board and to demand repayment from those among the vendor companies whose businesses had been overvalued and for which the new company had overpaid.

Matters came to a head in April 1902 at an Extraordinary Meeting called by the shareholders. Lawton presided defending his actions and those of his fellow directors as best he could; but there was no doubt how the contest ended; the board had been indicted as unfit to manage and Lawton, the man who four years earlier had been feted as 'one of the most astute business men in the country'[79] was now tainted by insinuations of fraud and false accounting.[80] The valuation of the 'Arkwright concern'[81] was singled out for particular comment. It included one mill.[82] 'actually lying in ruins...having been previously burnt down. Another mill was let as a laundry; and at the one Arkwright mill which [was] in operation, the sewing cotton part of the business never paid, and yet a very large sum was given for plant and machinery and goodwill for these firms.' Diamond also accused Lawton of excessive claims for his expenses on the visits he made to the United States amounting to about £2000 and, in a single week £200 and of doubling the salary due to him even demanding a contract of £6000 per annum for ten years.[83]

Diamond supported his claim that the company had overpaid for the Masson Mills with evidence of their profitability since 1897.[84] Losses of 3% in 1898 and 2% in 1899 had been followed by profits of 6% in 1900 and 3.6% in 1901. This did not justify the £123,000 purchase price nor the £12,000 spent on it since 1897. Not content with informing his fellow shareholders of his findings Diamond had taken it upon himself to write to those he considered to be the guilty parties appealing to them on behalf of the shareholders to return part of the purchase money they had received.

On 17th April 1902 F. C. Arkwright was among the recipients of the following letter.[85]

Dear Sir

I send you herewith a statement showing the heavy losses that have been sustained by this company in the working of the mill at...which you sold to it some time ago.

I would invite from you personally, the fullest investigation of all the circumstances connected with the sale, and of the price paid for the property. I am sure that a man of integrity and honour, such as yourself will very promptly come to the conclusion that it is a grave duty incumbent upon you to take some steps to readjust the price

*that has been paid for these mills, so that unfortunate shareholders of the English
Sewing Cotton Company may have restoration made to them of anything found
to be over and above a fair and reasonable price for the land, buildings, plant,
machinery or goodwill.*

*The deplorable condition of a large number of very poor investors, whose money is
in this concern, must surely appeal to you, and if there is any responsibility upon
you in the matter I must earnestly ask you to take such steps in the matter as justice
and honour dictate. This I believe, you will do, for I have always heard you spoken
of as a gentleman of the highest probity, I am sir.*

Yours faithfully
C. Diamond

He did not have long to wait for a reply:

Willersley Castle
21st April, 1902

Sir

*In reply to your letter of the 17th inst. enclosing a statement showing the unsatis-
factory working of Masson Mill since the English Sewing Company bought it, I beg
to state that I do not consider that I am in any way responsible for that, but I think
it is a matter for which those in whose hands the business has been are responsible,
viz the Directors. Mr Lawton will give any information you require, as he has it all
at his finger ends.*

I am yours faithfully
F. C. Arkwright

Perhaps because he was aware that the full correspondence would shortly appear in the
press and he wanted there to be no doubt in readers' minds of the case he was making for
the shareholders, Diamond pressed home his point that too much had been paid for Masson
Mill and, if it were not so, it was for Arkwright to prove otherwise.

He wrote once again.

Sir,

*I am in receipt of your letter, and note its contents. While it is perfectly true that you
have no responsibility for the management of these mills, or for the losses that have
taken place since you sold them, permit me to suggest that it is surely incumbent
upon you to show conclusively that the very large price you received for the mills
was in any way justified by the profits of the previous years. This is a matter upon
which you must have accurate knowledge, and I think it demands your attention.*

If there were no profits being made at Masson Mills, then to have taken the large amount for goodwill of the business[86] *was surely a terrible injury to the people who were called upon to pay that money. Will you therefore, be good enough to let me know whether there were really any profits for several years on Masson Mills precedent to the sale, and, if so, what these profits amounted to annually?*[87]

Yours faithfully

C. Diamond

It is not known whether Arkwright replied to this letter though it seems unlikely. By the time he would have considered a reply he would have realised he was dealing with a journalist whose intention from the outset had been to make public whatever passed between them.

Lawton's defence was unconvincing. He had been challenged by a man with a coherent argument supported by factual evidence. He replied with assurances of good faith, evasion and promises of future investigation. The valuations had been conducted by an eminent firm and the principal shareholder considered the amount to be moderate and reasonable or he would not have been the first to subscribe. The mill referred to as burnt down had been sold to the company at a valuation which took into account the actual condition of the property and the valuation was mainly based on the water rights with nothing included for goodwill;[88] and the adjoining mill, let as a steam laundry yielded a fair return. In defence of his own salary and expenses and the salaries paid to other directors and officials he denied overpayments had been made or that Diamond's assertions were correct. Never had he spent £200 in a single day though his expenses had been heavy. America was a very expensive place to visit. He denied absolutely seeking a £6000 p.a. ten year contract; and the payments received from the American Thread Company would have to be looked into by others.

Part of Lawton's difficulty was the common ground shared with Diamond. Both agreed the company lacked central control and a united board focused solely on the company's interests rather than a board of individuals, permanently interested in one or other of its constituent parts. To what extent Lawton felt able to welcome the decisions made at the end of a meeting that had so publicly questioned his integrity as a step towards this shared goal is unclear. But for Diamond it was a triumph. It was agreed that a committee of shareholders chaired by Mr Otto Philippi[89] of J. & P. Coats should confer with the board over the creation of a new smaller body to run the company. And at a further Extraordinary General Meeting in October 1902 the committee recommendations were adopted and the old board with 17 members was replaced by a board of 7.[90] For the next three years Lawton, though no longer a director, continued to make his voice heard at shareholders' meetings.

Diamond, now a member of the new board, renewed his appeal for action to be taken against the vendor directors to recover the money he believed they had misappropriated. In 1902, exasperated, it was widely understood he himself would serve writs on all the original board members.[91] Then a month later his targets were revealed to be the three original managing directors[92] Dewhurst, Lawton and Manlove.[93] The case was heard in Chancery in February 1903 Diamond alleging fraudulent conspiracy by selling businesses far above their value. The judge ruled the case should be struck out; not for any lack of merit but on the grounds it should have been brought by the directors of the company.[94] This might have been the end of the matter but Diamond would not let it rest and, six months later at the company's annual meeting, he was still urging the shareholders to consider a further lawsuit. His persistence now seemed vindicated. One of the actions of the old board in September 1902 had been the appointment of auditors to examine the prices paid for the constituent companies and their findings were now available[95] in the report[96] Alfred Butterworth presented to the meeting. There were cheers when he said too much money had been paid for the concern and further cheers when he went on to say everything beyond a 20 years purchase ought to be refunded. In some cases amounts equal to more than 30 years purchase had been paid; only two transactions were deemed reasonable. Diamond's response was predictable. A grave fraud had been perpetrated on the shareholders. 'Scandalous prices were paid which would not have been paid in the open market.' The shareholders should now consider a lawsuit along the lines he had attempted.

This was not an easy meeting for Lawton. He no longer held office[97] but remained a voice the shareholders were prepared to listen to. Still a prominent figure it was he who welcomed the company's improved performance attributing it to the efforts of Waterhouse, the new chairman, and the two leading directors, Morgan and Bowker. In the face of the auditors' report and Diamond's call for litigation, he was on the back foot. In a lengthy speech he claimed the present 'angry feeling' had arisen only because the company was not profitable. If it was paying 10 per cent 'the vendors would be called decent fellows. Well, they were decent fellows and the position was not their fault.'[98] He spoke, he said, 'as a man bred and born in Manchester... he did not feel he had done any injury to anyone. The auditors' report only told them that which they had known all along, the original capitalisation, in view of the earnings of the company, was far too high. The reason they had no dividends was because of competition outside and incompetence inside.' With regard to the alleged fraud he said 'there was not a statement in the prospectus of the company that was not well within the truth, and if there was he was prepared to take the consequences.' He ended on a defiant note 'Not a single vendor got a penny more than he should have done.'

Following the meeting three board members were appointed to meet the vendors to see if some money might be recovered; 'not on the grounds of misrepresentation but from the fact that the combination of sewing cotton interests had not shown the result of increased profit and diminished expenditure which had been expected by the various firms.' This approach, appealing to the vendors' sense of decency but of course with Charles Diamond's strident voice audible in the background, calling for action in the courts, delivered a positive response from at least five of the vendors.[99] The exact terms of the arrangements made with these vendors have not been identified but some details are available. Arkwright, Dewhurst Manlove, Strutt and Ermen and Roby all entered into agreements of one sort or another.[100] Arkwright agreed to take back the two unused buildings at Cromford and the 19 acre Mellor site[101] on the same terms as the purchase made in 1897. Dewhurst took back Airton Mill, one of the Skipton mills and arrangements were made with Manlove and Strutt.[102] The payments were made by adjustments to the debentures held in ESCC by the respective vendors.[103]

This was not the end of Lawton's association with ESSC. In 1905 a group of shareholders campaigned to bring him back to the board. Charles Diamond was due to retire and Lawton, his adversary, was seen as a suitable replacement. This was a serious bid. News of his candidacy was sent to the shareholders and regional meetings followed. In Manchester[104] support for Lawton was unanimous but he lost narrowly at a similar meeting in Glasgow, an event recorded in some detail in the *Yorkshire Post*.[105] Lawton presented himself to these shareholders as a practical, experienced business man intimately familiar with the sewing thread trade and aware of the obligations incumbent on those running a public company to create a return for their investors. If the account we have of the meeting is accurate his description of his part in the company's short life was shamelessly selective; even tendentious. There was no mention of Diamond's charges of fraud by now largely vindicated by the company's auditors nor any apology for his part as vice chairman in the poor governance of the combine in its first years. His audience heard he had been one of the 70 founders of the company; that he 'had lived his life in the business' which had never been managed as it ought to have been; the industrial businesses 'being left in the hands of the gentlemen who had sold them'. 'These gentlemen, each of them a little king in his little kingdom, did not keep before their minds in the new circumstances the fact that the business had passed out of their hands, that capital had been created which required a return, and did not take those steps which were promised in the prospectus.' Despite the current prosperity of the cotton trade the company was working at no more than three eighths of its capacity. Practical men were needed on the board.

The directors alarmed at the prospect of Lawton's return, issued a circular to their shareholders supporting Diamond and at the annual meeting two directors formally proposed his election. After a stormy debate, Diamond, though by now seen as a contentious figure, was re-elected.[106] Lawton, recognising imminent defeat, withdrew his nomination[107] complaining the board's circular 'had worked unfairly against him.'[108]

So Lawton, part visionary and optimist, part self-interested opportunist and pragmatist, finally parted from the sewing thread combine he had helped conceive and bring into being.

FIGURE 121. **Masson Mill, 1946.**

A leaflet promoting work opportunities at the mill stated that it offered 'particularly attractive prospects to women, and to girls and boys leaving school',reassuring parents that girls and boys 'are well cared for by a Welfare and Labour Officer'. Hours of work, over a five day week, were 7.30 a.m. to 5.30 p.m., a fifty hour working week, though, as the leaflet emphasised, 'leaving the whole week-end free'. The canteen provided snacks and full mid-day meals which cost 10d, or 6d for those under 16, (respectively just over 4p and 2.5p in decimal coinage). A trolley service delivered tea and sandwiches mid-morning and in the afternoon.

Private collection.

CHAPTER TWELVE

The Local Board and Urban District Council

Nature had done all for them, but they had done nothing for themselves. Now however, there was no reason why Matlock Bath should not become a perfect model of a watering place.[1]

The ratepayers elected to the Matlock Bath Local Board of Health who began their work in 1865 were confident of the transformational powers placed in their hands and proud of the new status their community had achieved. It had not been easy. At the end of 1862 a Local Board had been formed for Matlock which included Matlock Bath, an arrangement the resorts' ratepayers regarded as intolerable. They responded by petitioning the Home Office for a Board of their own. This was opposed by the Matlock Board and the Bath's residents found they were asked to pay rates to Matlock which would fund the Board's £200 legal costs to oppose their own independence. A number refused to pay and, in May 1864 23 were summonsed for non payment.

The optimism of the new Board would soon have been tempered by the day to day realities of the administrative functions dealt with at the Board's monthly meetings. The meeting in June 1871, described here, see panel, was unusual in having on the agenda a proposal of such strategic importance, the provision of urinals; mostly their time was spent in a monthly round of routine administration.

A Meeting of Matlock Bath Local Board held in June 1871[2]

The business after the minutes had been approved. The Board signed the licences for the hackney carriages and donkeys granted at the last meeting. It was reported that some of the donkey boys had no badges. The Inspector of Nuisances said they had been lost. Mr Green, the Clerk, said there were none in stock. The Clerk was ordered to see that some more were obtained. Mr Newbold proposed and Mr Holmes seconded the proposal that 'Matlock Bath be provided with urinals for the convenience of excursionists'. Mr Parkin [a member of the Board] quite saw the necessity for such places being erected as at present there were no public conveniences whatever. The motion was carried unanimously. A committee was then 'chosen to inquire as to the best mode and places of erection and to report progress'. Mr Hardy's tender for watering the roads during the summer months was accepted. After several cheques were signed, the meeting broke up.

The provision of essential services to the resort could not be put off indefinitely and required action which could only be taken by the Local Board; and from 1894[3] the Matlock Bath and Scarthin Nick Urban District Council. The needs of the settlement were complex, compounded in the season by the influx of visitors[4], the day trippers and the bed and breakfast clientele. Whatever solutions were delivered had to provide for Matlock Bath's swollen summer population yet remain within the capacity of the residents who paid the rates.

As the sanitary authority the Board could not ignore indefinitely the major responsibilities it faced. It might immerse itself in routine tasks, watering the roads, or exposing and resolving nuisances; or waiting to see if a solution might emerge from another quarter, but sooner or later something had to be done. It seems to have taken about twenty years for the Matlock Bath Board to recognise these realities. The perennial constraint for the Local Board and its successor the Urban District Council, was the size of the district they administered. With only 337 acres Matlock Bath was no more than a village and with many properties of low rateable value there was never sufficient income to undertake major works without substantial borrowing, followed by a consequential increase in the rates. Nor was there money in hand to cope with unforeseen events and periodically the authority found itself at odds with its ratepayers when they felt the rates they were being asked to pay were unaffordable. Two, among the several occasions when this line was crossed, occurred in 1885 and 1907. In 1885, a special meeting of the ratepayers held in the skating rink, called the Board to account over a proposed additional rate of 1/4d in the £ to meet the costs of a lawsuit the Board had lost. With the best of intentions it had erected a much needed urinal; unfortunately it turned out to be on property which belonged, not to the Board, but to a Mr Sellors of Tewkesbury. The Board had lost the legal action which followed and was now liable for their own and Sellors' costs, costs which the ratepayers must now meet. For the ratepayers it was a step too far; already the rates had risen from 2/- in the £ in 1883 to 3/- in the £ the following year, to support the £6-7000 spent on securing an improved water supply. Now the rate would be over 4/- in the £. F. E. Leggoe, an accountant, who had called the meeting claimed he would be paying £15[5] and accused the Board of acting illegally by not consulting the ratepayers before embarking on litigation.[6] In this instance there was a tangible outcome to the meeting in the formation of a ratepayers' association.

In 1907 the ratepayers expressed their displeasure through an election. Rates had reached 7/11d in the £, and Lawton the charismatic chairman of the UDC since its formation, lost his seat.[7] His mantra 'that no ratepayer would begrudge a reasonable rate if it were seen that the money was well and efficiently spent' had sustained his high spending strategies over many years but it had offered no protection against Charlie White's challenge. Claiming that working class ratepayers were going without necessities to pay the rates, in packed meetings in the Temperance Hall in Scarthin and the Assembly Room at Matlock Bath,[9] White was able to drive home the fundamental point; the rates had become too high.

The Board and the UDC were also delayed and sometimes obstructed by the oversight exercised by the Local Government Board. It generally took months to reach a decision on their loan requests and on occasion frustrated their plans by an outright refusal or unsympathetic quid pro quo. A notable case arose in 1882 when in response to local demand, and evident need, the Board attempted to utilise the powers it held under the 1848 Public Health Act to establish public pleasure grounds. An application was made to the Local Government Board for a provisional order which would enable the Board to purchase the land needed for a promenade and the pleasure grounds it had in mind. In May 1882 a response was received. It came from the appropriately named J. R. Rotton; the Board's representative, a Captain Hildyard, had inspected the proposal and while the Local Government Board would normally have agreed to the request, he said it must refuse on this occasion because Matlock Bath is 'not in a satisfactory condition as regards its sanitary arrangements.' 'Before any expense is incurred for purposes chiefly of an ornamental character, the more important requirements in the district, from a sanitary point of view ought first to be made.' And this was to remain the position until a sewerage plan acceptable to this central authority was in place. There had been a fundamental misconception of the importance of this scheme for the local economy, but the Board, lacking the leadership Lawton would later provide, allowed the decision to stand without challenge.[10]

Even locally the Board did not always receive the support it might have expected as it attempted to exert its authority and bring order and regulation to the resort, where previously there had been none. In July 1870 the Local Board summoned Francis Anzani Buxton for offences against the bye laws in having erected a building not constructed of 'brick, stone

Transport Matters

A scene between rival bus proprietors at a meeting of the Local Board, Tuesday, 2nd June 1891.[11]

There was a complaint against Mr H. Briddon for allowing unlicensed vehicles to ply for hire. The Board recommended 7s 6d to be paid on the recommendation of the Committee.

Mr Briddon asked to give a word or two of explanation. He said he was quite pleased to go before them. There were brakes running to Matlock Bridge, Haddon Hall, Chatsworth and Dovedale. Those brakes should be on the stand at a certain time and if they did not load up should go away. But there was a party who kept the brakes on the stand one or two hours.

Mr Leggoe: [a member of the Board][12] I rise to a point of order.

Mr Briddon: Allow me to have my say and he can do as he likes.

Mr Leggoe: I object to the time of the Board being taken up except what Mr Briddon is asked to be here for.

Mr Briddon: I wish you would hear me.

The Chairman: Deal with your own cases Mr Briddon.

Mr Briddon; When these brakes are on the stand are they licensed.

Mr Leggoe: I object to this altogether.

Mr Rowland [a member of the Board] It seemed to the Committee that Mr Briddon had broken the bye-laws on three counts.

Mr Briddon: I admit I had four licenses and six vehicles out, but I have done this to bring it before your notice. I have complained and complained until I am tired. [He explained that if he did not take a certain number of people Mr Leggoe would.]

Mr Wheatcroft [a member of the Board] Mr Leggoe does everything with impunity.

Mr Briddon: There is no one comes to Matlock Bath unless they are touted by Mr Leggoe to take his milk, go to Haddon Hall, Chatsworth, or take refreshments at his place.

Mr Wheatcroft: He is a professional tout.

Mr Leggoe to Mr Briddon: You are half drunk; no sober man would say what you do.

[Mr Rowland proposed Mr Briddon be fined 7s 6d.]

Mr Briddon: Next time I come here I shall have a hearing. [And later] I most reluctantly broke the bye-laws to bring the matter before you. If the touting is not stopped I shall put another on at the side of one you all know.

or other hard and incombustible' material without its consent. It turned out, that for several years, Buxton had 'been in the habit of coming to Matlock Bath and erecting a bazaar of wood covered with canvas for the sale of Derbyshire spars, marbles and other fancy goods.' He would generally erect the building at the latter end of May and remove it about the beginning of October and had had no objections from the Board until 14th June when he was given notice to remove the structure. Buxton had paid the rates required of him but did not apply for consent because he did not know it was required; nor could the Board supply him with a copy of the bye laws when asked to do so. The magistrate, at the Matlock Bridge petty sessions, dismissed the summons, rebuking the Board for its negligence in allowing the matter to continue for so long and offering the advice that the parties 'better try to settle matters betwixt themselves'. It was a setback for the Board which would seem to have had the law on its side and to have been acting in the best interests of the resort, but a fair decision. How could years of customary behaviour be reversed by an agency so ill equipped it could not produce a copy of the regulations it sought to enforce.

With limited funds, constrained by delay and unsympathetic decisions from London, and led by men of limited experience and vision, the Board had no alternative but to confine its activities to building and sanitary controls, to regulating cabmen, naming and maintaining local roads and serving notices on those who committed nuisances.[13] And while some residents and visitors condemned the Board for its apparent failure to deal with the bigger issues, these day to day matters were by no means trivial. Licensing the cabmen and later the boats; controlling the hucksters and maintaining the roads and footpaths; all these actions were essential if a safe and pleasant environment was to be offered to the visiting public. But it was not sufficient to satisfy the critics and no doubt more might have been done. At the same time the Board did have admirers, even of its road maintenance, in the hands of its surveyor Mr Speed. A report in 1887 described Matlock Bath's roads 'a few years back [as] proverbial as being amongst the very worst in the county;' [now they] 'have been put into really first class condition; a credit to the Board and the inhabitants generally.'[14]

One who was not an admirer of the Local Board, expressed his frustration and despair at its inactivity, in an eloquent if waspish letter to the *Derbyshire Times* in 1881. He concealed his identity within the enigmatic pseudonym VISITOR while from his acute observation of the resort's predicament revealing insights that could only belong to a local insider. We print the letter as it appeared to the paper's readers on 22nd October of that year.

Degenerate Matlock Bath, *Derbyshire Times*, October 22, 1881

'As a visitor at Matlock Bath I am somewhat amused at the ways and means of the resident public headed by the Local Board to cater for the amusement and enjoyment of visitors [who] from time to time make this place their rendezvous. Without an exception the cry of the residents is the degeneracy of the place. They complain that the palmy days of yore which so brightened their prospects and brought the coveted silver-lining to their pockets, exist only as relics of the past." O ye gods why have ye forsaken them! Why this awful dispensation of providence?" The answer is

not far distant. It lies in the lethargy displayed by those who ought to be foremost in every attempt in improvement. What inducement is there for visitors to spend their leisure moments in Matlock Bath? Absolutely none! Nature in all her boundless ramifications has endowed the place with everything that is pleasing to the eye and congenial to the taste. The visitor for the first time is amazed at the grandeur spread out before him in such panoramic fashion. The inhabitants on the other hand have done all they could to mar and neutralize the results which Nature has been at such trouble to develop, and by vigorous onslaught have converted this earthly elysium into a scene of despair. Ten minutes in the locality will convince the most sceptical on this point. We come here not only for the benefit of our healths, but for the enjoyment which changes of scene naturally gives; for a time we are pleased with the natural display of beauty as afforded by the majestic rocks covered with the ever-changing verdure; as the eye becomes accustomed to the change, and as one's blood receives more of the purifying element engendered by being trotted out up and down those rugged cliffs, we long for some of those social and health giving amusements which are the concomitants of every well arranged place of resort. Not a bit of it, we look in vain; no gardens, no promenade, no pavilion or music, no public institution of any kind not even a library where we can meet for a friendly chat. Even this could be endured for a time were it not that one's domestic comforts were imperilled. Water in abundance can be seen running to waste, yet it is with the greatest difficulty that the supply to the houses can be kept up. Look at the drainage. A positive disgrace to any civilised place, fortunately the super-abundance of rain which proved so disastrous to other parts of the country, is a perfect God-send in this vicinity, for by this means, the velocity of the river is such, that the filth is swept away or so diluted that it is rendered powerless to generate disease. Not until Matlock Bath has been decimated by typhoid fever or some of its allied diseases will attention be turned to ordinary sanitary arrangements. Look again at the streets, especially during a dry and hot season. If the wind is at all boisterous, everything is immediately covered with dust; as compared with which the howling winds and blinding dust and storm of the desert scarcely bear comparison. It is true that a water-cart is occasionally seen being lazily dragged about, the horse and driver alike being affected with the contagion so typical of the surroundings; but even this village commodity does not make its appearance until one is almost blinded, and one's suit of clothes, or what is worse, ladies' dresses have become seriously deteriorated by the small particles of lime which are so characteristic of the place, and which are ever and anon on the aggressive. Can it be supposed that ladies will turn out for a promenade under such circumstances? If they do, their feelings soon find vent in disgust, which end in their packing up their traps until a more favourable season. They arrive full of hope, they leave in despair and wend their way to Buxton or some other locality, where they at least, have attention paid to their little wants and weaknesses. Take another view of the case equally gloomy as the one just depicted. It had been raining some hours, at last dear old Sol breaks out shedding glory all around and giving the beautifully tinted leaves a splendid appearance; the air in places where defective drainage had not asserted its sway, is laden with perfume. Ah, now we shall enjoy a walk, what disappointment? We turn out, and if perchance our steps are directed through the streets, we are assailed by the fern-basket vendors or petrifying-well croaksters, In some places so narrow are the pathways that on meeting anyone, especially those who do not understand the ordinary ways of civilisation, we have to step aside into the street, to emerge bespattered with an adhesive substance akin to mortar and being known in common parlance as mud. A carriage dashes by, and we find ourselves spotted with a solution of lime, which to say the least of it, is antagonistic to silks, satins etc. If the puny pipings of those in authority were directed more to the furtherance of the true interests of the place than to such absurdities as "Cabmen's Badges" or whatever they are designated, we might hope for better things. The cab-proprietors headed by the valiant J. W., are a credit to the place, for nowhere can better appointed vehicles and cattle be found. These indispensable adjuncts to pleasure are certainly a step in advance of the civilisation of Matlock Bath, and did others who have the catering for the public amusements etc, improve the means at their disposal in the same rate, Matlock Bath would speedily assume a different aspect. I am advancing the truth, deny it who can, when I state that if the supine inhabitants of this beautiful and so naturally gifted place do not bestir themselves, it will eventually become a tenth-rate resort, to be frequented only on excursion days, by Jack, Bill, "Arry" and people of that class. So delightfully situated as Matlock Bath is, and acknowledged by all who visit it to be all absorbing in grandeur; its accessibility from Manchester, Sheffield and other large centres; there is no reason why it should not become one of the most fashionable resorts in England, not only in summer, but also in winter. It is well sheltered and might well be converted into an "Inland Torquay". To do this, it is requisite that public requirements and taste should be met and fostered, this of course means money; ergo are the inhabitants prepared to abandon their state of "Masterly inactivity", if they are let them, like some species of snakes leave behind their old mantle of sloth and put on the new one of activity, bearing in mind that their reward will be dependent on their zeal. If it is true, as I hear, that they purpose making some sort of promenade in front of the parade, it is a step in the right direction; but the area is so limited that it is barely sufficient "for one dawg to make the acquaintance of another dawg." It is the half-hearted policy which is so detrimental to the growth of this place. A few go ahead spirits led by Mr B, are hampered by the stern decrees which emanate from the older but not wiser ones. It must not be forgotten that this is a progressive age, and just now Matlock Bath is under a cloud, but nevertheless one which would speedily disappear, were the right spirit to pervade the corporate body. These remarks are made in good faith, not with the interest to cause offence, but if possible, to ameliorate the condition of those vegetating in this particular vale of tears.

Believe me.

Yours faithfully
Visitor, Matlock, October 13th, 1881.

Water

Ultimately the Local Board had to address the issues that were central to its function as the sanitary authority for the Matlock Bath district. Its first major challenge was the resort's wholly inadequate water supply. Until 1862 Matlock Bath's water supply depended on springs and communal taps and tanks, an unreliable combination subject to seasonal fluctuations and worse. In that year a water company was formed and the following year a site for a reservoir was chosen, outside Matlock Bath, beside Hackney Lane on Darley hillside, in a field called Derbyshire Ground. Pipes were laid from there terminating, 'at or near the Toll-gate' at Artist's Corner, from where it was distributed. In 1883 the Board bought the Water Company for just over £1900; it extended the works, borrowing the money from the Public Works Commissioners on a thirty year term. Two years later the ratepayers were complaining £6-7000 had been spent, with a further £600 committed, for a water supply that delivered only 14 gallons a minute which was quite inadequate.[16] It was at its worst in summer when the demand was highest and the supply weaker, at no more than 11 gallons per minute; so poor that the taps were open for just a few hours each day.[17] In 1890 an engineer's report confronted the Board with the stark reality of the problem. The actual summer need, when the resort might have to cater for 15-20,000 visitors in a day, was he estimated, 41.7 gallons per minute. Something had to be done and three years later a reservoir, fed from Brown's Spring, was built on F. C. Arkwright's land in the Birchwood, above High Peak Junction, to the south of Matlock Bath. This supplied 150,000 gallons a day six days of the week, the seventh serving Cromford Canal. Mrs Rebecca Arkwright formally turned on the supply on May 18th, 1893.

But this was not the end of the matter. In 1900, in its review of the end of the century, the *High Peak News* noted the record amount of building in Matlock Bath. The need to secure an increased water supply could not be ignored and the UDC reached the decision to pump water up to a reservoir on Ember Farm, above Upperwood. A site for a pumping station was earmarked at the end of Music Row on Temple Walk but complications about acquiring the land caused delays. Meanwhile, the seriousness of the situation became increasingly apparent. By early 1903 water in Matlock Bath was again being rationed. Unless the Darley reservoir was full, Upperwood and Masson roads could not be supplied at the same time as Clifton Road, the New Bath and Woodbank and in 1904 it was claimed that half way up Waterloo Road a supply was available for an average of only half an hour per day[18] and that water had to be carried up to Woodbank, Lawton's palatial new house. He was vociferous in his condemnation of the situation. Relief came at last at the end of 1906 when the Ember Farm reservoir scheme was completed.

Poacher turned gamekeeper.[15]

The Matlock Bath Local Board complain about touting. It is done at every watering place. Mr Leggoe is the first man to lift his voice about importunating. He can afford to do it now. Having left his business on the most prominent street in Matlock Bath he feels free to descry an evil, of which he was the chief ornament and choicest specimen. Last summer his voice could be heard in songs of praise about his 'dinners,' 'teas,' 'beautiful refreshment room,' and 'the way to every popular drive within a score of miles from Matlock.' Now he wants to commence a violent process of extermination of all who open their mouths in attempting to catch a customer. He is not a competitor and the familiar voice is lost on the parade.

A letter received by the Local Board March 7 1890[19]

M.Sir, I yould your gentelemn be kinde enough to grant mee liceness for two poneys and two donkeys. I have lent miss Smedley one of my donkeys for the summer sesern, and I have only two donkeys now. Mr Smith, the town concler, as towled mee to take a house in matlock parish and they wouled grant mee licnens at once and they granted mee my licnens and my sun as shifted his goods to the house in matlock parish and I want tow be in matlock bank half-a-day and half-a day in matlock bath and I want to be in the after noon in matlock bath with my donkeys and ponies and I hope your gentelemen I have been on a grate expense all winter ceeping my donkeys and poney and where hever your gentelemen wishes mee to stand I will stand with my ponies and donkeys and I will drive cromford way all they time. I ham at work till 8 o'clock.

James Rouse.

Mr Rouse subsequently attended a meeting of the Board on April 1st hoping to receive licences for his ponies. The chairman told him *'we have come to a decision that your ponies [are] too vicious to be on the streets...we cannot give licences to any one for them.'*

The 'presidency'

In April 1893 at the beginning of its last term before replacement by the Matlock Bath and Scarthin Nick Urban District Council, the Local Board elected a new chairman, John Edward Lawton. He was new to the Board though familiar with its role from his service with the Dukinfield Local Board. He described himself as 'a stranger among them;'[20] this was not assumed modesty for though he had worked in Matlock Bath since 1879, during the intervening period, he and his family had made their life in Dukinfield. He owed his instant appointment to the chair as much to the impasse between two factions which threatened to paralyse the Board as to his personal qualities. He was seen as the man who would command the respect of both parties and after a lengthy meeting in which he more than once declined the nomination that was being thrust upon him, he was elected to the chair, in preference to the previous chairman, Mr Lennox, a local draper.

Matlock Bath responded enthusiastically to the prospect of their village having its own council and when the time came in December 1894 to elect the members of the new body there were 21 nominations for the 11 seats.[21] Lawton topped the poll with 174 votes, 42 ahead of his nearest rival Dr J. E. Innes, a local surgeon. A 'presidency' had begun; it was to last until 1907. With Lawton at its head Matlock Bath felt good about itself. Always ready with an

FIGURE 122. **The road roller and crew posing outside Mr Scorer's draper's shop in Derwent Parade.**

The *High Peak News* report of the MBUDC meeting in March 1903 noted that a tender from the Oxford Steam Roller Company for 20 shillings a day (1s less than last year) had been accepted; the work to commence April 20th and last 5-6 weeks; the Council to provide the fuel. Was this picture taken then or in another road rolling session?

Private collection

FIGURE 123. **The MBUDC watering cart, photograph, early 1900s.**

In periods of dry weather it was customary to employ the watering cart to lay the dust. In 1866 a visitor, 'almost blinded by dust' wrote to remind the Local Board of Health that they owned a watering cart which had been paid for by public subscription but claimed 'for what purpose it is now used I cannot learn.' He was 'at a loss to understand how the Board 'without experiencing qualms of conscience apply to these injured persons [the ratepayers] for the payment of rates.' There were limited experiments with ashphalting and tar spraying from 1886 onwards but apart from one ringing endorsement in *The Lady* magazine in 1887 'The famous Matlock dust has been conspicuous by its absence', the complaints according to season, were continuous. The cart was not needed in December 1909 when mud, mud, mud was the cry. Having 'a job to cross the street' was blamed on the big steam and motor wagons drawing stone.

Greatorex family collection.

emollient if lengthy speech he seemed to know intuitively what his listeners most wanted to hear and to have the words to indulge them. Here he is in November 1894, shortly before the UDC election, addressing the annual dinner of the Matlock Bath Military Band. His message was actually an unwelcome one; he was there to say the Board would not be funding the band but wrapped in his warm words, where there might have been a frosty silence, he was rewarded with applause.[22] First he assured them 'he was on their side. He yielded to no man in his anxiety to aid and establish good music everywhere.' Then the bad news, sweetened a little by his assurance that 'if the law had given them power to make a contribution out of the rates', they would not resist. And finally, to send them home happy and proud, he told them; 'this year he had covered forty thousand miles in the Eastern and Western hemispheres, but had never seen in any country a more beautiful spot than this one of Matlock Bath.'

Lawton did not deny or disguise his enjoyment of the role in which he had cast himself. It is evident from the words he chose when greeting the party of 6-700 Liberals from north Salford who, in September 1900[23] enjoyed a day out in the resort at his expense. They were welcomed with the words; 'the town over which [I have had] the honour to preside for a considerable number of years [has] in its own way done what it [can] to make the visit pleasant.' It certainly had. Matlock Bath was en fete, with ceremonial arches, lights on the trees and illuminated boats on the river. There was no doubting who ran the village in these years. It is also apparent that the 'presidential' family played its part. In May 1897, in support of the Fund for the Diamond Jubilee, at the Bath Assembly Room in North Parade, all his children performed in their own dramatic production. It was judged a brilliant success.[24] Lawton explained his motivation in a lengthy speech at the ceremony to mark his silver wedding. 'He happened to be one of those Englishmen' he said, 'who believed that no matter what station of life he happened to be in, it was his duty, and no more or less than his duty, to do whatever he could for his neighbour, and for the community in which he happened to be.'[25]

Frequently prolix, often pompous and not always to be believed, Lawton was the leader Matlock Bath needed at a difficult time in its development. His energy, experience and courage in addressing major issues, was evident in the Council's successful litigation with Derbyshire County Council. The UDC had repaired the footpaths which ran alongside the main highway but the County Council refused reimbursement and there the matter might have rested had Lawton not seen it as a challenge to be fought and won.[26]

Gas

With the highways dispute yet to be resolved, Lawton turned his attention to the problem of Matlock Bath's gas supply. The Matlock Gas, Light and Coke Company had been formed in 1853[27] to supply the whole of Matlock parish from works sited at the foot of Bath Fields, to the north of the railway station, from where at that time it was considered most demand would come. In 1857 more shares were issued and a second plant was added in the Darley Road, just north of Matlock, to better supply Matlock and Darley.[28]

The supply of gas was erratic and all too often the pressure fell below the required level. In 1896, in response to public demand for a more reliable supply and despite opposition from Matlock Bridge UDC, the Matlock Bath and Scarthin Nick Urban District Council obtained the Matlock Bath Gas Act which empowered them to compulsorily purchase the gas company's plant at Matlock Bath for just over £16,726.[29] Additional costs including claims by the parent Company, Matlock Bath's expenses incurred in securing the Act of Parliament, and for the arbitration which had to be sought to fix the price, brought the total expenditure to well over £20,000. A small number of other Councils had purchased their gas works but these had been in towns of some size; for Matlock Bath, more village than town, this was a decision of extraordinary courage. The equivalent value in modern terms adds a helpful perspective. The village had spent more than £2 million. But Lawton's judgement was sound and it proved to be a good investment, the profits after covering the loan charges providing an income that could be offset against the Council's expenditure, so reducing the rates.

The Act also authorised the company to supply gas to Cromford and Bonsall and though an application was made in 1896 to the Board of Trade for a Provisional Order to extend the supply it was not until 1906 that a loan of £3,000 was sought to fund laying pipes to Bonsall. Lawton had been instrumental in nursing the Council's case through the parliamentary process. His claim for expenses indicates the scale of the undertaking involving no less than 24 days of hotel and travel expenses.[30] These and his other expenses amounted to £76-4s. The purchase of the gas works was judged to have been a huge success the profits enabling Lawton to claim the rates had in effect been substantially reduced.

By 1900 the council faced a dilemma. More capacity was required and in 1901 plans were passed to extend the gas works. The extensions and renovations were undertaken at a cost of £2000, ignoring a clause in the 1896 Act which required the works to be moved within the next two to three years, to a place where smoke and fumes would cause less public nuisance. The council's decision not to re-locate the works meant that it had to secure another parliamentary bill to obviate this clause from the 1896 Act. This was not sought until 1909, by which time improved methods of gas production had reduced the nuisance so that the works could stay in its original place.

FIGURE 124. **A Midland express passing through Matlock Bath railway station, around 1900, photograph.**

The Matlock Bath Gas Works gasometer appears in the background to the right of the train.

Private collection.

There are indications Lawton's success in the business world and as chairman of the council, in the courts and in Parliament, bred an overconfidence which, particularly if it was coupled with the deep suspicion felt for their neighbours Matlock Bridge, led the council into fighting battles they could not win. So it was in 1904. The now separate Matlock Company promoted the Matlock Gas Bill to extend its area which already included Matlock Dale, to reach Rowsley and Winster. Matlock Bath Council opposed the application unsuccessfully. There the matter should have rested but despite this setback, a public meeting was called to seek authority to obtain compulsory powers for Matlock Bath to supply gas to Matlock Dale. A letter to the *High Peak News* calculating the likely cost to Matlock Bath ratepayers for such an action, compared with what the writer considered would be an annual profit of £10 on the gas sold to the Dale, asked 'are we so utterly foolish, so insane, as to give our Council a mandate to go again to London to further oppose the passing of the Matlock Gas Bill?' There was a response. The Matlock Bath Ratepayers' and Property Owners' Association was formed[31] and a petition of 139 names, along with letters from F. C. Arkwright, who was abroad, and Mr Quilliam, were presented in opposition. Lawton in his one and a half hour address to the meeting which had been called to discuss the matter, 'contemptuously refused to admit or consider the petition.' The Council went its own way - back to London where it was again unsuccessful; the ratepayers were faced with another bill for expenses. The *Journal of Gas Lighting* reporting on the case described the council as litigious, and commented 'The Chairman's pleasant and offhand deftness in dealing with awkward matters cannot always succeed.'[32]

Sewerage

Of all the major infrastructure issues facing Matlock Bath's Local Board and Council sewerage had the longest record of debate, and inaction with inevitably a gradual worsening of the situation. We do not know when the Board first considered the management of sewage. Despite the Rivers Pollution Prevention Act of 1876, the river continued to provide part of the local solution. In February 1879 the Matlock Bath Local Board meeting was informed that '109 large and moderate houses emptied into the river' and was reminded that even one house discharging to the river was a breach of the Act. A year later the Board was considering 12-15 plans from engineers for sewerage schemes but there would seem to have been no tangible outcome which may explain why, in about 1883, the Local Government Board began its campaign of threats and persuasion which was to continue for the next 25 years. It was to take until 1908 for an agreed and fully funded scheme to emerge.

There were two problems. One was the cost of a comprehensive scheme which would have been far beyond the ratepayers' means an additional burden on top of the rates they were paying already to service the investments in water and gas.[33] The second, the nonsense, as it appeared to Matlock Bath residents, of dealing with their sewage while Matlock and other settlements upstream continued to pollute the river with theirs. There were also some who saw no reason to improve the resort's sanitation. They had a strong voice in the Reverend R. Nicholson, (1842-1916) a member of the Board who opposed a proposal in 1893 on the grounds of cost, lack of need and risk of sickness. The cost, he argued, would be 'suicidal to the interests of the place;' rates would increase to at least 4s-3d in the £, an impossible figure for ratepayers; nor was there a need 'on the score of health, because their own bill of health was one of the finest in the kingdom, and much better than Buxton;' and there were risks. Schemes of this sort he claimed 'resulted in epidemics of fever'.[34] It is not clear how many other ratepayers shared these views but as the proprietor of two hydropathic establishments some will have seen him as professionally qualified in medical matters and followed his lead in casting doubt on the need for improved sanitation. Irrational as Nicholson's views may appear today, he was

Mistaken Identity: a costly health scare

Just how important its reputation as a healthy place to visit was, as a component of the resort's success, was demonstrated in April 1882. A case of smallpox was reported in the *Sheffield Daily Telegraph* said to have been contracted in Matlock Bath. On the day the paper appeared the news reached Manchester, Derby and Birmingham. The Midland Railway cancelled its special trains and hundreds of people were prevented from visiting the Bath. The case had actually occurred in Matlock Bank but the damage was done. Telegrams were sent and letters written to the newspapers across the region quoting the memory of the oldest inhabitant who affirmed there had never been a case of smallpox in the resort. The Local Board was told of a similar situation in Southport where it took three and a half years to rebuild public confidence.

in fact expressing what for many would have been the conventional wisdom of their generation. Since the days of Edwin Chadwick's first sanitary reforms in the 1830s the driving force behind improvements in sanitation had been the response to outbreaks of disease; and while the local medical officer confirmed in his regular reports to the Local Board that

Matlock Bath was a healthy place in which to live and to visit, what need could there be for expensive sanitary engineering? Even those among Nicholson's fellow Board members who recognised the case for improvements seem to have been moved more by the external pressures from the LGB than from a concern to update the primitive facilities the resort offered its visitors and residents.

In 1888 a scheme was devised by Mr Speed, the Board's surveyor, which envisaged separating the district into five sections and in each one laying drains to a septic tank. His report refers to 463 houses of which only about 165 had water closets[35] and to the extensive use of privies. These he wished to replace with earth closets[36] which would be emptied weekly so leaving only surface and slop water to drain as best it could. His proposal was a stopgap measure and at an estimated cost of under £700 likely to be attractive to the Board, appalled by the 'gigantic expenditure' a comprehensive scheme would involve; in the chairman's words '£9,000 for the sewage of 463 houses was too great a cost.'

Speed's plans for Scarthin offered little more than the replacement of privies by earth closets but with an estimated cost of £120 it was a solution the Board subsequently may have wished it had taken up. Five years later, in November 1893, its contribution to F. C. Arkwright's sewerage scheme for Cromford and Scarthin had cost £450 with a further £90 expected for the completion of the outfall works.[37] How much of Speed's plan was implemented is not clear but whatever improvements there may have been they did not satisfy the Local Government Board which continued to press for an overall plan.

The shadow cast by the Local Government Board was a continuing presence in the Local Board's deliberations. For a while it might seem to have gone away and the Board could relax into its housekeeping agenda; and then it was back, always the same question. When will you commit to a comprehensive sewerage scheme? A snapshot of this unhappy and unequal dialogue, typical of many other exchanges involving these two parties over the years, is provided by the range of views expressed in the Board's meeting in August 1890. Mr Peters, the chairman, told his colleagues he'd received a personal letter from the LGB complaining of three unanswered letters about the need for a sewage scheme. He had replied blaming the clerk, telling them the 'matter had perhaps better be dealt with by the fresh clerk.' Clearly the Board now had to come up with a response for Mr Lymn, the new clerk, to deliver. It would prove to be an impossible task. Mr Lennox thought they had better deal with the problem because he knew other Boards had made a start and 'if the LGB saw they were doing something it would meet them.' But they had made a start, said Mr Rowland. 'They had made a cess pool in connection with the Clifton Road drainage, and in connection with the house by Mrs Shepherd's, and ... the LGB ought to be informed of that.' It was a brief moment of hope in a meeting where all the participants knew the only honest response to the LGB would be to tell them nothing was being done, the Board having neither the financial or political capital to promote or deliver a scheme. It was Mr Lennox who came closest to this admission. He suggested 'putting a sum of money by for the purpose of doing a little bit of a sewage scheme regularly; now that they were in a good financial position' they could afford it. Mr Lymn confirmed the LGB 'would allow them to do it in bits, if they put before them a general scheme'. And that was the rub. As Mr Wheatcroft said 'they had had plans'. They had paid a surveyor from Stockport £50 and paid a fee to another but the lowest estimate was £10,000 [about £1 million in modern value] not including the purchase of land. 'It was a moral impossibility for the place to undergo a great sewage scheme, because it would not be possible for them to pay the rates.' Mr Lennox remained optimistic and focussed on placating the LGB. They could 'carry out a scheme on a small scale which would be sufficient for the time being and would be able to drive matters on and show the LGB they were willing and intended to do something. They could not afford a £10,000 scheme and they never could afford a scheme that would be perfectly satisfactory to the Bath.' And the conclusion? A special meeting of the full committee would be held in a fortnight's time.[38]

In 1891 a scheme was prepared by another local engineer, J. R. Parkin of Idridgehay and an application to borrow £9,000 was submitted to the Local Government Board which sent an inspector to report on the proposal. His enquiry in October 1890 was attended by deputations from Matlock Bath and Matlock Bridge Local Boards and representatives from the County Council and from Cromford. It was in this forum that the first serious steps were made towards a joint scheme in which the effluent from both districts would be piped to outfall works near High Peak Junction. It was recognised on all sides something had to be done; the resident population in both districts was growing, more in Matlock than in the Bath, though it made its own special contribution to the problem, given that on a well attended Bank holiday, sewage from 20,000 visitors poured into the Derwent.[39] But while an amalgamated approach solved one problem the issue of cost remained. This was a bigger problem for Matlock Bath where the rateable value had barely increased wheras in the same period Matlock Bridge was enjoying growth of about £100 per year. There seemed to be no way forward for Matlock Bath on its own; and even a joint scheme might require more than the modest population could sustain.[40]

Lawton attempted to address the funding problem as part of his Improvement Bill which was before Parliament in May 1905. Matlock Bath's population of about 1,830 inhabitants and current rateable value of £11,092, carrying a debt of £25,451, largely from the gas purchase, could not repay the loan required for a sanitation scheme within the usual LGB term of thirty years. To do so would inflate the rates, already at 6/- in the £, to an intolerable level. However if Parliament would agree to a term longer than the Local Government Board's limit then the matter might be resolved. He asked for fifty years for lands and forty years for works, to cover both a new gasworks and the sanitation scheme. For Parliament this was a step too far and both the gas and sanitation sections of the Bill were lost.

It was not until towards the end of 1908 that the Council, now led by Charlie White, signed an agreement to seek Local Government Board sanction for a joint scheme with Matlock Bridge, with an overall cost of £40,000, to which the Bath would contribute no more than £10,000.[41] A year later it received approval. Progress of the scheme was seriously affected by World War I when limited manpower was available for such work. There were long periods with half-finished trenches in the road which exacerbated the already existing problems for traffic and pedestrians in Matlock Bath. The work had reached North Parade by May 1915 and the pedestrian bridge across the river opposite Brunswood Terrace was being erected carrying a sewer pipe beneath it to the east side of the river. Proceeding 'at the pace of a snail' was the report in July 1917; the suggestion then that the scheme should have been delayed until after the war came rather too late. Tenders for its completion were submitted in September 1922 and four years later that objective was achieved though cess pits and night soil collection continued to be part of sewage management in some places for many more years.

At a more personal level a problem for day visitors before the first World War, was the shortage of public toilets especially for females. Two urinals, one at the end of the Promenade, the other at Fishpond Hill gave provision for men, but ladies sometimes had to rely on private houses which touted 'Wash and brush-up for a penny'.

Charles Frederick White, Chairman of Matlock Bath UDC 1908-1914

If Lawton was a man of business, White was a man of the people. He was the Bath's second outstanding council leader, following Lawton after an interval of a single year. Though lacking Lawton's polish and with none of his patriarchal style, his courage and direct, uncompromising approach to the flagrant inequalities and abuses he saw around him, won him the loyalty and trust of his electorate. In the pages that follow we offer a brief description of an extraordinary life.

Charlie White, (1863-1923) was born in Tetbury, Gloucestershire in March 1863, His parents were poor[42] and he started work aged 10 as an assistant to a cobbler, earning a shilling a week. About 1880 he came to Bonsall[43] and in 1881 was living in Yeoman Street working as a boot and shoe maker. In October of that year he married Alice Charlesworth, raising a son and four daughters in a partnership that endured, despite the many challenges his life choices, frailties and temperament imposed on it. His political career began in Bonsall in 1898 with his election to the Urban District Council and he continued in this role until 1903. Already there are signs of the contentious figure he was to become. As a fellow UDC member complained 'Mr White only comes [to Council meetings] to kick up rows.' In 1906-7[44] the family moved to Chapel Hill, Scarthin, within the Matlock Bath UDC district and in 1907 White stood for election. His 'trenchant, scathing and fearless criticism of the then council created a sensation' and he headed the polls. Years later the *Derbyshire Advertiser*, in an obituary,[45] offered this description of his oratory. 'He possessed a voice of pleasing timbre and by no means uncultivated: a voice which lent itself to those emotional appeals which sway large audiences, over which Mr White exercised a truly magnetic influence, his oratory owing we fancy at times rather more to emotion than to facts and logic.'

A year later in 1908 he became Chairman of the council and, by virtue of this office, a J.P. On the bench, he soon became the scourge of the local police force[46] attacking their behaviour in cases brought against working men; this added to his growing reputation as a man of the people. In the council elections of 1910 he secured more votes than had ever been received before and subsequently was re-elected chairman. In February that year he also gained a County Council seat standing for the Winster division. He soon made his presence felt, fighting to secure better wages and terms of employment for the roadmen and other low paid workers employed by the Council. It was said on his death that his 'pronounced radicalism [had] caused many a flutter among the conservative members' of the council. By 1903 he was already active in the Liberal Association and in 1905 accepted his first paid political appointment as assistant registration agent, a year later becoming agent. His work for Edward Himmers, the Liberal candidate, in the elections of 1906 and January 1910 was so admired that when Himmers stood down shortly before the election of December 1910, White was seen as the obvious replacement. In a campaign of about a week he was judged to have done well in holding Lord Kerry, the sitting member, to a majority of 1,060 votes; now well known throughout the district he was seen as the coming man.

In May 1914 his promising future in public life was snatched away from him. He had been declared bankrupt and unable to meet his creditors' demands there was no alternative but resignation from all the public offices he held.[47] His financial ruin was the result of an ill judged resort to the courts to settle a longstanding feud with two local adversaries whom he accused of libel and slander. The case, heard in London, lasted four days, involved costly legal teams and expenses for numerous witnesses and was followed by a fruitless appeal. Family and supporters rallied round but despite generous public subscriptions White's liabilities amounted to £1,198-18-5. His financial embarrassment was accompanied by the humiliation he had endured at the trial at the hand of the celebrated barrister Marshall Hall K.C. as he proved to the satisfaction of the jury that White was a gambler, womaniser, drunkard and pub crawler who had used the pubs of Cromford, Wensley, Winster, Elton and several others to treat his friends and constituents to encourage them to support his cause. The case was reported verbatim; page after page in the local press, exposing him to ridicule and concluding with a jury verdict that left no doubt they considered him a liar.

White's recovery from this crushing setback was achieved in 1918 through the financial support of unnamed political friends[48] in Matlock and as a result of his war work. In August 1918 his debts were settled and his bankruptcy annulled, the judge commenting on his 'substantial service to the country during the war'. He had had a good war, serving first as substitution officer for Chesterfield during which time he is said to have addressed over 300 meetings; and then as distribution officer for the Ministry of Food in which capacity he devised a rationing system which was so successful it was adopted nationally. He had remained a figure in the public eye and, as subsequent events proved, lost none of his popularity. By early December 1918 he was fighting his old opponent Lord Kerry for the Parliamentary seat of West Derbyshire.[49] He stood as a man of the people on a radical platform; homes for the lads who during the war he had persuaded to enlist; nationalisation of the railways; disputes to be settled by arbitration rather than strikes; and free trade. He would, he said, like a woman to be Minister of Health and believed the old age pension should be 10/- a week from age 65. With a backward glance at his previous misfortunes he promised his nemesis, his trial judge Mr Justice Darling, 10/- a week instead of his £3,500 a year.

The class card also had a place in the mix and it was played with some dexterity. White knew about food rationing as did his audience but could they 'imagine Lord Kerry standing in a queue at five o' clock in the morning?' He won handsomely with 54% of the vote and a majority of 2,160. Four years later, standing against the Marquis of Hartington, he won again, narrowly this time, his majority reduced to 87.

By the time White embarked on his parliamentary career he had moved to Matlock.[50] He was active in the questions he asked and in the constituents he supported[51] and the causes he upheld but the House heard little of the oratory that had inspired the ratepayers of Matlock Bath and the West Derbyshire electorate. Overawed and for much of the time unwell he was perhaps worn out from decades of overwork. Old age pensions and pensions for ex-servicemen were particular concerns of his; but as a member of Parliament without private means or the trades union support enjoyed by many Labour members he also argued for increased allowances for M.P.s. He had only the £400 then provided from which he was expected to find rail costs, administrative expenses and living expenses. Even though he lived in London for 12/- a day, how was he and others similarly placed supposed to manage? He was nominated to join a committee to look into the matter but no real progress was made.

His political career might have extended to a third term but fighting the 1923 election he was taken ill and on December 4th he died.[52] His funeral attracted a crowd estimated to be around 7000. His supporters were present in force many of them wearing yellow ribbons; so also were his opponents including Lord Hartington. There were many tributes and from Hyda Cross these words 'The old pensioner, the ex-serviceman, the widow, the oppressed, they have lost a champion, a friend who understood their needs, and fought for them against tremendous odds.'

Talking to some of his supporters in the 1960s, the fondness and passion with which they venerated his memory was matched in equal measure by their disappointment in his son, Charlie White junior, (1891-1956) who had deserted his father's cause and joined the Labour party.

A judge encounters a strange working class habit.[53]

In the four days of the case White brought against Barnes and Rose for libel and slander in March 1913 much time was spent describing White's drinking habits in the Bell in Cromford and in pubs in Winster and Elton. White told the court his usual drink was port wine and lemonade. 'A small port in a village is 2d,' he said, 'so you don't get very much for it.' Again and again refuting allegations of drunkenness, White claimed to have had just two or three drinks of port wine and lemonade.

Finally the judge, Mr Justice Darling, could conceal his curiosity no longer: Excuse me Mr White, how do you drink port wine and lemonade?' Mr White: 'Mix it my Lord.' (laughter).[54]

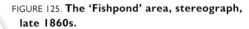

FIGURE 125. **The 'Fishpond' area, stereograph, late 1860s.**

On the left of this view is part of the property purchased by William Pearson at the Old Bath estate sale in 1864, now modified to form The Fishpond and the shops at the southern end of South Parade. Of particular interest to us is the 'shed' in the furthest angle of the yard (see enlargement). It appears to have people standing in front of it under an awning and with a signboard above. We believe it to be the type of temporary construction for the erection of which Francis Anzani Buxton was fined by the Local Board in 1870, see page 170.

John Bradley collection.

CHAPTER THIRTEEN

Matlock Bath in the 20th century

At the beginning of the twentieth century, Matlock Bath continued to be a busy seasonal resort but to the north Matlock, as we know it today, had become the faster growing and more important settlement. Signs of this change in status, each a blow to Matlock Bath's pride are seen in the railway company's decision in 1905 to change the name Matlock Bridge Station to Matlock and in 1912, the opening of a purpose-built Head Post Office in Matlock.[1]

As World War I engulfed the nation local matters became subordinate to national priorities as the late Charles Berresford in his comprehensive account *Matlock Bath at War* has recorded in touching detail. The British tourist resorts with their capacity to house large groups of people made a significant contribution to the war effort and Matlock Bath was no exception.[2] It received its first detachment of troops from the Army Service Corps early in

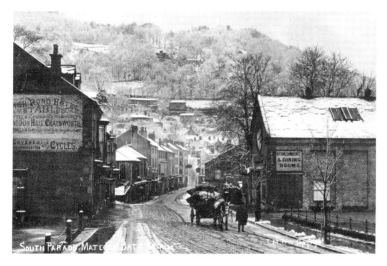

FIGURE 126. **South Parade in snow, photograph about 1905.**

John Boden is taking his cart loaded with rag waste from the station to Dunsley paper mill in Bonsall Hollow. The name South Parade replaced the earlier Museum Parade sometime in the 1880s.[3] Well before 1900, it had developed into a street of shops offering a wide range of services for residents and for visitors. At this date these included businesses selling shoes, china, fish, meat, groceries and confectionery, as well as tea rooms, a harness maker, a druggist and a photographer. At Hodgkinson's and the Fishpond Hotel and several other addresses accommodation was available. The former Central Museum, now assuming the title Royal Museum, Buxton's and the petrifying wells continued the tradition of selling spar goods and petrified objects to the visitors. Boden's Refreshment and Dining Rooms on the right offered seating for 120, one of several establishments meeting a demand to cater for large organised groups at one sitting. The Central on North Parade offered 'seats for 500' and later, the largest of them all, the Royal boasted capacity for 800. On the right, note the railings which have replaced the wall against the fishpond and the trees that had been planted there in 1896.

Private collection.

1915; later men of the West Yorkshire regiment arrived but the influx which seems to have left the strongest lasting memory in the village was towards the end in Spring 1918, when 210 beds were made ready in the Royal Hotel Figure 80 for the Canadian Convalescent Officers' Hospital; 200 orderlies and other staff took over the Bath Terrace Hotel Figure 89. Maybe they were remembered best because they contributed so much to the community; they were fit enough to join in village events; their August Bank Holiday was the busiest for the last ten years; the reopened Pump Room sold 1,396 glasses and 86 bottles of water in the month. And perhaps most importantly, they were there to share the celebrations for the end of the war in November 1918.

Throughout the war years visitors still came to Matlock Bath though not in such high numbers as in the past. Trains were commandeered to move troops around the country and cheap excursion trains were lost though some full price specials still ran; but by 1914 huge numbers now arrived by motor transport. This trend had been foreseen by Mr Ashby, a whitesmith and bicycle builder, who had set up his business at the foot of Green Lane where he advertised as 'Official Repairer to the Automobile Club of Great Britain and Ireland' and by 1902 had been granted a petroleum licence. By 1907, the year Matlock Bath considered introducing a speed limit, this business had closed but motorists continued to be served by E. Williams & Company's motor garage on South Parade. Williams also sold cars. In August 1910, for the sum of £286-17-0 he sold Edward Caudwell a 'BSA motor' which became part of the transport fleet at his mill at Rowsley[4] as he gradually replaced his horse drawn carts and wagons with steam and motorised vehicles. Cycling was also very popular; at several sites, visitors' cycles were stored at two pence a time leaving their owners free to explore the resort on foot. In 1916 when military demands on petrol supplies caused the use of motor driven charabancs to be banned, horse-drawn charas reappeared in the village. The Royal, the Temple and the New Bath were reported busy; it seemed guests were favouring inland resorts over their coastal rivals where German attack was feared.

With petrol supplies restored early in 1919, motor traffic returned; the Canadian Government returned the keys of the Royal to its owners in July; the Venetian Fete was reinstated in September and entertained huge crowds. Trade picked up.

FIGURE 128 (top left). **Cyclists relaxing outside Frosts' Refreshment Rooms, South Parade, snapshot, about 1900.**

Cycling was thirsty work on unsurfaced roads especially in the summer dust and many inns and refreshment houses advertised for the cyclists' trade. Victoria House (now 122-124 North Parade) still displays its Cyclists' Touring Club badge.[5] The building shown here can be placed in the next view. It adjoins Howe's and is now 178 South Parade.

Ken Askew collection.

FIGURE 129 (top right). **South Parade, photograph, before 1882.**

The roadways of crushed limestone in Matlock Bath were a notorious feature for the dust which arose from them in dry weather. Generations of visitors complained; amongst the earliest Joseph Farington recorded in his diary in August 1801 'The dust at Matlock exceeds whatever I

remember to have met with. The date of this photograph is uncertain but is not later than 1882 when Howe's business was transferred to the newly rebuilt[6] Fountain Baths.

Ken Askew collection.

FIGURE 130 (bottom left and right). **Charabancs in Matlock Bath, photographs.**

Outside the Fishpond Hotel, about 1910, a group poses for the camera in a vehicle marked Joseph Tomlinson & Sons Ltd, Sheffield. The proprietor of the Fishpond is shown as E.F. Martin.[7] The group outside the Grand Pavilion in July 1925 is the Langley Mill Baptist Pleasant Hour outing en route to Ashover. This picture was taken by Edgar Wright, a local photographer who lived at Speedwell Cottage, Upperwood. He took photographs of groups as they set out on their excursions around the area to sell to them when they returned

Ken Smith collection.

But by 1921 post war optimism had dissolved. It was replaced by a mood punctuated by complaints about high prices and the slump in trade. In Matlock Bath the rise in the price of gas by 9d to 6s 3d per 1000 cubic feet was a particular bone of contention. It was claimed that it was largely because Masson Mills was taking just over a third of the supply at below cost price, a contract entered into before the war. This drew a swift riposte from the Secretary of the English Sewing Cotton Company correcting the claim and condemning the council's inefficient, unbusinesslike management of the gas works.[8] Percy Rowbottom, the photographer, who was then managing the Fountain Baths described the 1921 season as 'ghastly…never in my life saw the place so absolutely stagnant' but he found some hope in Masson Mills 'once again doing full time' and the glove factory 'doing a bit'.[9]

Matlock Bath War Memorial. No. 1721.

FIGURE 131. **The War Memorial soon after its erection.**

May 1921 saw the unveiling of the Matlock Bath War Memorial on the Promenade.[10] It cost £700 which, despite the hard times, had been raised by public subscription.

Tony Holmes collection.

1922 was little better, the excursion trains brought no more than a 1000 visitors compared with up to twenty times that number in the past. There was some cheer with the reopening of the refurbished Royal Hotel at Easter and of the Royal Pavilion on Whit Monday. The *High Peak News* described thousands of vehicles making the valley a halting place on the first Sunday in May but even that was not entirely good news. The following week's paper recorded a visitor's lament 'charabancs, private motor cars, motor bikes and side-cars, all [combining] to swirl up the limestone dust from the dishevelled roadway until you could hardly breathe or see or smell.'[11] The problem was exacerbated by local quarrying.

FIGURE 132. **Harveydale Quarry, Matlock Dale, 1920's.**

The entrance to the quarry and some of its plant is shown on the right hand side of the picture with its sign board advertising Greatorex and Sons Ltd Limestone and Tar Macadam Works. The Dale's quarries provided employment but added unsightly plant at the roadside and much dust and noise which did not go unnoticed by travellers approaching Matlock Bath from the north. There were 5 limestone quarries working in Matlock Dale in 1922 but the stone trade was flat and early in the year notices appeared in several of them announcing a ten shilling per week reduction in wages for all grades.[12] A year earlier Messrs Smart & Co's quarry near Matlock Bath station had closed 'till more normal times'.[13]

Tony Holmes collection.

FIGURE 133. **Before and after, 1922.**

The pictures illustrate the change at the foot of the Pitchings which took place in 1922. The new building is in sharp contrast with the horse-friendly surface of the Pitchings, the route to the New Inn stabling which was created about 150 years earlier. The flat over the bank became the new Police House.[14]

Tony Holmes collection.

FIGURE 134. **The menagerie on Lover's Walk.**

In 1922 a new visitor attraction, a troop of monkeys and a den of wolves was introduced on Lover's Walk and gradually a small menagerie was developed. The children's playground occupies the site now. Occasional escapes added excitement to the enterprise and overwintering the animals was a problem. The winter of 1927 saw them housed in the Pavilion; and in December 1928 the lemur, opossum and macaw were lodged in the glove factory but the twelve monkeys were sold for thirty five shillings each and for only £1 in 1929. The two small bears shown in the summer of 1930 'grew too big' and in November were offered for sale at the reduced price of £28-10s each while the small birds, monkeys and lemur went to the public shelter on the Prom.

Tony Holmes collection.

Alongside the increase in motor transport, Matlock Bath continued to be served by special trains; the August Bank Holiday in 1923 brought 20 specials carrying 6,730 passengers with a further 1,500 on the timetabled services. They came from the same wide catchment as before the war, though in more modest numbers, from as far as Liverpool and Barnsley to the north and Lincoln and Birmingham to the east and south. The railway had an added significance now as a local employer, of station staff and of platelayers and shunting yard workers.[15]

There is abundant evidence for the difficulties the resort faced in the inter-war years. The Venetian Fete was a great success in September 1926 but at the same time Frederic Dalton was advertising Osborne Manor, a new name for what was formerly Clarence Boarding House, free for the winter if the tenant would keep it for the summer. Two Miss Osbornes who may have been tenants then or earlier had walked out of the building one morning leaving the breakfast tables laid and beds made up. Some twenty years later they reappeared to visit a neighbour, with their explanation - they had just had enough.

The Pavilion was and was still seen as a problem[16]; by 1929, its cinema was back in use but losing money. Councillor Charlie White (junior) asked was it ever likely to pay in 'its present unattractive state' and claimed that, as with the tram in Matlock, which had stopped running in August, 1927, if it was losing money, it had to go. The cinema was given a reprieve for four months but closed the following year. The Pavilion's fate was no longer in the hands of the Matlock Bath UDC. In 1924 this council had been abolished and Matlock Bath was now under the control of a new Authority which brought together the two districts of Matlock Bridge and Matlock Bath as the Matlock Urban District Council. It was not a development for which there was much support in Matlock Bath. It had been rejected by 98.7% of the Matlock Bath ratepayers in the referendum held on its adoption but despite this opposition it went ahead. For some years afterwards the amalgamation contributed to the difficulties of the period as local government was characterised by continuous wrangling between members of the old council bodies with Matlock Bath portraying itself as the Cinderella of the council wards.

FIGURE 135. **Demolition of the Royal Hotel in progress, c. 1937.**

On the left, the main building of the Royal Hotel is being demolished. On the right hand side the surviving west wing was converted into flats which survived in use until the 1960s. Now the Temple Road Car Park occupies most of the site's level ground and Gulliver's Kingdom the hill slope above it.

Ken Smith collection.

In 1929 major fires in the district affected both employment and local morale. In Matlock Bath the fire at the Spa Glove Company, in the former Boden's café building, brought attention to the inefficiency of the Fire Service and led to the glove business, and some staff, moving to Chelmsford. The Matlock Bath premises were demolished. Much more serious for the resort, was the fire at the Royal Hotel at Easter, the beginning of the 1929 season, leading to its closure. At first there was the expectation that the Royal would rise from the ashes and hopes were buoyed when an advertisement hoarding appeared announcing that a replacement was to be built. Over several years various plans were considered and rejected when funding could not be found. The new Royal was not to be and finally John William Wildgoose's Matlock building firm was contracted to demolish the building. The loss of the Royal was a huge blow. It was Matlock Bath's only serious competitor to the Matlock hydros which continued to be busy; its demise coincided with the Great Depression; it was the end of an era for Matlock Bath. It was here that Matlock Bath's history had begun; where from the late seventeenth century visitors to the valley had been offered some form of water cure. In the eighteenth century its mineral water baths had given Matlock Bath its name; it was the focus for the social life of the resort well into the nineteenth century and later it had adjusted, albeit slowly, to embrace hydropathy, the new fashion in water treatment.[17]

FIGURE 136. **Matlock Bath's Cricket Pavilion, Upperwood.**

In 1924, Matlock Bath formed a cricket team but for the next 5 years played all its matches away until, on a more or less flat field in Upperwood, a home ground was created. A small black and white striped wooden pavilion in the corner of the field advertised its role. Later the club fielded a ladies' team and years later, Matlock Bath School's football teams trekked up the Wapping to the ground to play their home fixtures.

Ken Smith collection.

FIGURE 137. **LMS poster c. 1935, Artist George Ayling (1887-1960).**

National Railway Museum / Science and Society Picture Library.

The **MATLOCKS**
FOR A RESTFUL HOLIDAY
EXPRESS SERVICES & CHEAP FARES
BY
L M S
GUIDE FREE FROM TOWN HALL MATLOCK

The need for more effective publicity and promotion had long been recognised. In the 1930s advertising in conjunction with the London Midland and Scottish Railway, the LMS, was seen as particularly valuable but various bodies had campaigned to bring the Matlocks and Derbyshire to the attention of a much wider public. The Matlock Publicity Association formed in 1925 and based at Matlock Town Hall published a guide which was distributed nationally and to Europe and the USA. A year earlier, in Derby, the Derbyshire Rural Community Council had been formed and in 1931 launched the *Come to Derbyshire Guide*. Separately, the Matlock Bath Spa Advertising Association made a short lived attempt to publicise the health benefits of the resort.

During the 1930s the Pavilion found a new audience as it became an events venue open to private organisations. So it was, in 1932 when the Matlock Cinema House was closed while the 'talkie' apparatus was being installed, the Matlock and District Operatic Society brought its production of Yeoman of the Guard to the Pavilion.[18] It was promoted as warm and comfortable; buses were laid on for its patrons. The review of the event claimed that it had opened the eyes of local residents to the fact that they themselves were shareholders in a commodious and well situated building', albeit rather neglected, but which 'should be made a distinct acquisition to the twin health resorts.' The message might have been more persuasive had it left out the summary of the old public view of the Pavilion as 'a large, cumbersome and somewhat rheumatic "white elephant", cold, ugly, a drag on the local rates and a blot on the landscape'.

It was a good summer in 1933 with a glorious Whitsuntide when 'shorts and beach pyjamas [were] popular among the ladies'. Casual clothing became an issue in the resort three years later. Women visitors, particularly the cyclists, were wearing shorts leading the Matlock Bath PCC to brand the town 'one of the wickedest spots in England'. Sixty years later this accolade might have been embraced with some relish; not so in 1936. It was a charge vigorously denied by those who made their living catering for the visitors. As ex Councillor Harry Boden of the Arcade Restaurant said to the *Sheffield Independent* 'you see the sort of thing they complain about...much more blatant at any seaside place if you walk along the beach and watch the sun-bathing. Personally I think it is all piffle.' Nor was the Matlock Cycling Club pleased. 'Of course they wear shorts' an official said 'but there is nothing immodest about that. No one complains about men and women wearing shorts for tennis. Why bring cyclists into it?'[19]

Nationally things began to pick up. Locally the Matlock Bath Gas Company was purchased by the Matlock and District Company. This was significant for Matlock Bath because some of the money raised by the sale was earmarked for the compulsory purchase of Lover's Walk which was achieved in 1936. It was a critical move. But for the Council's action this historic pleasure ground may not have survived. George Drabble, a timber merchant, had purchased the woodland at the Willersley estate sale, and when the Council stepped in the Lover's Walk was protected only by an existing lease which was close to expiry.

1934 saw the paddling pool replace the Pavilion pierrot stand and in Matlock the construction of the boating lake, both supported by some funding from the Playing Fields' Association. The same year the outdoor swimming pool at the New Bath Hotel was opened and the Matlock Police Ball was held at the Grand Pavilion, highlighting the shortage of a venue for such an event at Matlock.

Four years later in the shadow of the darkening international crisis, life in the resort continued after a fashion. Trade was reasonable, buoyed up by the largest bank holiday crowds for a number of years but the year also saw the loss of another of the resort's bath sites. Since 1926 the Fountain Bath had been in the hands of Frederick Godfrey.[20] For some years he kept the baths open to the public and ran his other business from the site but in 1938 the bath closed. The decision may have been influenced by the opening of the Lido swimming pool at Matlock in May that year. With its indoor and outdoor pools and modern facilities it would have offered additional competition to a site which was already challenged by the New Bath's new pool.

The second world war saw many buildings in Matlock and Matlock Bath requisitioned for military uses; once again the Pavilion was an army billet, the Palais Royale became a training school, the Parochial Hall a canteen. Evacuees arrived and mostly left again. Some visitors came and ration books were juggled to cater for them. But the village suffered no physical damage and gradually after 1945 life without the army or blackout curtains was rediscovered.

As cars and coaches became the predominant form of transport and rail travel ceased entirely from 1967 until 1972, the excursionist hordes of the past were replaced by coach parties of more manageable size and the catering establishments adapted their premises to suit the new market. The Pavilion accommodated changes too, the County Council using the ground floor as a book store; the Matlock Bath Attractions Committee managing the upstairs from 1949 to 1971 as a venue for music festivals, dances, local theatre performances, the Miss Derbyshire competition and, from 1974, it was leased as a privately managed Entertainments Centre. From 1957 for twenty years the Pump Room became a café and now it is used by the Peak District Mining Museum which was formed in the Pavilion's large downstairs room in 1977/78.

Happy memories

A personal memory of the first 30 years of the century from Charlotte 'Lottie' Farnsworth,[21] a local poet, offers a perhaps rose tinted view of the place but from a good vantage point, having spent her working life in Matlock Bath's tourist industry, most of it in the Council's pay boxes.

'I remember coming over the fields from Bonsall when I was a girl and watching the crowds streaming down from the station on a Bank Holiday from the excursion trains.

I remember the crowded ferry boat and the merry crews on the river in the rowing boats and especially I remember the Good Friday when four young people were drowned in the flooded river at the weir.

Matlock Bath was a popular place in those days with the Royal Hotel in full swing, with a wonderful Italian Band playing out on the terrace each evening and dances and concerts in the lovely old Pavilion.

Then the new Grand Pavilion opened and I remember many of the plays, concerts and pictures we had there. We ran for nearly two years on Stoll's wonderful British productions, featuring all the best books and actors, also many popular musical comedies such as "The Quaker Girl", "Tons of Money", "Paddy the Next Best Thing".

Matlock Bath was really 'with it' in those days and I remember meeting many well known artistes at the Pavilion, also among the pierrot troupes who had a pitch behind the Pavilion and were greatly appreciated on a wet day as they had shelter for the crowds.

I remember the days of the first World War when the Canadian officers were billeted in the Royal Hotel and old Pavilion as a Convalescent Hospital. I think they had nearly 200 permanent staff to wait on them. These men got to know the local people well and even fell in love and married some of the local girls and took them back to Canada.

I remember the fire at the Royal Hotel also the one that destroyed the engine room at the Pavilion and put an end to the silent pictures there, for the talkies came in before we could get started again.

In spite of all the sorrow and trouble of War, there are many pleasant incidents to remember and there were no Mods and Rockers in those days.

Matlock Bath is a beautiful place and thousands of people know and love it and I hope it will be ever more popular in the future.

My thanks go to those who have tried to make it and keep it a charming holiday resort – the Switzerland of England.'

With the growth of supermarket shopping and private car ownership Matlock Bath, like towns and villages all over the country, gradually lost its specialist shops. A roll call along the Parades from the 1950s would have included - the Post Office and two Banks, two green-grocers, four grocers, two off licences and the sweet shop, two dress shops and a hat shop the fancy goods shop, the haberdasher, insurance agent, baker, butcher, cobbler, fishmon-ger, chemist, tobacconist and two newsagents as well as five public houses and more than half a dozen cafes; Holme Road boasted its own butcher, grocer and greengrocer. Few have been replaced. Several formerly licensed premises have been closed, the Prince of Wales, the Vaults, the George Hotel and the County and Station; the Rutland Arms; the Roadside bar and the Devonshire have been demolished. The long serving Fishpond and the Midland have survived in the trade and in modern times have been joined by the Princess Victoria and Rose Cottage.

As visitors have become more demanding, expecting higher standards for overnight stays the number of places advertising such accommodation has shrunk. Many of the private houses which had offered a room or two were much too small to be adapted to offer en suite rooms or car parking or both; the greater freedom to travel about to find a job has provided alternative ways to supplement the family budget. The Midland and the High Tor Hotel still offer accommodation for overnight guests and from the eighteenth century, the New Bath and Hodgkinson's have maintained the tradition; the Temple is being refurbished. Holiday Lets, a style of visitor accommodation that would have been entirely familiar to

Matlock Bath's eighteenth century clientele, is available at Portland House.

The most significant alteration in the appearance of the built village in the twentieth century was the concession to 'progress', the Matlock Bath road widening. The Ministry of Transport's improvement to the London to Carlisle A6 Trunk Road was regarded by many as a necessary modernisation which would help to to bring the village into the twentieth century, the age of the motor car. The loss of buildings, the development of car parks and the pall of air pollution have all been part of the price that has had to be paid for the survival of Matlock Bath as a resort and as a commuter village. The upheaval seems to have been passively accepted by the residents though for one at least the speed with which traffic could now hurry through brought to mind John Ruskin's response to the destruction of the beauty of Monsal Dale when the Buxton to Rowsley railway was built through the valley. He wrote 'now every fool in Buxton can be in Bakewell in half-an-hour, and every fool in Buxton at Bakewell'.

FIGURE 138. **Before (in about the 1930s) and during the road widening at Cromford Tors in 1961-2.**
Private collections.

Effects of the A6 Road widening scheme; demolition of property in Matlock Bath

The Ministry of Transport began buying property,[22] for demolition as early as 1939; Glenorchy house and chapel were demolished in 1957 but the first phase of widening was at Cromford Tors in 1961-62. This was followed by the Fishpond to Jubilee Bridge section in 1968 and a year later, Jubilee Bridge to Holme Road. The Wapping to Clifton Road alterations were made in 1973-74 and finally Masson Mill to the Wapping in 1974-76. The missing section Clifton Road to the Fishpond was considered too expensive to undertake because of problems with the churchyard at Holy Trinity Church and the Temple Road junction. In 1984 the Temple Road retaining wall was rebuilt. A prize-winning scheme restored a petrifying well to the riverside land opposite South Parade in 1970. It was demolished and replaced by shops in 2000. On both occasions the opportunity to turn back the clock and open up the view across the river from a promenade was missed. The pictures which follow show some of the properties which were demolished for the scheme.

Hand-made Hosiery
DIRECT FROM THE MANUFACTURERS

S. SKIDMORE & SON,
(Near the New Bath Hotel)
MATLOCK BATH

ESTABLISHED 1784.

LADIES', GENTLEMEN'S and
CHILDREN'S HOSIERY
in Silk, Silk and Wool, All Wool,
and Merino in every texture.

DURABLE, UNSHRINKABLE,
ECONOMICAL

Price List and Patterns
sent Post Free on application.

ALL GOODS CARRIAGE PAID.

FIGURE 139 (top left / right). **Before and after demolition of Masson Terrace, in the period 1974-76.**

FIGURE 140 (middle left / right). **Snapshots, about 1969, on the left Mount View and Weirside; on the right the red brick block, at this date named Linacre, Vale House and Weir Café.**

The buildings on the left[23] were on the Wapping, and the red brick block, on the right[24] adjacent on New Bath Hill.

All Ken Askew collection.

FIGURE 141 (bottom left). **Woodland House, postcard, about 1960.**

The house stood at the junction of the original road through Matlock Bath, turnpiked in 1759 (on the left) and the turnpike diversion of 1819 now the A6 (bottom right). The New Bath Hotel is visible in the background.[25]

Ken Askew collection.

FIGURE 142 (bottom right). **Advertisement from "Souvenir View Album" published in 1904.**

FIGURE 143 (top left). **Snapshot, about 1969.**

This property stood opposite the original Matlock Bath school building. The steps led up to Beck's bakehouse, derelict here, and beside them to the left in the dark opening steps led down to a petrifying well. This was Boden's well, Matlock Bath's first petrifying well, an important feature in the village's history.[26]

Ken Askew collection.

FIGURE 144 (top right). **Matlock Bath Filling Station, guide book advertisement, 1920s.**

The Secretary of State for the Environment purchased the property from Dyson and Clough in 1975 prior to its demolition.[27]

FIGURE 145 (bottom left). **The start of the demolition of Win Tor (see Figure 60) in 1939.**

Beyond is Dyson and Clough's garage and at the bottom of the original road which served the New Bath the building[28] with the large central 'showroom' window, believed to be where Richard Brown, the eminent statuary and spar turner from Derby, set up his first museum in 1810 in partnership with John Mawe. Note the church spire is just visible behind the lamp post on the right.

Harry Gill collection.

FIGURE 146 (middle right / bottom right). **The south end of North Parade, postcard, about 1915.**

This post-card shows the beginning of North Parade. The Devonshire on the right was built between 1822 and 1832.[29] The picture below records its demolition.

Ken Smith collection / Harry Gill collection.

FIGURE 147 (top left and right). **Front and back views of houses and shops on North Parade, snapshots, about 1960.**

This pair of double-fronted houses stood almost opposite Rose Cottage, now 2019, Riva, on riverside land called The Green.[30] The block was purchased by the Ministry of Transport in 1966.

Terry Moore collection.

FIGURE 148 (bottom left and right). **Reconstruction of the river bank after demolition.**

After each phase of demolition of riverside properties work was done to re-align the river bank in its new position, as shown above, after 1957 viewed from the site where Glenorchy stood and below, just south of the Jubilee Bridge, after 1968.

Harry Gill collection.

Conclusion

The eighteenth century leisured elite, taking the waters and cultivating an appreciation of English landscape gave way long ago to the car and motor bike traveller and the lycra clad cyclist. They stay now for no more than a few hours and if they are inclined to stay overnight, as some are, their choice of hotel or bed and breakfast accommodation will be very much more limited than the resort offered their Edwardian forebears. The railway, back in use since 1972, but only from the south, still drops visitors at Matlock Bath's Swiss style station where two of the five original buildings survive though no longer in railway use. The W.H. Smith's bookstall, prize winning gardens, signal box, goods yard and the dozen staff are all gone; and not even on bank holidays are its passengers counted in thousands.

The late eighteenth century saw Matlock Bath briefly join the ranks of the pedigree English watering places but in the century that followed this 'perfectly romantic place', despite the attraction of its incomparable scenery, found itself unable to compete with the larger resorts. At 68 degrees F Matlock Bath's thermal waters, tepid rather than warm, placed the resort at a permanent disadvantage to Bath or Buxton. It was a burden from which there was no escape. Had Matlock Bath been able to emulate Matlock Bank and adopt hydropathic treatments in the 1870s and 80s, rather than a generation later, the resort's life and reputation as a health centre, might have been prolonged. But it would have been a palliative and no protection against the relentless force of excursionism unleashed by the development of the railway network.

In 1840 when the station opened at Ambergate and the first day trippers found their way to Matlock Bath the seeds were sown for the growth of an economy now so familiar to the modern visitor it seems endemic. And once the railway reached Matlock Bath itself and the Midland Railway company had recognised the potential of its excursion business the trend towards Matlock Bath becoming a weekend resort for the day visitor had been set in motion. There could be no return to the pastoral life, the quiet gentility of the refined watering place which for so long had attracted the well born, the wealthy and the aspirant middle class. Increasingly Matlock Bath belonged to anyone who could afford the price of a day out and thanks to philanthropy, some who could not.

Several decades had passed between the early days of the rail excursions when the arrival of a horde of trippers had been a novelty and their social class and demeanor worthy of comment before the local press began to remark on the absence of staying guests and the poor condition of the resort. If the newspapers offer an accurate measurement of public opinion it was not until the 1880s that this was seen as an existential issue. Of course the problem had been identified years earlier and solutions proposed. As a local observer of Matlock Bath's predicament wrote to the *Derbyshire Courier* at the end of the 1869 season; that summer had seen the resort 'inundated with excursionists 'who only spent the day, and their ephemeral visit' brought no profit to the inhabitants. And the reason they had not stayed 'for weeks and months as at other places' was that when they [had] spent the day in sight-seeing they [had] no place where they[could] rest and enjoy themselves in the evening, as they [have] at Scarbro.'[sic] His remedy a promenade 'with suitable walks, seats, shrubberies etc' and a building 'to serve as a concert hall or ball-room.' So equipped he was confident Matlock Bath would be able to compete with her 'more popular sisters'.[31]

But as this correspondent predicted nothing was done. Some thought the resort could cater for both markets unable or unwilling to recognise the inherent incompatibility between the two; the one offering visitors tranquillity; fashionable pastimes and social intercourse with like-minded people of their own class; the other tea rooms, trinkets and a cheap day out. But for decades the old and the new co-existed, a co-existence we suspect which depended on the absence of day visitors throughout the working week and, as Colonel Newnham-Davies was to argue a generation later, because of the appetite shared by so many of the day visitors to find their pleasures among the many attractions outside the resort, returning to Matlock Bath only to eat and catch the train home. The absence of trippers during the day made the resort safe and available to their social superiors; or so the readers of the *Pall Mall Gazette* were invited to believe. That he needed to reassure his middle class audience they could visit the Royal, confident of not having to rub shoulders with people they would regard as socially inferior, is evidence in itself of how perception of the resort had been transformed during the course of about sixty years. It would seem that the Colonel was right. The town's new persona as a weekend leisure resort did not entirely extinguish the older tradition. This was kept alive and taken forward into the twentieth century by the Royal and the New Bath until fire destroyed the former in 1929. This year, 2019, the refurbished New Bath has re-opened its outdoor swimming pool for some public use as well as for its guests.

It would be misleading however to suggest that the dislocation of the resort's traditional business as a watering place was caused solely by the impact of the new market catering for day visitors. Like many of the other smaller spa resorts Matlock Bath gradually fell behind its larger better financed competitors in the facilities it offered its staying guests. It was slow to adopt the fashionable new treatments that brought such prosperity to its neighbour Matlock Bank. As a health centre it came to appear outdated and by the early 1880s its image was no brighter as a leisure resort. It was in the words of one critic brash, noisy, dusty, polluted and without a reliable water supply. There were 'no gardens, no promenade, no pavilion or music, no public institutions of any kind not even a library.' As the *Leeds Mercury* saw it Matlock Bath had 'relied too much upon her wealth of scenery; while such resorts as Buxton, possessing fewer natural advantages, but developing more artificial attractions [had] outstripped her in prosperity.'[32]

Something had to be done but the voices identifying these shortcomings were less vocal in recognising causes and solutions. Herbert Buxton, chairman of the Local Board, believed the town had been held back by it having so much land owned by non residents who had not been prepared to invest. Speaking in January 1878 he hoped, now most of this property had been 'bought up', things would change.[33] Fingers were also pointed at the Local Board, more adept it was said at regulating the cabmen[34] than in delivering substantial improvements. There was some justification in this accusation the Local Board having been in existence for nearly twenty years before it addressed the deficiencies in the local water supply in 1883-86 and it was not until 1895 when the Urban District Council began its work under the inspired leadership of John Edward Lawton that sustained attempts were made to resolve the major issues of gas supply, sewerage and the investment of public money in new facilities. Lawton was prepared to take on external authorities if they stood in his Council's way, even at considerable expense and was not afraid to turn to the courts and to Parliament to achieve his goals. Even with such a leader the Local Board and its successor the UDC failed to address the manifest needs of the resort. As the temperature of the thermal spring water hampered the growth of the resort so the limited size of the administrative district and the low rateable value and rate income constrained its local authorities. Physically constrained by its location in a valley where settlement was confined to the western slopes the Bath was just too small and too poor to fund the essential investments when they were needed. For years the water supply was pitiful; the roads dusty when dry and filthy when wet and the sanitation was deplorable. Nor was the Board able to contribute to the enhancement of the facilities for visitors even though the creation of walks and pleasure grounds was within its legal capacity.

The other apparently immutable constraint which the resort had to contend with and which, though reduced, remains a fact of life to this day is the seasonality of its trade. Earning a living between May and September proved impossible for many business ventures and even today the predominantly weekend trade pattern remains seasonal. The businesses along the Parades which catered for visitors rather than residents closed down for the winter and except for weekends many still do. As a result competition was fierce, condemning some of those caught up in it to a brutally hand to mouth existence.[35] Sir George Head recognised the reality in 1835 in his account of the show caves. 'These caves', he wrote, 'were it not that supply is fully equal to the demand, would yield an ample harvest to the proprietors; but, as it is, there are so many that competition has effectually kept down the price of admittance. One shilling is the stipulated charge.'

Matlock Bath never enjoyed the benefits of a long term wealthy investor such as Buxton found in the Cavendish family, and consequently, without such support, there was no masterplan or consistent investment. Few fortunes were made here; investors appeared from time to time sometimes, as in the case of those who put money into the Matlock Pavilion and Gardens Company, years too late and most left without the expected financial return.

In the later years of the nineteenth century (and it may have existed earlier though we have not found it)[36] there emerged a collective will to get things done for the benefit of the community. Whether it was subscribing for the purchase of a water cart, the creation of a promenade, the jubilee bridge, the establishment of Venetian Fetes or forming a band, there were residents who were prepared to step forward and contribute their time, money and skills for a cause they believed in and without this element of self help the Bath today would be a very different physical shape and its life as a resort might be no more than a memory. In modern times the same collective spirit has created the Mining Museum, is rescuing the Pavilion and helps to maintain the annual illuminations.

Many English towns experienced profound change in the years following the second world war and their historical context is lost or obscured by modern development. Not so Matlock Bath. The essence of George Vernon's estate still forms the heart of the settlement against its backdrop of the Heights of Abraham; Blake's Victorian terrace survives at the northern end though now with a diminished riverside promenade. The natural topography of the pleasure grounds of High Tor, Lover's Walk and the Willersley estate still protects the east side of the valley. Underground there are old mine-workings forming one of the most important historic mining sites in Britain. There remains much to admire.

It is our hope this book will enhance a growing awareness of how far Matlock Bath's history defines it as a place to visit and contributes to its many qualities as a place to live.

Appendix: Population Figures

The information about the growth of visitor accommodation in Matlock Bath between 1789 and 1802 comes from guide books and topographical works and none of it is likely to have been the result of counting actual bedrooms. It suggests capacity trebled from 150 to 450 and the evidence of new buildings in these years supports such growth. It is reasonable to suppose that this growth would have been matched by some increase in the population of the settlement so feeding the service industry required to manage greater visitor numbers, but of course the demand would have been largely seasonal and much of it may have been met from adjacent settlements such as Bonsall or one of the Matlocks. Firm information is simply not available.

Even in the nineteenth century, changes in population in Matlock Bath are difficult to establish. This is in part because the census figures for 1801 -1831 were collected on a different basis from the later ones and record the total population parish by parish so Matlock Bath and Scarthin were included with Matlock. The timing of the census is also important as it would determine whether the totals included a significant number of visitors. The dates on which the counts were made and the available figures registered are shown in the table below.

It is likely that most of the increase shown between 1801 and 1831 is due to growth in Matlock Bath rather than in Matlock itself. At the time of year when counts were made, 1811-31, the visitor season would be underway and temporary residents would have been included but this is not the whole story. Contemporary evidence of visitor growth in Matlock Bath and of the houses built after the break- up of Vernon's estate suggest that the resort enjoyed real growth during this period.

The 1841 to 1891 census enumerators' returns divide the area into districts so for this period it is possible to assess the population for a particular district. If we choose the heart of Matlock Bath as it is recognised today, the area from just south of Masson Mill to the site of the first Vicarage, west of the footbridge to Starkholmes, enumeration district Matlock 11, and exclude Scarthin and Matlock Dale, the figures are as shown below. For comparison the figures for Matlock and Matlock Bath together are also shown. Note that the figures for the 1901 census for our chosen Matlock Bath area have been calculated from the census return because the former Matlock Bath district 11 was formed from parts of 2 enumeration districts, Matlock Bath 14 and 15 at this date.

MATLOCK PARISH INCLUDING MATLOCK BATH					MATLOCK BATH			
DATE	POPULATION	% CHANGE	HOUSES	% CHANGE	POPULATION	% CHANGE	HOUSES	% CHANGE
10/03/1801	2,354		475					
27/05/1811	2,490 [+136]	6%	523	10%				
28/05/1821	2,920 [+430]	17%	605	16%				
30/05/1831	3,262 [+342]	12%	673	11%				
6/06/1841	3,782 [+520]	16%	752	12%	827		143	
30/03/1851	4,010 [+228]	6%	845	12%	792 [-35]	4%	153	7%
7/04/1861	4,252 [+242]	6%	878	4%	755 [-37]	5%	162	6%
2/04/1871	5,220 [+968]	23%	1,049	19%	884 [+129]	17%	190	17%
3/04/1881	6,093 [+873]	17%	1,215	16%	1,063 [+179]	20%	229	21%
5/04/1891	7,131 [+1,038]	17%	1,424	17%	988 [-75]	-7%	233	2%
31/03/1901	7,798 [+667]	9%	1,630	14%	1,105 [+117]	12%	248	7%

The combined figures for the period from 1841 to 1891 show modest growth between 1841 and 1861; a major increase in the decade 1861-71 which was sustained until 1891 and then much reduced. During the same period the Matlock Bath figures are more irregular with periods of stagnation between 1841 and 1851 and again in the following decade. It is not until 1861-71 that there is significant growth. This coincides with the construction of North Parade. The difference between the two settlements is considered to be largely a reflection of the success of the promotion of hydropathic treatment in Matlock after John Smedley opened the first hydro in 1853 and encouraged others to follow his example.[1]

It is also possible to compare the growth in the number of houses within the same two settlements. A similar pattern emerges. In our chosen Matlock Bath area the period of major growth was between 1861 and 1871 sustained until 1881. But then, unlike Matlock, where growth continued, Matlock Bath suffered a reversal though growth had returned by 1901. The census information also includes the number of uninhabited houses and as many as 14 were recorded in 1861, nearly 9% of the total number of houses, which taken together with the 5% reduction in population and negligible house building, underlines what a difficult period the 1850s were for the resort during its transition from spa to a day visitor, residential and commuter economy.

In the next decade 1861-71, there was an improvement which at first sight is remarkable as this was the decade which witnessed the cotton famine. As we have shown much of the mill workforce came from neighbouring villages though it is reasonable to suppose some families left Matlock Bath and Cromford in search of employment. The tourist trade in its new form, on the other hand was unaffected and it was this which provided the buoyancy to the economy and supported the resort's expansion to the north. The highest number of new houses built was in in 1871-81 and much of this later expansion was on the plots, now more readily accessible, as advantage was taken of the new link via Holme Road to Upperwood.[2]

Notes and references

Abbreviations for references

CER	Census enumerator's return
DA	Derbyshire Advertiser
DA&J	Derbyshire Advertiser and Journal
DC	Derbyshire Courier
DT	Derbyshire Times
DT&ChH	Derbyshire Times and Chesterfield Herald
DDT	Derby Daily Telegraph
DM	Derby Mercury
DRO	Derbyshire Record Office
HPN	High Peak News
LM	Leeds Mercury
LG	London Gazette
MBA	Matlock Bath Advertiser
MC	Manchester Courier
MC&LGA	Manchester Courier and Lancashire General Advertiser
MG	Matlock Guardian
SI	Sheffield Independent
SDT	Sheffield Daily Telegraph
YP	Yorkshire Post
YP&LI	Yorkshire Post and Leeds Intelligencer

INTRODUCTION
PAGES 1-12

[1] It is expected to be covered in detail by a forthcoming publication by Roger Flindall.

[2] Phyllis Hembry *The English Spa, 1560-1815,* 1990, pages 356-357. There were by 1699 an additional 5 for which Hembry had no date.

[3] Sir John built his own baths at Unite's Well about a mile from Lichfield, sometime between 1697 and 1702. Hembry describes it as 'a prototype for small bathing spas'. It consisted of two baths, each 16 feet long and about 10 feet wide, one for men and one for women each with a dressing room. In 1780 the baths were acquired by Erasmus Darwin though by this time the baths may have been converted to a single cell; certainly this is the form in which the structure exists today measuring about 15 feet square and about 3 feet deep. Darwin incorporated the bath house within his botanic garden. He put the bath up for sale in February 1800. Hembry op. cit., page 162, King-Hele, *Erasmus Darwin,* 1999, page 134; King-Hele, *The Collected Letters of Erasmus Darwin,* 2007, pages 540 and 541.

[4] Rail against it they certainly did. Here is the Reverend Henry Bourne, curate of the Parochial Chapel of All Saints in Newcastle upon Tyne in 1725. 'In the Dark Ages of Popery, it was a Custom, if any Well had an awful Situation, and was seated in some lonely melancholy Vale; if its water was clear and limpid, and beautifully margin'd with the tender Grass; or if it was look'd upon as having a Medicinal Quality; to

gift it to some Saint, and honour it with his Name. Hence it is, that we have at this Day Wells and Fountains called, some St John's, St Mary Magdalen's, St Mary's Well etc. To these kind of Wells, the common People are accustomed to go, on a Summer's Evening, to refresh themselves with a Walk after the Toil of the Day, to drink the Water of the Fountain, and enjoy the pleasing Prospect of Shade and Stream. Now this Custom (tho' at this Time of Day, very commendable and harmless, and innocent) seems to be the Remains of that superstitious Practice of the Papists, of paying Adoration to Wells and Fountains: For they imagin'd there was some Holiness and Sanctity in them, and so worshipped them.' He continues. 'To give Names therefore to Wells, is of an ancient standing; but to pay Homage and Worship to them was never heard of among the People of GOD, till they sunk into gross Idolatry, and became Worshippers of Stocks and Stones.' But the practice continued. Large and sometimes vast numbers of people visited these holy wells as for example the immense crowd of invalids who flocked to the Glastonbury spring. Here in May 1751 it was said there had been 10,000 visitors. It was Vaux's belief, writing in 1894, that faith in the miraculous powers of such wells had continued until 'comparatively modern times'. *Observations in Popular Antiquities* including Mr Bourne's *Antiquitates Vulgares,* John Brand, 1810, pages 90-93; *Church Folklore,* Edward Vaux, 1894, page 277.

5 Thomas Short, *The natural, experimental and medicinal history of the mineral waters of Derbyshire, Lincolnshire and Yorkshire* (abbreviated title), 1734, pages 92 and 360, A Table of the Waters examined. The entries for Derbyshire are:- Ashover, Beighton, Beauchief, Buxton, Buxton chalybeate, Burgh, Cawley, Castleton, Chesterfield, Dofield [sic], Eagles-ster [sic], [Youlgreave], Hope, Kedleston, Matlock, Matlock Bridge, Middleton Bath,* Stoney Middleton, Stoney Middleton Chalybeate, Quarndon, Rousley Bridge [sic], Rumley, Shuttlewood, Tibshelf, Wirksworth two warm brooks and a third sulphur spring at the south end of the town and Whittington. Short identifies 6 locations at which there were baths in use. By 1811 Farey lists 12 though he indicates that 4 were out of use. Farey *General View of the Agriculture and Minerals of Derbyshire, vol I,* 1811, pages 502-506.

*The Middleton bath is marked on the Bonsall Leys Enclosure map, 1774, a few hundred yards west of today's Via Gellia Mill. William Bray, *Sketch of a Tour into Derbyshire,* 2nd edition, 1783, page 124, describes it as 'chiefly used to cure mangey horses and dogs but is fit to be employed to much greater purposes.' By 1789, as a consequence of lead mine drainage, the bath had disappeared. J.H. Rieuwerts, *Lead Mining in Derbyshire, Part 4,* 2012, page 36.

6 There were of course exceptions. Cold water bathing did not die out. It continued at a reduced level of popularity. For example the cold baths at Cold Bath Fields which claimed to be the coldest spring in London; these were established in the 1690s and survived until the 1870s. James Stevens Curl, *Spas, Wells, Pleasure Gardens of London,* 2010, page 77.

7 King-Hele op. cit., *Letters,* 72-3, 30/9/1772.

8 *Encyclopaedia Britannica,* 1797, *vol. XII,* Mineral waters. This of course was a selective list. Hembry identifies 173 spas in existence by 1815 and there were certainly more than 7 with active baths. Nevertheless it is indicative of the overall decline in the popularity of cold water bathing. The centres on this list with operational baths were Borrowdale, Bath, Buxton, Clifton (Oxfordshire), Malvern and Matlock (by implication). In other cases it is noted that water is used externally for washing sores, the water delivered 'at the spout' or by some other means. At Loansbury in Yorkshire the only recorded use of the water was for washing mangy dogs and scabby horses.

9 John W. Williams, *The Bathers New Medical Guide.* The book is undated but from the dedication to Queen Adelaide it was evidently published between 1830 and 1837. See pages vi and 216-217.

10 This account is based on Hembry, *British Spas from 1815 to the Present,* 1997.

11 Hembry 1997, op. cit., page 6.

12 Ibid, page 242; Curl op. cit., pages 25 and 175.

13 As for example John and Caroline Smedley. The Smedley's system combined a strict regime of diet and exercise supported by a number of set procedures all involving water, sometimes hot, sometimes cold, and often bandages and wet sheets. In his manual he gave each of these treatments a number, 242 in all. He

claimed to cure cancer, consumption, deafness, diabetes, dropsy, paralysis and smallpox; and the list goes on. He did not believe vaccination offered protection against smallpox though his hydropathic remedy could cure it. *Smedley's Practical Hydropathy, (Not the Cold-Water System),* 1868 and Mrs Smedley's *Manual for Ladies and Children, (Not the Cold-Water System),* 1878.

[14] Hembry 1997, op.cit., page 2.

[15] In Matlock Bath, albeit years too late, ownership of the problem was finally taken up by the council, see chapter 8.

[16] As for example Bath Street at Bakewell which still has a surviving bath house or Water Lane and Coldwell Street in Wirksworth.

[17] Hembry 1997 op. cit., page 157; and for examples of other spa towns in this period see Chapter 9.

[18] Of the five best hydropathic establishments known to the author T. O. L. writing in 1912, who contributed to the Chapter on this subject, three were in Matlock. They were Smedley's, Rockside and Matlock House. Nine others are described as adequately equipped and under proper supervision. *Health Resorts of the British Isles,* page 123.

[19] The climate of Buxton and Harrogate was considered 'tonic' or 'bracing' in contrast to Bath and Cheltenham 'ennervating' or 'relaxing'; Matlock Bath 'partly stimulant' and 'partly sedative' according to the season. *Health Resorts,* op. cit., page 3.

[20] Hembry 1997, op. cit., page 24.

[21] This account is based largely on the advice offered by Ephraim Chambers *Cyclopaedia, Vol IV* under the heading Waters Mineral. The book was first published in 1728 and reprinted many times until towards the end of the century it was revised and enlarged to 4 volumes by Abraham Rees. Volume IV appeared in 1783. Extracts from Thomas Short's recommendations for drinking Matlock Bath water are produced on page 49. Note the areas of disagreement between Chambers and Short, indicative of the contentious nature of this subject within the medical fraternity.

[22] 1 pint = 0.568 litre, 2 pints or 1 quart = 1.136 litres, 2 quarts = 1/2 gallon

[23] Curl, op. cit., page 93.

[24] Benjamin Bryan, *Matlock Manor and Parish,* 1903, page 132.

[25] See chapter 9 for a discussion of Matlock Bath's failure to invest in a pump room.

[26] Hembry 1990, op. cit., pages 79, 116, 122 and 220.

[27] Curl, op. cit., pages 98 and 215. Dr Johnson patronised Streatham Spa towards the end of his life and praised its waters. The spa was near the house of his friend Hester Thrale.

[28] Short, op. cit., page 305. Of the Kedleston water he writes. 'The drinking water is exceeding clear but stinks intolerably.'

[29] This appears to have been the case at the Nevill-Holt Spa in Leicestershire. It was discovered in 1728 by a farmer searching for water for his cattle and opened up by the Nevill family who owned the land. A spout channelled the spring water into a stone cistern 'with a strong stone arch, and a stout oak door [with a] lock on it. Here [people] may gather and bottle water either from the spout or cistern, equally good.' Thomas Short, *A general treatise on various cold mineral waters in England,* (abbreviated title), 1765, page 138.

[30] In Tunbridge Wells these women were known as Dippers. Hembry 1990, op. cit., page 79.

[31] He writes 'a nearly decrepit old woman seated before the scanty stream, with her shrivelled hands distributes [the water] to the applicants as they approach her.' He remarks waspishly 'it is one of the great attractions of the German Spas that smart female attendants are provided, and ever ready to supply the limpid and sparkling water in crystal or china beakers...without fee or reward.' See Granville, *Spas of England, vol. 2,* page 30.

[32] Granville, op. cit., page 70 'The mineral water here rises fountain-like out of a circular basin of durable limestone placed upon a pillar and is allowed to overflow.'

[33] Curl op. cit., page 94. Later when a tea garden was added the admission price increased to six pence.

[34] Epsom water. Hembry, 1990 op. cit., page 366.

[35] Hembry 1990, op. cit., page 110.

[36] Hembry 1990, op. cit., page 177.

[37] Hembry 1990 considered the market for bottled water to have peaked by the 1780s. Hembry, op. cit., page 178. Improved transport having enabled so many people to visit a local spa their appetite for bottled water had diminished. Hembry seems to have been unaware of Matlock Bath's bottled water.[38] Streatham wells. Their water sold in bottles at 1/6d per dozen or delivered at 2/6d. Curl, op. cit., page 215.

[39] Some bottled waters were marketed using their alleged palliative quality; for instance Powis Water 'medicinal for sore eyes; and Highgate eye water'. Curl, op. cit., pages 162 and 166; and Hembry 1990, op. cit., page 367.

[40] Short, op. cit., page 91.

[41] Erasmus Darwin not only sent patients to Matlock Bath, on occasion he accompanied them. In November 1796 he was there with Thomas Coutts (1735-1822), banker to King George III, and his daughter Fanny who was seriously ill. King-Hele, op. cit., Letters, letter 96.14.

[42] Bryan, op. cit., page 215.

[43] Ibid, page 214.

[44] After all if you were going to take all your clothes off to bathe with strangers you wanted some reassurance as to their status and probity.

[45] This is the fate which befell the Temple of Apollo near Westminster Bridge; once renowned for its fine music, old wines, chastity and dignity; it subsequently acquired a reputation for rowdiness, thieving and lewd behaviour until it was suppressed by the magistrates in 1793. A trepanner; someone who ensnares or beguiles another for a criminal purpose. Curl, op. cit., page 194.

[46] The Gentleman's Magazine in May 1820 credited Lady Mary Wortley Montagu with convincing society that natural mineral waters were best; her endorsement of Islington Spa is said to have ensured its success as a fashionable resort. Ibid page 39.

[47] Curl, op.cit., page 36.

[48] Hembry 1990, op. cit., pages 194 and 218.

[49] As for example Dr Erasmus Darwin who wrote to his patient, a Mrs Arden, in August 1787. 'The season is yet rather too warm for [B]ath, nor would it perhaps be safe for you to bathe in your present situation in a bath so hot as the public baths there, which are much above the heat of the human body. Perhaps bathing and drinking the water at Buxton might at this season of the year be of equal service to you, as there is a greater similarity in the waters of Buxton and Bath than has been generally supposed.' King-Hele, op. cit., Letters, 87.13.

[50] Curl, op. cit., page 94.

[51] Bryan identifies ten. Bryan, op. cit., page 213. The assessments of the therapeutic value of the water came from Dr John Medley in 1730 and Dr Thomas Short in 1733.

[52] Chaplet; a wreath for the head or garland.

[53] Thomas Short, op. cit., page 73. In 1789 in part II of his major work, The Botanic Garden, Erasmus Darwin, recognised at the time as the leading poet of the day, added his paean to Matlock, see page 36.

[54] Roy Porter, Health for Sale, Quackery in England 1660-1850, 1989.

[55] As for example Dr Trigg who offered for sale his Golden Vatican Pills: Famous for the Cure of Most Diseases in either Sex. Porter op. cit., page 114.

[56] Porter identified numerous examples including Horace Walpole's father, Lord Chesterfield, Henry Fielding, Sylas Neville. Ibid, pages 53-54.

[57] Ibid, page 25.

[58] The water of Acton Spring was so strongly purgative it caused 'a soreness in the fundament.' Enc. Brit.1797, op. cit., Waters Mineral.

[59] King-Hele, op. cit., Letters, page 387 note 5. See page 37 for details of how they spent their time in Matlock.

[60] Curl, op. cit., page 267. The diseases and conditions claimed by the London Spas to be cured or alleviated by their medicinal springs.

CHAPTER ONE
PAGES 13-26

[1] William Woolley, History of Derbyshire, Derbyshire Record Society, Vol VI, 1981, page 199.

[2] John Medley, *Tentamen Hydrologicum or An Essay on Matlock Bath*, 1730, page 39.

[3] DRO Wolley *Mss* 6667 ff 176d.

[4] Wolley, op. cit.

[5] DRO Wolley *Mss* 6668 ff 175-180.

[6] John Macky *A Journey through England in familiar letters... Vol II*, 2nd edition, 1724, page184. Macky's preface dated 1723 (3rd edition) explains the volume would have been finished some years since but was delayed by the death of Queen Anne and the 1715 rebellion and only finished when Misson's *Observations through England* was published in 1719 'stuffed with the greatest Absurdities imaginable'.

[7] Ibid, page 183. 'I my self, when there, saw the Hostler who had been there some time so Lame of the Rheumatism, that he was incapable of any Business, so bad that he was with much Difficulty brought thither in a Cart, but in less than a Month was perfectly cured, he said, as I then saw him.'

[8] Daniel Defoe, *A Tour thro' the whole island of Great Britain, Vol III*, 1st edition, 1726, reprint 1927, page 567. It would be unwise to regard this description as indicative of the bath in 1726. It could be a decade or more earlier. Scholarly analysis of Defoe's Tour reveals it to have been a skilful amalgam of other texts, not always acknowledged, outright plagiarism, notes worked up from visits made years earlier and in some cases accounts of recent tours. Pat Rogers identifies the third volume which included the Matlock visit as complex citing as an example the Buxton entry which dates from a visit made in 1712. Rogers, editor, *Defoe A Tour through the whole island of Great Britain*, 1992, *page 9; Richetti, The Life of Daniel Defoe*, 2005, pages, 323-336; *Rogers, Defoe's Tour and the identity of Britain in Richetti, The Cambridge Companion to Daniel Defoe*, 2008, page 102.

[9] The spring still flows strongly and supplies the ornamental pond cut into the tufa bank below the car park and, on the other side of the A6, the fish pond in front of the Pavilion car park. The twentieth century drinking fountain which was fed by the spring, now stands in the Peak District Mining Museum.

[10] 'You go from the Bath (where there is no Entertainment, saving a Dram or so when you come out of the Water) along the Meadows for some Space, and then you ascend a Derbyshire-Hill; I suppose every one who has been in the County, will readily understand what I mean, to the House which stands on the Middle of the Hill.' Macky op. cit., page 207.

[11] The road is marked as the Pitchings on the fold out map at the end of the book.

[12] Wolley *Mss* op.cit. A neighbouring landowner, William Richardson claimed that the bath 'began to grow to greate fame' and could have been let for £50 or £60 per annum. He was 'unwilling the said New Building should be erected' alleging that, in building on and enclosing the waste ground on Masson, Pennell had interfered with Richardson's rights to graze cattle there. He sought legal advice from Mr Abney and Mr Holden in 1727 and early 1728 as to how he might 'lawfully prevent the carrying-on or Building of the said House or Bath.' This appears to have been a last ditch attempt. Despite his interfering with the work and being responsible for 'the buildings or some part thereof being pulled down' Pennell completed the development.

[13] Two, Samuel Clarke, gentleman, and Richard Milnes, mercer and grocer, held quarter shares; three, Adam Slater, apothecary, Richard Slater, mercer, and Godfrey Heathcote, gentleman, held a one eighth share and Joshua Jebb, hosier, and his brother Samuel, Doctor of Physick, from Stratford, Essex, a one sixteenth share. DRO 1859M/T3.

[14] Mixed bathing was very much an English practice in contrast to continental Europe. As early as the 1560s William Turner implored his countrymen to mend their ways and give up 'beastly Filthiness' [there being] no Partition between the Men and the Women whilst they are bathing, but suffer them contrary both to the law of God and Man, to go together like unreasonable Beasts.' But the habit endured or, as at Buxton c.1700, the men and the women bathed at different times. Each bathed naked. We have not discovered whether Matlock's bathers wore drawers and shifts as Sir John Floyer advocated or were also unclothed. Hembry 1990, op. cit., pages 6 and 94 and Short, op. cit., page 51.

[15] These are large sums of money. The regular cockfights held in London at the Restoration Spring Gardens all through the week offered 2

guinnas per battle. Curl, op. cit., page 186.

[16] If Hembry is correct this puts Matlock Bath decades ahead of Buxton which was not trading its water until the 1780s. Hembry 1990, op. cit., page 366. The price Bestall charged, two pence per quart would appear to equate to two shillings per dozen assuming the bottles used in the trade held a quart. This would place Matlock Bath at the lower end of the price range see page 8 though comparison is difficult as the other prices available include the cost of transport to London, a much greater distance than the twenty miles to Derby.

[17] *DM* 19 & 26/8/1742; *London Evening Post,* June 1743.

[18] Timothy Clayton in *The English Print 1688-1802,* 1997 comments 'In stimulating an appetite for British beauties, Thomas Smith of Derby was a pivotal figure' and adds 'Smith's prints emerge as one of the earliest manifestations of the vogue for romantic scenery and as exerting a profound influence on later patterns of tourism.' It is difficult to believe that the inclusion of Matlock Bath in Smith's series of engravings was not in some way linked to the Bath proprietors' desires to market their new acquisition. Evidence that it contributed to the areas growing popularity may be seen in the announcement of the opening of another Bath in the settlement in 1745. Smith published four more Derbyshire views in 1745 and a further set including High Tor in 1751, Figure 4. In 1748, John Boydell of London was advertising his own 'remarkable VIEWS' which included Matlock Bath and Cromford and in 1769, by then a dominant figure in the print business, he republished Smith's earlier views.

[19] This was a feature of many of the spas in London and this provision is a further sign of the settlement equipping itself as a fashionable resort. Many of the greens in London were established early in the seventeenth century, Coke and Borg, *Vauxhall Gardens, A History,* 2011, pages 17 and 77 and Curl, op. cit.

[20] It was arranged that during the bathing season, May 1st to November 1st, each partner should visit the Bath for one 24 hour period in every fortnight 'to see the business of the place regularly carried on and to examine the accounts'. They were to have their 'eating and stay' free and pay only for liquor and corn. DRO 1859M/T3.

[21] From *Four topographical Letters,... from a Gentleman of London to a Brother and Sister in Town,* 1755, pages 47-48.

[22] *DM* 28/6 and 5/7/1751.

[23] Evening balls were held there. Powys P. L., *Passages from the Diaries of Mrs Philip Libbye Powys* edited by E. V. Climonson, (London, 1899) pages 30-31; and concerts.

[24] From *Four topographical Letters* op. cit., pages 44-45.

[25] *DM* 4/5/1770. It is not known if he was the first tenant nor whether the change was driven by increased patronage or increased competition.

[26] Matlock Enclosure Act 1780, enacted 1784.

[27] This addition to the spa's infrastructure was not to the taste of the Hon John Byng, later Lord Torrington, who in 1789 wrote disparagingly of the development 'Just below the great house at Matlock, are new stables &c built, much to the disfigurement of the place, and to spoil the view.' But he was no better pleased with the Duke of Devonshire's great stables at Buxton, which he described as 'a most ill contrived, magnificent mews, where all things are common; and where they and their furniture must be hourly watched: nothing like a quiet stable to call your own.' *The Torrington Diaries, Vol II. 1781-94,* 1935, pages 41 and 167.

[28] Hembry 1990, op. cit., page 47.

[29] Borsay in *The Pleasure Garden from Vauxhall to Coney Island,* edited by Jonathan Conlin, 2013, page 54; Coke and Borg, op. cit., Curl, op. cit. Ranelagh Gardens, on the site of Ranelagh House, opened to the public in 1742; the older Vauxhall Gardens had opened about 1660 and were further developed in the 1730s.

[30] *Gentleman's Magazine,* October 1793.

[31] This suggestion was made by Mark Girouard, cited by Borsay, op. cit., page 58.

[32] The first known written use of the name is in the cartouche for Thomas Smith's print of 1742.

[33] Arthur Young, *The Farmer's Tour through the East of England, Vol I,* 1771, page 209.

[34] William Bray, *Sketch of a Tour into Derbyshire and Yorkshire,* 1st edition 1777, page 77.

[35] The land on the east bank of the river did not belong to the Bath. The woodland there was the

Hagg Wood, part of the Willersley Farm Estate. It had belonged to descendants of the Pierrepont family of Nottingham before passing by marriage in 1746 to Edwin Lascelles, who later became Lord Harewood. Wolley *Mss* 6687 ff109-113. Benjamin Haywood's son Wigley Haywood, who lived at Senior Field, (now Cromford Bridge House), was a lessee of the estate.

[36] Christopher Hussey, *The Picturesque,* 1927, page 128.

[37] Susan Lasdun, *The English Park,* 1991, page 96.

[38] *The Poetical Works of Jonathan Swift, Vol. 2,* 1833, page 354.

[39] From *Itinerarium Curiosum,* William Stukeley, 1724, quoted in K. Sloan and P. Joyner, *A Cozens Album in the National Library of Wales,* Walpole Society, Vol. 57, 1995.

[40] Horace Walpole, *Journals of Visits to Country Seats etc.* 1768, Walpole Society, Vol. 16, page 65.

[41] Arthur Young, op. cit., page 209.

[42] It seems likely that Walpole and Young are describing a later lessee than Mr Ashe. So perhaps our best conjecture is that the Walks were planned by Mr Ashe and that the boot ketch, one Adam Walker, laboured to realise his vision, later taking over the tenancy himself. This proposal is supported by a retrospective comment from William Adam which implies that the walks and the boats were in the hands of the Walker family since about 1760, a view supplemented in 1837 by Henry Moore who comments that Richard Walker was renting the walks 'which were originally laid out by his father.' This is also consistent with the sale and lease history of the site. In 1778 Lascelles sold his Willersley Farm Estate including Hagg Wood to Edmund Hodgkinson, Wigley Haywood's son-in-law (DRO, D7573). At the time of the sale Hagg Wood Walks were the subject of a 40 year lease of which 24 years remained indicating that the lease had begun in about 1762, a close fit with William Adam's account. Further support for this explanation is found in Josiah Wedgwood's attribution of the walk pages 37-39 to the ingenuity of a man called Adam, a name commonly used by the Walker family. What happened to the features such as urns and ballustrades when the Walker family took over is not known. They are not mentioned later and do not appear to have been retained.

[43] Ebeneezer Rhodes, *Peak Scenery,* 1824, page 250, surely expressed the exasperation of generations of visitors to Matlock Bath when he wrote, 'one would not be much surprised if the good folks of Matlock Bath were to place a door in some part of the dale to admit people to High Tor, and this they would probably not hesitate to do, if they could profit by it.'

[44] Henry Moore, *The Stranger's Guide,* 1837.

[45] The term hotel with its present meaning did not come into use in England until the 1760s, See *Dictionary of the English Language,* 1818, Dr Samuel Johnson.

[46] Thomas Short, op. cit., page 73.

[47] This was promoted by Isaac North with the offer 'that a Gentleman (by waiting a little) may have it all let out and filled again with fresh Water', *DM* 16/5/1745. William Lovatt 'late Servant to William Fitzherbert Esq' succeeded North in 1766, *DM* 28/2/1766 and when he retired in 1787 was able to reflect upon 'the splendid and numerous Company who have for many Years honored LOVATT's NEW BATH with their Patronage and Support.'

[48] DRO Q/S Turnpike plan No. 15.

[49] William Adam, *Gem of the Peak,* 1st edition, 1838, page 31.

[50] Adam, op. cit., pages 31-2.

[51] The fact that the announcement of the opening included the reference to Isaac North's wife's past employment at the Old Bath surely indicates it was perceived to be successful.

[52] H. Moore, *Picturesque Excursions from Derby to Matlock Bath,* page 28.

[53] Notably Albert Goodwin (1845-1932) and Arthur Severn (1842-1931).

[54] This account is taken from *John Ruskin,* Tim Hilton, 2002.

[55] White's Directory, 1857, describes it as 'recently enlarged and refurbished in a very superior manner.'

[56] Rev. R. Ward, *Matlock, Buxton and Castleton Guide,* first edition, 1814, page 19.

[57] At this date it is occupied by Ellen Smedley, the widow of John Smedley, son of William Smedley. It was known as Elm Cottage and the area as Win Tor when the property was

demolished in the 1930s.

[58] George Lipscombe, *A Description of Matlock Bath,* 1802, page 66, credits William Smedley with making spar ornaments from about 1770.

CHAPTER TWO
PAGES 27-40

[1] *Four topographical letters,* op. cit., page 44. This is an example of the letters and diaries which were occasionally published and which, along with the visual material introduced the valley's charms to a wider public.

[2] From *Sonnets and other Poems* by a resident of Sherwood Forest, published 1825.

[3] British Library Add. MS 42,232. Tyler was accompanied by Thomas Sandby RA, artist and architect, Theodosius Forrest, artist and musician, Captain Robert Elwes and Samuel Coles.

[4] *Morning Chronicle* 29/8/1782. Perhaps this was the occasion when the street of high quality houses which Richard Arkwright had built for his weavers and their families in 1776 acquired its name, North Street. But if that is the case courtesy might suggest it would have become Lord North Street.

[5] Letter from Joseph Spence to W. B. Massingberd, 2/10/1752, Yale University Library.

[6] Letter from Joseph Spence to Lord Lincoln, 12/8/1752. Ne C 4132, Nottingham University Library.

[7] *Four topographical letters,* op. cit., page 46.

[8] 'for the comfort and convenience of those visitors, who wished to be out of the noise and bustle of a crowded inn'. Adam, op. cit., 1838, page 35.

[9] The Enclosure Commissioners meeting to determine the ownership of property built on common land referred to it as 'heretofore a cottage' which now occupied 1 acre 1 rood 35 perches.

[10] Before this development the carriage access to the Temple would have been by Green Lane.

[11] Joseph Pearson's Original Museum was founded on Temple Walk c. 1790 and the 1814 edition of Ward's *Matlock, Buxton and Castleton Guide* draws attention to 'Miss Millns's long established Repository containing an elegant assortment of female attire…and a Circulating Library' also located there.

[12] *DM* 19/3/1807. The practice of visitors buying their own food and having it cooked in their lodgings to eat in their rooms was widespread and existed alongside the food offered in the dining room at communal tables.

[13] The assemblies which were advertised in the resort were held at the Old Bath, where the room was described as admirably adapted for the purpose, superbly fitted up, and of noble dimensions, being 51 ½ feet long, 22 feet wide, and the height in proportion. In 1809 for example the season commenced on Friday 30th of June offering 'Subscriptions for the season £1 15s, for each Assembly 2s 6d. There will be three assemblies each week on Monday, Wednesday and Friday.' Earlier Lipscombe, op. cit., page 75, described them as regulated 'by the inclination of the Company'. Barker, *The Panorama of Matlock Bath and its Environs,* 1828, described 'balls and assemblies twice a week but it is universally allowed with regret that the music might be better.'

[14] *DM* 31/7/1794.

[15] Tea, see Chambers, op. cit. *vol. iv,* 1783; coffee, see Chambers, op. cit. *vol. i,* 1786; and chocolate, Chambers op. cit. *vol. ii,* 1786.

[16] Charles Cotton, *The Wonders of the Peak,* 1725, page 64.

[17] *The Journey of Celia Fiennes,* 1697, page 101.

[18] *A Tour through the Northern Counties of England…Vol. 1,* Revd. Richard Warner, 1802, page 138.

[19] Macky, op. cit., page 184.

[20] Defoe op. cit., 1st edition reprint, page 567.

[21] Letter from Edmund Evans to Madam Turner, 10/7/1736, DRO Wolley *Mss* 6692 ff 91-92.

[22] William Stukely, op. cit., 'we are now got into the very Peak of Darbyshire, the British Alps, where the odd prospects afford some entertainment to a traveller, and relieve the fatigue of so tedious a road. Now you pass over barren moors in perpetual danger of slipping into coalpits and leadmines, or ride for miles together on the edge of a steep hill on solid slippery rock or loose stones, with a valley

underneath where you can scarce discover the bottom with your eyes...Instead of trees and hedges they fence their poor meadow or arabl [sic] with walls of loose stones pickt up from beneath their feet. The extended sides of the mountains are generally power'd over as it were with rocks, streams of water dribbling down every where, and now bolder cataracts diversify the romantic scene...'.

[23] DRO D1053 Z/P1.

[24] DRO D1053 Z/P1; *Cromford Revisited,* pages 141-143.

[25] In the distance Cromford bridge is shown with rounded arches on the 'up' side, a form which was adopted when the bridge was widened in the eighteenth century; the gothic arches of the original fifteenth century bridge survive on the downstream side. Smith has given the bridge an extra arch. The J. Smith from whose drawing the print was made is believed to be John 'Warwick' Smith who visited Derbyshire around 1775 and again around 1784.

[26] William Bray, op. cit., page 75.

[27] Barker, op. cit.

[28] He commented in his diary 'The Pass into Matlock Dale is what must arrest the attention of every Visitor – the most incurious mind cannot but be struck with a defile through a solid mass of Rock...but if he shall learn (as is the fact) that by human labour and perseverance the opening was effected to render the admission to the Dale more safe and commodious the sensations with which he has been imprest [sic] instead of decreasing will rise to a higher pitch of astonishment.'

[29] *DM* 26/9/1821.

[30] The original toll-house was on the opposite side of the road near the bottom of the slope leading up to the New Bath. It was re-modelled as a cottage, known in 1974, as Weirside Figure 140. *DM* 22 and 29/4/1774, advertised the auction of tolls quoting 'the amount produced last year (above expenses) for Warmwalls was £50-17-9 ½'. The toll-gate posts shown in this view now stand beside the New Bath Hotel.

[31] This new gate had more than one name. It was referred to as Matlock Bridge Gate in the 1851 census and on the Matlock Bath Waterworks map of 1863 as the Holt Lane Toll Bar. One toll-gate

post now stands on Old English Road in Matlock. Adam, 1843 edition, referred to the cottages beyond as 'several small but heavy looking houses' having been recently erected here. To the north Stephen Glover, *Peak Scenery,* 1830, draws attention to 'two beautiful cottages' built by Mr Chenery [sic], surgeon and illustrates Dale Cottage, date-stone 1820, as one. Primrose Cottage on St John's Road is considered to be the other. This part of the valley is Common Wood but now is usually referred to as Artist's Corner. The riverside land here was threatened with development in 1889 and laid out in lots for the erection of cottages. An appeal led by Mr Peters of Guilderoy, Matlock Bath, raised subscriptions to buy it so that it could be dedicated to public use. There was an expectation that it would form part of the long considered riverside promenade linking Matlock to Matlock Bath.

[32] Three years later, in 1780, Richard Arkwright (1755-1843) married into the Simpson family of Bonsall and subsequently became a partner in the Toplis bank at Wirksworth. The Evans's, developers of the Darley Abbey Mills, and the Strutts, of the Belper mills dynasty, also intermarried.

[33] Ten of them were Fellows of the Royal Society. John Brewer, *The Pleasures of the Imagination,* 1997, page 599.

[34] Jenny Uglow, *The Lunar Men,* 2002, page 139.

[35] King-Hele, *Letters,* op. cit., page 303.

[36] J. Pilkington, *A View of the present state of Derbyshire, Vol I,* pages 256-75. Darwin contended correctly that the springs are warmed by subterranean heat rather than chemical action as had been supposed previously.

[37] King-Hele, *Biography,* op. cit., page 181.

[38] James Watt (1736-1819) had described Arkwright as 'one of the most self-sufficient ignorant men I have ever met with'. Arkwright won his case, though he lost at the subsequent trial in June of that same year. At the second trial his witnesses included Darwin and Watt. See King-Hele, *Biography,* op. cit., pages 189 and 205-6.

[39] The reference to the water cure appears in Part II where he argues that the story of Aeson recovering his youth from swimming in the medicated bath of Medea teaches the reader the efficacy of warm bathing in retarding the

progress of old age. *The Botanic Garden, Part II, The Loves of the Plants, canto I* lines 387 and 388 (with the explanatory note).

[40] *The Botanic Garden, Part II, The Loves of the Plants, canto II,* lines 85-104.

[41] *The Botanic Garden, Part II, The Loves of the Plants, canto IV,* lines 171-190.

[42] Brewer, op. cit., pages 633-4. The obsession for travel books in search of the picturesque became a target for parody. In the best example Dr Syntax, an impoverished cleric and his nag Grizzle complete an arduous tour but on presenting his journal to the bookseller for publication he is told:

> *We can get Tours, - don't make wry faces-*
> *From those who never saw the places.*
> *I know a man who has the skill*
> *To make you books of Tours at will;*
> *And from his garret in Moorfields*
> *Can see what ev'ry country yields;*

W. Combe, *The Tour of Dr Syntax in Search of the Picturesque,* 1809, page 206.

[43] His poetic style became unfashionable and a subject for parody and his personal reputation never recovered from the publication of his poem *The Temple of Nature* in 1803 in which he expressed his belief in the evolution of life. His work was seen as an insult to both Christianity and human dignity and he was branded an atheist. King-Hele, *Biography,* op. cit., pages 346-352.

[44] *The Botanic Garden* also refers to Buxton and Chatsworth, *Part I, canto III;* and other locations including Dovedale and Thor's Cavern *Part II, canto III.*

[45] He was in England between 1757 and 1774 representing the Pennsylvania Assembly. His friendship with Anthony Tissington began in 1760 after which they began a correspondence. Franklin visited Tissington in Derbyshire more than once. Tissington's brother George was also a mine agent and both were friends of Darwin who called them his 'subterranean Genii' after they took him exploring 'the Bowels of old Mother Earth'. King-Hele, op. cit., *Letters,* 67-3.

[46] All quotations from the Wedgwood manuscripts by permission of the Trustees of the Wedgwood Museum, Barlaston, Staffordshire.

[47] Uglow, op. cit.

[48] Patty Fothergill's diary, 1793, Uglow, op. cit., pages 139 and 459.

[49] Adam, op. cit., 1838 edition, page 30. They were cousins and their family estates Newstead and Annesley were close to one another in Nottinghamshire. She was his first love but her affections were already bestowed on Jack Musters, the man she would marry in 1805.

[50] Bray op. cit., 2nd edition, 1783, page 125.

[51] Hembry 1990, op. cit., page 202.

[52] *The Torrington Diaries,* op. cit., page 40.

[53] *Four Topographical letters,* op. cit., page 47.

[54] *Camden's Britannica,* 2nd edition, 1806.

CHAPTER THREE
PAGES 41-50

[1] The Hotel deeds, DRO, D161 Box 1813.

[2] The cause of his financial distress is unknown. He may have over-reached himself in this development; or it may have been the failure of another of his businesses.

[3] The landscaped walk was made possible by the Matlock Enclosure Award from which Stephen Simpson acquired allotment 335, a steep, narrow strip of land on the south facing slope of Masson Hill above his Hascom Leys Farm property. At the end of 1786 the development of the estate remained incomplete and advertisements for a tenant offered the inducement of the premises rent free until Lady Day 1787.

[4] *A Description of the Country from 30 to 40 Miles around Manchester,* Aitkin, 1795 describes the view as taken from Mason's Inn, the Miner's Arms. Views of the north end of the Old Bath in the 1790s do show a new building or a remodelling of an existing one which support the idea that Robert Mason opened such an amenity there Figure 17. Edward Dayes, (1763-1804), was a leading topographical watercolourist of his time. His views often contain carefully drawn figures.

[5] The tenant in 1830 was Thomas Robinson who made his own important contribution to the landscape of Matlock Bath when, in retirement, he built Tor Hill and landscaped the hillside around it. Job Hodgkinson succeeded him as inn keeper and in 1846 purchased the property which still bears his name.

[6] There is no evidence that Simpson extended the landscaping scheme from his original plot.

[7] The Heights of Abraham, like the Lover's Walk, is an early historic pleasure ground which has remained in continuous use since its creation. The importance of both sites has been recognised by their inclusion in the Historic England Register of Historic Parks and Gardens.

[8] Calamine (zinc carbonate) was mined locally and had been processed at Cromford for example, since the 1760s and earlier at Bonsall. It was exported from the district to be used with copper in the production of brass.

[9] It seems the Old Bath was similarly divided between separate suites and individual rooms. In 1843 it contained 'about twelve sitting rooms.' *The Scotsman,* April 5, 1843.

[10] It is significant that Vernon called his new accommodation the Hotel. The term conveyed an element of superiority; a cut above an Inn or lodging house; better furnished and serving food. The same source *Dr Johnson's Dictionary,* 1818 edition, quoted a Mr Malone as having stated that in 1810 there were above 100 hotels but by 1818 the designation was 'very common'.

[11] See the advertisement for its sale, pages 75-76.

[12] Pilkington, op. cit., page 225. Perhaps as much as two thirds of the available accommodation was at the Old Bath though a precise figure is not available for this date. By 1843 it had the capacity to 'make up about 100 beds' and may have already reached that size by 1806 when Cumming took over the lease. *The Scotsman,* April 5, 1843.

[13] Lipscombe, op. cit., page 7.

[14] Thomas Potts, *Gazetteer of England and Wales,* 1810.

[15] Ward, op. cit., page 43. For comparison Hembry 1990, op. cit., page 308, gives figures for Buxton in 1806, 700 rising to 8-900 in 1813 while Bath allegedly drew 10,000 in the 1812-13 season.

[16] *Barclays Dictionary,* published c. 1812, Matlock. Potts described the Hotel as 'one of the most commodious in England.' His commendation indicates the impact of Vernon's investment bringing high quality accommodation to the resort.

[17] *Matlock and Bakewell Directory 1893.*

[18] J. H. Manners, Duke of Rutland, *Travels in Great Britain, Vol. II,* (pub.1813), page 280, describing Oct. 1796.

[19] *DM* 6/3/1800.

[20] Benjamin Wyatt (1755-1813) had a significant role in the Wyatt's 'design and build' dynastic empire which was active across the Midlands with family members in Burton, Sutton Coldfield, Tamworth and Lichfield. In the early years of the nineteenth century he was in charge of the building firm Benjamin Wyatt and Sons developed by Benjamin Wyatt (1709-72) James Wyatt's father, executing plans created by James and other architect members of the family. He was the grand nephew of the founder of the firm. John Martin Robinson, *The Wyatts, an Architectural Dynasty,* 1979, and by the same author, *James Wyatt, Architect to George III,* 2012.

[21] *Matthew Boulton,* 2013, Jennifer Tann and Anthony Burton, pages 168 and 169.

[22] The term dasher may need some explanation. There is on the one hand the obvious and relatively innocuous implication of 'one who cuts a dash' or in today's parlance 'a show off' or perhaps even a 'chancer'. But both Partridge's *Dictionary of Historical Slang and the Oxford English Dictionary* are clear that at this date it was a term especially used to describe 'a showy harlot' or a 'fast young woman'. Vernon would have had good reason to take offence whatever he is alleged to have said about it in public.

[23] *DM* 31/6/1799.

[24] *DM* 15/8/1799.

[25] *DM* 11/9/1806.

[26] The particulars of the resulting sale of Thomas Froggott's Matlock Hotel furniture and furnishings which began on April 29th, 1805 provide some interesting details. Five days were taken up with furnishings from bedrooms, 10 on the first day and later from 10, 7, 5, and 6 more, (a total of 38), the numbers no doubt reflecting bedrooms in the individual buildings along the terrace. There were 80 Four Post Camp and other Bedsteads', 40 woollen mattreses and Irish linen sheets, the elegant assembly and card room curtains as well as Dining, Assembly, Card, Drawing Room and Parlour furniture. There

were Kitchen, Dairy Hall and Laundry Utensils and on the last day, May 9th, the new built Billiard Table, Post Chaises, Sociable, Water and narrow wheel carts, 3 Horses and a Milch Cow, Harness, gearing &c, &c.

[27] *DM* 14/5/1807.

[28] *DM* 9/7/1807.

[29] Hembry 1990, op. cit., page 311. With reference to heating baths in this period Hembry comments that the rural spas 'primitive cold baths so extolled by Floyer, were now out of fashion … Contemporary visitors … expected a complex of different kinds of baths, hot, tepid and cold, with better quality fittings instead of a simple one room structure.' She associates success in meeting the expectation with the greater production and easier transport of coal. The mention of 'Italian Marble' in Varley's advertisement suggests Matlock Bath was aware of the trend to provide better quality facilities for its patrons.

[30] Dr Thomas Short, op. cit., pages 90-91. The rules for diet and recreation he also applied to bathing. Bohea Tea - a form of black tea; gleets - phlegm; fluor albus - white vaginal fluid; King's Evil - scrofula.

[31] Granville, op. cit., page 73.

[32] Nephritic; of the kidneys.

[33] Rhodes, *Derbyshire Tourist Guide,* preface.

CHAPTER FOUR
PAGES 51-62

[1] Revd Richard Ward (1758-1845) was appointed by Richard Arkwright junior as the first curate of Cromford Chapel when it opened in 1797. For more than twenty years he lived on Museum Parade close to what is now Hodgkinson's Hotel and between 1814 and 1827 he produced several editions of a well written and perceptive guide book *The Matlock, Buxton and Castleton Guide.* Over the years this recorded the changes in Matlock Bath which he was so well placed to observe. In 1835 he gave up his curacy at Cromford and moved to Brandon in Essex.

[2] Somewhat remodelled, it still stands near the children's playground. Its original more gothic style shown here is confirmed by Joseph Farington's view published in 1817 Figure 20 and, a year later, by Henry Moore's description

'the old alcove, a Gothick arch of rude stones, patched with moss'. Moore, op. cit., page 33.

[3] Oxford University, Bodleian Library, Gough maps 41A ff 53-81.

[4] Britton J. and Brayley E. W., *The Beauties of England and Wales,* 1802, pages 522-3.

[5] William Adam, op. cit., pages 71-74.

[6] Lipscombe, op. cit., page 59.

[7] Ward op. cit., page 14, summarised the experience in 1814. 'These walks, by Mr Arkwright's indulgence, are open to all who choose to visit them, every Monday and Thursday… Views of the most striking and pleasing kind are to be met with here.' He added 'The house itself is not shewn, as its furniture is not selected with a view to splendour of appearance, but rather for the purposes of utility and comfort, which this mansion possesses in an eminent degree.'

[8] *The Gentleman's Magazine,* July 1793, page 426.

[9] Benedict Nicolson, *Joseph Wright of Derby Painter of Light, vol. I,* page 263 and *vol. II,* page 164. Mr Wright's Account book lists 'Two Views of Matlock' for Mr Emes, £63.' It is not known if this is one of them. Joseph Wright, (1743-1797) was not a member of the Lunar Society or of the Derby Philosophical Society which Erasmus Darwin founded in March 1783, see King-Hele, op. cit., *Letters,* 83-1. But he was, in Jenny Uglow's words a 'Lunar Man'. He knew almost all the members of the Society, shared many of their interests and painted portraits of a number of them. His particular friends were John Whitehurst, a near neighbour in Derby, and Darwin, his doctor from 1766. Wright painted numerous Derbyshire scenes and like so many other artists could not resist the dramatic scenery of Matlock Dale and Cromford. His attention to detail in his view of Cromford Mill by Day and its companion Willersley Castle lends them an important archive value.

[10] R. S. Fitton, *The Arkwrights, Spinners of Fortune,* 1989, page 73.

[11] H. M. Colvin, *Dictionary of British Architects, 1600-1840,* 2008. Maxwell Craven, *Willersley: An Adam Castle in Derbyshire,* The Georgian Group Journal, Vol. XXII and pers. comm. Undated drawing DRO D7573.

[12] The Reverend James Pilkington, 1803. Sir Uvedale Price, 1810; and Lord Torrington 1790. R. S. Fitton, op. cit., page 83.

[13] It is unfortunate that Arthur Young visited Matlock Bath too early in the century to see Masson Mill. In Coalbrookdale the juxtaposition of wooded hills and the forges, furnaces and lime kilns he found 'altogether sublime'. He would not have been alone in viewing the Matlock gorge of the 1780s in much the same way. Roy Porter, op. cit., page 315.

[14] In the early years this was taken as Richard Arkwright's unwillingness to risk his inventions being spied upon. Later Ward explains that 'Many persons would be much gratified, if permission were given to inspect the mills; but as, in such a situation, a general permission would be attended with much inconvenience, and a partial one would be offensive to those who did not obtain it, it has therefore been determined that no application for leave shall be complied with.'

[15] Wolley *Mss* 6671 ff 310-313.

[16] This land is thought to be an area of just over three acres described as 'two Mason [sic] Closes, North and South' in an undated list of property in the Lordship of Crumford. The list is believed to refer to William and Mary Milnes property and to date from the 1760s. DRO D7573.

[17] Wolley *Mss* op. cit.

[18] Hodgkinson was the tenant of Edwin Lascelles' Willersley Farm Estate on the opposite side of the river Derwent. It is unlikely that this is the unusual convex weir which exists at Masson now which would have been an unnecessarily expensive construction to serve this paper mill; but a rather less ambitious forerunner which was later modified or replaced when Arkwright built his cotton mill close by.

[19] DRO 1859M/F25.

[20] From papers, at the time uncatalogued, at Chatsworth House.

[21] BM *Add Mss* 6670 f 239. Fitton records that in October that year Richard Arkwright agreed to buy the land Masson Close and the paper mill built on the adjoining Upper Masson Close, a purchase which would appear to include George White's interests in the property. It is likely that this was the case though no definitive evidence has come to hand.

[22] DRO D7573. Adam Wolley's summary of the Abstract of Title describes the property as being the same as for the Lascelles to Hodgkinson sale but with the addition of 'all other his Estates in the Parish of Matlock'. This is thought to include additional land at Masson.

[23] William Stretton suggests in a manuscript note now in Nottingham record office that his father, Samuel, built Arkwright's first Cromford Mill and he is known to have been the builder Arkwright used for his earlier mill in Nottingham. Dr S. D. Chapman also considers Haarlem Mill at Wirksworth to be his work. Stanley D. Chapman, *Sir Richard Arkwright's Masson Mills, Matlock Bath, Derbyshire*, 2015, pages 22 and 24.

[24] Warner, op. cit., page 144.

[25] By 1800 the mill was in the hands of Anthony Debanke who continued the business until 1817 when it was taken over by John Skidmore. He retained the lease into the 1830s.

[26] It enjoyed a right of water from the Derwent but not on Sundays and a share of water from the New Bath stream. This was used for washing paper and drawn from the thermal spring which supplied the bath at the New Bath. A dwelling house was included in the lease.

[27] *DA&J* 12/6/1868.

[28] *LG* 1/1/1874 and 19/12/1879.

[29] In style and in scale at this early date of Matlock Bath's development the building he erected, later known as Glenorchy House, was comparable only to Cliffe House which had been built in the previous decade by Thomas Leacroft of Wirksworth high on the hillside at the northern end of the valley.

[30] *Harrison's Derby and Nottingham Journal*, 7/8/1777.

[31] Bryan, op. cit., page 180.

[32] Bryan, op. cit., pages 177-180; *DT* 30/12/1938.

[33] Warner, op. cit., page 144.

[34] DRO D7573.

[35] By the mid-1800s a building had been added either side of the stable block. All three were in use as two-storey cottages Figure 139 when they were demolished before the 1970s road widening.

[36] Defoe describing the river in flood at Derby in the 1720s called it 'so frightful, that we contented ourselves with hearing at a Distance its shocking roar'. *Tour through... Vol III*, 1742, page 71.

[37] It is shown on the Matlock Tithe Map of 1848.

CHAPTER FIVE
PAGES 63-74

[1] J. Barnatt and R. Penny, *The lead legacy: The prospects for the Peak District's lead mining heritage*, 2004.

[2] Macky, op. cit., page 208.

[3] Rogers, *Defoe*, op. cit., pages 163-4.

[4] William Hauptmann and J. Harald Waber, *John Webber (1751-1793), Pacific Voyager and Landscape Artist*, Exhibition Catalogue, 1996, page 203.

[5] British Library ADD. MS 42,232, 1774. William Tyler RA, visiting Matlock Bath with friends is describing 'the most noble Rocky Mountain' opposite the Old Bath see also Figure 35.

[6] Several visitors mention them, see Torsten Althin, *Eric Geisler and his journey of 1772-1773*, 1971; Thomas Quincy, *A short Tour in the Midland Counties of England performed in the year 1772...*, 1775, page 57; Bray, op. cit., 1777 page 77; Josiah Wedgwood, see panel, page 38; Revd John Swete see next footnote; and William Tyler see panel, page 66. Several illustrations of them are known of which this is the clearest.

[7] The picture shows the rods above the river and on the opposite bank, at the left side of the building a roller on a post, (one of a series depending on how far away the mine entrance was) which directs the chain towards the mine entrance. In some cases, as later at Side Mine under High Tor, the wheel and the mine opening were on the same side of the river. At the pump shaft in the mine the connection was made via an L shaped joint fixed at the angle of the L so that as the crank moved the rods backwards the L rocked back and pulled the pump rod up throwing up 'a vast quantity of water at each stroke'. In 1783 at a site below the Masson weir, Swete recorded that he and the miners crossed the river on planks laid across the pumping structure; the engine he described was derelict when he visited again in 1795. *Diary of Rev. John Swete*, Devon Record Office Z19/2/19.

[8] As a consequence the river backed up forming a pond above the weir which was used for boating Figure 23.

[9] Ian Ousby, *The Englishman's England*, 1990, page 133.

[10] Matthew Boulton bought fossils for which he received a bill for 22s from Thomas Pearson of Matlock [Bath] dated 25 April 1783. His 72 fossils cost 3½ d each and he was charged 1s for the 'packin box.' *The Matthew Boulton Bicentenary Exhibition Catalogue, 2009*, exhibit 49.

[11] When Mary Shelley's fictional characters in her gothic novel *Frankenstein* visit Matlock [Bath] the book refers to mineral cabinets as 'little cabinets of natural history' and compares the scenery to Switzerland except for the hills being green rather than white with snow.

[12] From *Through Derbyshire to the Lakes*, 1797, page 221.

[13] The Heights of Jacob was at the top of Jacob's Steps which were built in 1882 to replace the footpath from Temple Road to Upperwood which ran across the land where the Matlock Bath Pavilion and Gardens Company had been given permission to build their Pavilion. In 1901 John Edward Lawton modified the route, replacing the top section of path, which wound across a steep field known as Tear Breeches, with the straight flight of steps in use today. An advertisement in May 1923 for the sale of Upper Wood Mine, whose adit entrance was in the side of Upperwood Road opposite the top of the steps, offers an explanation for the change. Tear Breeches and the field below were included in the sale as the tipping ground for the mine.

[14] *DM* 13-14/8/1823 and 11/8/1824; *Derby Reporter* 31/7/-1/8/1833; *The Caverns and Mines of Matlock Bath*, R. Flindall and A. Hayes, 1976.

[15] Potts, op. cit., the book does not have numbered pages. The entry is Etruria.

[16] *Matthew Boulton*, op. cit., page 70.

[17] Blue John is the rare form of fluorspar found only near Castleton in Derbyshire. In 1769 Boulton bought just over 14 tons from John Platt for £81-1s-6d.

[18] Quincey, op. cit., page 57, observed 'around

the baths many poor women are generally waiting with petrifactions, chrystals [sic], and other curiosities, the produce of the adjacent country'; by 1782 a visitor could report on 'spars and petrifactions…worked into various shapes for use or ornament and sent to many places in England for sale'; the Duke of Rutland visiting late in the 1796 season purchased various articles from the 'spar shops with which Matlock abounds'. J. H. Manners, op. cit., page 280; and the Museums of the nineteenth century offered elaborate displays using local and foreign materials. In 1826 John James Audubon, *The 1826 Journal of John James Audubon* (transcribed by Alice Ford, 1967), page 210 'fearing that I might forget them', listed his nicely packed up purchases to send to America. For £4-13-0 he had bought 1 fruit bowl, 1 bell vase, 4 boxes, 1 wafer box, 19 smelling bottles and 10 lockets. His friends added a black inkstand and a 'little box for little John. Matlock is nicely engraved on it'.

[19] As late as 1921 the Smiths (of the Royal Museum) were appealing to Mr Weston, their elderly, (over 90 years old), marble worker at Steeple House near Wirksworth for their 'goods as quick as possible, our customers are anxiously waiting for them.' pers. comm.

[20] Torrens, H. S., *The Early Life and Geological Work of John Mawe, (1766-1829)*, Peak District Mines Historical Society Bulletin, Vol 11, No 6, Winter 1992.

[21] *LG* 31/1/1818 reported that the partnership between Richard Brown of Derby and John Mawe of London, Derby, Matlock and Castleton, firm of Brown and Mawe, was dissolved by mutual consent.

[22] In December 1849 Adam, who had taken over the business at the Royal Museum was forced to sell up to meet the terms of a deed of assignment with his creditors. The sale, included furniture and spar and marble ornaments. *DM* 12/12/1849.

[23] *Pigot's Directories* of 1831 and 1835 advertise his showroom at 232 Regent Street, London.

[24] DRO D5991/10/27.

[25] Chambers op. cit., *vol. iii,* 1781. Internal evidence leads us to conclude that this entry dates from 1728 when the book was first published.

[26] Barker op. cit.

CHAPTER SIX
PAGES 75-92

[1] Lipscombe, op. cit., page 4.

[2] Heights of Abraham deeds, DRO D127/ MT/1-30; The Hotel deeds DRO D161, Box18/3; D. Palmer Pearson, *Matlock Bath, Its Hotels and Baths, HPN* 8/2/1919 and 15 and 22/3/1919.

[3] John Farey, General *View of the Agriculture and Minerals in Derbyshire Vol. II,* 1813, comments on Town Dung 'its price at Matlock Bath in 1808 weighed at the Road Engine was 7s per ton.' He reports that 'weighing machines were becoming common to weigh Coals, Hay, Straw, Manures. At Matlock Old Bath Mr James Cumming has a weighing machine in public use.'

[4] This is the name of the road today; we do not know when it came into use.

[5] Adit - a horizontal entrance by which a mine is entered or drained.

[6] The cavern is still open to the public.

[7] *The Times* 22/6/1825.

[8] Atkinson's later financial difficulties left Pechell as the most active partner.

[9] *DM* 26/7/1838.

[10] In 1860, Alfred Henry Pechell sold Guilderoy and the Heights estate to Thomas Wakley see also page 101. An advertisement for a 'Private and Select Ball' held at the house in December 1861 described it as 'a spacious and elegant mansion, beautifully festooned'. *Matlock Bath Telegraph* 11/1/1862. It was advertised for sale again on 19/5/1863. It was divided into two dwellings in 1898 and in the same year a pair of semi-detached villas, then called Sunbury and Ouida was built in the far west end of its grounds.

[11] J. Croston, *On Foot through the Peak,* 2nd edition, 1868, page 245.

[12] Built directly above Rose Bank, (today the site of the original lodge) this Octogon Lodge was later called Jessamine Cottage, then East Lodge and now the Round House.

[13] By 1864 Robert Chadwick owned the Lower Tower and the Heights and made the Lower Tower his home. He moved the public entrance to the Heights further away from the house to a new lodge, the North Lodge, later called the

East Lodge, on Masson Road. This entrance is no longer used.

[14] Granville, *Spas of England,* Vol. 2, 1841, page 71.

[15] DRO, Q/S Turnpike Plan No. 15.

[16] A. Jewitt, *Matlock Companion,* 1837, page 15.

[17] Bryan, op. cit., pages 127 and 128.

[18] *DM* 8/6/1815.

[19] The Old Bath offered two large rooms; the drawing room 50 feet by 22 and the dining room 45 feet by 23. Clearly neither would accommodate a substantial gathering but it was the best this 'village' resort could offer. *The Scotsman* April 5, 1843.

[20] A letter dated October 1795 from Peter Nightingale to Robert Mason complains of the 'company that comes to the baths' destroying pheasants on his estate near Woodend. DRO, D3585/1/1, page 75.

[21] Thomas Short, op. cit., 1734, page 72.

[22] See page 19.

[23] H. Moore, op. cit., 1818, page 31.

[24] Ebeneezer Rhodes, op. cit., The site which was known early in the nineteenth century as Dungeon Tors but later as the Romantic Rocks is now enclosed in the modern pleasure ground, Gulliver's Kingdom. From the Rocks, a steeply stepped path led to the Fluor Cavern which was opened to the public at about the same time Figure 37. The path has not survived.

[25] The content from the 6th Duke's diaries is printed 'By permission of the Duke of Devonshire.' Devonshire Mss., *Diary of 6th Duke of Devonshire.* 764.449, 25th August 1825. Britchka: an open carriage with a folding hood and space for reclining when on a journey. Droschki: a Russian low four wheeled carriage in which the passengers sat astride a narrow bench their feet resting on bars near the ground.

[26] *DC* 2/11/1839.

[27] H. Moore, *The Pilot,* 1818, page 4. It was situated on the hillside above the Temple Hotel and later described as Mrs Bown's Botanical Garden offering a fine collection of 'above seven hundred species of indigenous rare plants' any of which may be purchased.

[28] *A Home Tour Through the Manufacturing Districts of England in the Summer of 1835,* Sir George Head, pages 119 and 122.

[29] Head, op. cit., pages 117-122. The guide at the Fluor Spar cavern he found was 'an old woman who lived in a hut, or rather a den, at the mouth of the cave' and at the New Speedwell Mine he was 'suddenly accosted by a poor old woman, watching like a spider at the angle of the path … The ancient creature looked comfortless and exerted all her kindness and activity to please me.'

[30] Both of which survive in the garden of what is now a private house. The house originally called Fountain Cottage, but now Fernie Bank, was built by John Allen soon after he purchased the property in 1855.

[31] A. Jewitt, op. cit., page 24.

[32] Jewitt exhorted Matlock Bath 'GO! AND DO LIKEWISE.' There is no evidence that his cry was heeded.

[33] Bryan, op. cit., page 204.

[34] Bryan, op. cit., pages 177-180; *DT* 30/12/1938.

[35] The new church was committed to the same evangelical forms of worship that at this time were followed at the parish church, St Giles, in Matlock. This originated from the ministry of the Reverend Philip Gell (1783-1870), an extremely evangelical low churchman, who was resident curate to the absentee rector from 1806 until 1829 when he moved to the newly built, St John's, in Derby. He was not forgotten in Matlock and it was he who was chosen to preach when the foundation stone of the new church in Matlock Bath was laid. The *Derby Mercury* reported he 'delivered a lengthened, fervent, and energetic address', adding, perhaps with some relief, 'we regret our space precludes us from giving entire.' George Withers Saxton is commemorated in the church as one 'by whose unwearied perseverance in the service of his Lord and Saviour, the numerous voluntary contributions by which this church was built were chiefly raised.' The height of the clock in the church tower was raised by one foot six inches so that it was visible from the New Bath Hotel. Matlock Bath became a separate parish in 1843. Thirty years later the London architect T. E. C. Streatfield was engaged when the church was to be enlarged to increase

accommodation by about 130 sittings. The south aisle and a new vestry were added, the organ was moved from the organ gallery in the tower to a new setting in an extended chancel and the east window was installed. In 1875 Mrs Anne Clarke, a benefactress of the church presented a reredos and in 1885 a window was installed in her memory. Edward Greenhough and his family were commemorated by a window in 1923. Greenhough's memorial in the churchyard records his death in 1899 and acknowledges his role 'for 42 years Warden of this church'.

[36] *DM* 16/6/1841 and *DM* 12/10/1842.

[37] Revd. H. E. Brown, *History of Holy Trinity Church, Matlock Bath,* 1966. The building remained in use as a vicarage until its sale in 1946. Lyndhurst on Brunswood Road then served as the vicarage until a new house was built for the purpose close to the church. The first vicarage became a country club; was bought by the YHA in 1956; became the headquarters of the Probation Service in 1983 but is now a private residence.

[38] See frontispiece.

[39] Revd. H. E. Brown, op. cit.

[40] The deep eaves of the next to the last building on the right in Woodland Terrace mark the house which James Pearson built here for his own use some time before 1848 when it is recorded on the Matlock Tithe map; the rest of the terrace was built by 1851. A keen angler, Pearson was shooting otters from his property there in 1857.

[41] DRO D2929M /F1/1-3.

[42] The old school building is now in residential use; the present Matlock Bath Holy Trinity School was opened on Clifton Road in 1973.

[43] The War Memorial was erected in the space in 1920-21.

[44] *DA* 9/5/1890. The paper announced the arrival of telephones for 'business facilities' in May 1890. Matlock Bath is represented in the first Matlock telephone directory dated 1896-97 by Masson Mill No.3 and the Royal Hotel No.19. The Local Board had been unable to persuade the telephone company to bury the wires along the Parade so that the poles did not detract from the effect of its new Promenade and at the meeting of 13/6/1887 suggested the poles should be painted stone colour.

[45] N. Pevsner, *The Buildings of England, Derbyshire,* 1978. The reference is to the much copied architectural style which Horace Walpole (1717- 1797) made fashionable as he extended and decorated his house, Strawberry Hill at Twickenham in the third quarter of the eighteenth century.

[46] *Derbyshire Tourist Guide,* 1837, page 27.

[47] He is described as of Brighton.

[48] The pool in the foreground is now an ornamental fishpond.

[49] *HPN* 12/8/1871. Large crowds gave them 'a hearty welcome' at the station where the band played and an address was delivered. The road to the hotel was decorated; 'dinner was provided in the excellent style peculiar to that establishment, after which the green was illuminated.'

[50] *Derbyshire Independent* 26/8/1869. This attractive backdrop had been threatened by an advertisement offering land for sale for 23 building plots high on the hill; one used for Smedley's Cavern.

[51] Meanwhile in the 1860s ownership of the property passed from descendants of John Saxton to Philip Hubbersty, a solicitor from Wirksworth and in 1898 from his son, Albert Cantrell Hubbersty, to the recently incorporated New Bath Hotel Company along with the neighbouring Bath Terrace Hotel.

[52] Bryan, op. cit., page 206.

[53] The tufa bank was cut back and a swathe of property demolished Figures 140 and 145 including the Roadside Bar. The ends of the old road to the New Bath were reduced to footpaths and a new approach road was cut into the tufa bank.

CHAPTER SEVEN
PAGES 93-98

[1] East Midlands Group of the Railway and Canal Historical Society, A.K. Cheetham, 1987, *Tour No 123;* Dr Stephen Mann, *Sketches and Reminiscences,* 1856. He took the canal trip in May 1844 when on the return journey 'a number of juveniles taking the tow rope hauled us along … until weary of the toil they unanimously declared "they would na, could na, and should na pu honna more till peed".' A shower of nuts and

halfpennies answered this request.

[2] *DC* 9/7/1842.

[3] *DM* 3/7/1844.

[4] *DM* 30/6/1847.

[5] *DM* 3/7/1844.

[6] *DA&J* 14/5/1858.

[7] *DT* 11/4/1874.

[8] *WA* 10/7/1863.

[9] From Edward Bradbury's *Good Friday Sketch* in *Pilgrimages in the Peak,* 1879, page 44. This was Matlock Bath in 1879, thirty years after the railway station had opened. More remarkable, perhaps, was the speed with which the arrival of the railway transformed visitor numbers to the resort and its wider neighbourhood, as these two accounts from the summer of 1850, just a year on from the first trains, confirm. In July trains from Sheffield brought 1700 scholars and teachers from St John's and St Paul's church schools. A month later, '47 first and second class carriages' from Birmingham, Gloucester and Cheltenham, delivered a 'highly respectable party' en route for Chatsworth and Haddon. *DC* 27/7/1850 and *Buxton Herald* 17/8/1850.

[10] 'The Midland Company carried heavy human freight.' *DM* 24/5/1865.

[11] *Cambridge Chronicle and University Journal* 7/9/1867. The reference to covered would have reassured potential customers that the journey would not have to be made in the open carriages often used for excursion traffic. Simon Bradley, *Railways,* 2015, page 65.

[12] *DA&J* 8 and 15/7/1853.

[13] J. B. Firth, *Highways and Byways of Derbyshire,* 1903, page 390.

[14] In 1867 the railway line through Matlock Bath became part of the Midland Company's main route from London to Manchester. It was closed from Ambergate to the north in 1967 but in 1972 was reopened from Derby to Matlock and now offers a valuable service for travellers through the Derwent Valley Mills World Heritage Site.

CHAPTER EIGHT
PAGES 99-112

[1] This is the view expressed by G. C. R. H. who contributed the chapter on Matlock and Matlock Bath in *Health Resorts of the British Islands* published in 1912. He dates the Spa's decline from 'towards the middle of the century'.

[2] Hembry 1997, op. cit., page 134.

[3] Granville, op. cit., page 37.

[4] Bryan, op. cit., pages 153 and 154. In addition to those dignitaries, listed on page 83, Bryan describes visits from Duke Nicholas of Russia in 1815; the Dowager Queen Adelaide in 1840 accompanied by the Duchess of Saxe Weimar; and in 1856 ex queen Marie Amelie of the French.

[5] Granville, op. cit., page 71.

[6] Among these short stay visitors in 1838 was George Gilbert Scott (1811-1878), who visited Matlock Bath as part of his honeymoon tour. He visited again in 1856, by then an established architect. He arrived by train and posted on to Chatsworth and Haddon and then to Buxton. *Personal and Professional Recollections*, edited by Gavin Stamp, 1995, pages 251 and 466. How long Lord Barham stayed is not known but the *Cheltenham Chronicle* 8/8/1833 announced 'Marriage at Matlock, Lord Barham to Lady Francis Jocelyn, second daughter of Earl Roden. It is the fourth marriage of his lordship. 'He is in his 52nd year and his newly married lady in her 19th.'

[7] Bryan considers 1835 to have been the high point for the locally crafted marble products and notes that when the railway brought 'its thousands of excursionists' the industry declined through lack of customers who could afford such items. Bryan, op. cit., pages 160 and 161.

[8] The quarry face is still visible behind the former Chapel and 44 North Parade; and at the northern end of the Upper Holme is the weathering scar of Blake's Long Tor quarry.

[9] Most of the rest of the frontage to the main road as far as Holme Road was completed between 1864 and 1869 except for what still exists as a single storey block, now no. 26-28 North Parade, the dining rooms which F. E. Leggoe built in 1890.

[10] *SI* 24/3/1893.

[11] DRO D161B/ES109. September 10, 1850. Francis Blake's daughter, Harriette Anne, married Thomas Wakley's son, Thomas.

[12] Adverts appeared in the *Wolverhampton*

Chronicle and Staffordshire Advertiser 30/9/1857; and *Birmingham Journal* 7/10/1857.

[13] *MBA* 18/6/1858.

[14] The ratepayers of Matlock Bath agreed to the old road's closure on May 17th, 1860 and the New Road was completed the following year, see DRO Q/SB 9/207. The original route of the old bridleway leading across the hillside to Bonsall, the Key Pasture Wood Road, ran from the valley bottom near the present Brunswood Terrace, up behind the former vicarage and over ground where later Brunswood House was built. It levelled out just below the Birklands and crossed the hillside to continue past the Round House to Upperwood as now. Near the Round House the Matlock Enclosure map records an ancient gate, the Key Pasture gate, which may once have defined the boundary of the Key Pasture with Masson common land and provided a barrier to prevent animals straying into areas of cultivated land. A small obelisk stands there today; it is possible this marks the location of this gate.

[15] David Sharp, *Thomas Wakley (1795-1862), a biographical sketch,* 2012; and op. cit., Heights of Abraham deeds.

[16] The early twentieth century local historian David Palmer Pearson explains that Thomas Robinson of Torr Hill built Derwent House in the Dale for his son-in-law Thomas Smedley. The house does not appear on the Matlock Tithe map of 1848 but Smedley is listed there in Melville's Directory in 1853. By 1857 Smedley is described as at a spar shop near the railway bridge. Pearson explains that when Francis Blake began to work a quarry at Long Tor, Robinson complained of damage to his property there. Blake's solution was to build the shop for Smedley in exchange for him giving up Derwent House. Blake sold the Long Tor hillside including the quarry to Samuel Claye of Long Eaton in 1858.

[17] *Enlightenment,* 2000, Roy Porter, page 226; *Philosophical Inquiry into the Origins of our Ideas of the Sublime and Beautiful,* Edmund Burke, 1756; *Observations, Relative Chiefly to Picturesque Beauty,* 1786, Reverend William Gilpin; *An essay on the Picturesque as compared with the Sublime and Beautiful,* Uvedale Price, 1794. In his definition, of the sublime Dr Johnson used the words 'exalted by nature'.

[18] Matlock Bath's scenery, as with its spa treatments, accommodation and social facilities later suffered in comparison with mainland Europe and the accolade of which it was apparently proud, the Switzerland of England, should surely be seen as the resort acknowledging its inferior position in relation to the more sublime Alpine landscapes.

[19] In 1869 the Midland Railway set out the proposed route for a railway along the west side of Matlock Dale opposite High Tor. The Company feared it might lose the right to use the existing line on the east side of the valley which it leased jointly with the London and North Western Railway Company (L&NWR). The new line was not required when the L&NWR gave up its lease in 1871. The deposited plan for the proposed line helps to date the development of this part of Matlock Bath.

[20] Stukely, op. cit. He added 'And enter'd another hermit's cell, who had a mind if possible to get quite out of the world; 'tis hewn in the rock, with a most dreary prospect before it. On one end is a crucifix and a little niche where I suppose the mistaken zeal of the starv'd anchorite, plac'd his saint or such trinket.'

[21] It was a popular attraction, much more conveniently placed than many of Matlock Bath's show caverns and it remained open until at least the 1940s.

[22] A year later he was advertising his hydropathic establishment at Matlock Bank managed by Mr and Mrs Stevens charging 3/6d per day. *DC* 11/11/1854. If an unnamed witness whose testimony is recorded many years later is to be believed, Smedley first sought to establish his hydro in Matlock Bath but was rebuffed, telling his work people at Lea, with tears in his eyes that Matlock Bath had refused him the Royal Hotel and 'they would live to regret it'. How this might have changed the life of the resort! *HPN* 13/2/1904.

[23] *DM* 17/6/1865.

[24] The Arkwright family may also have been responsible for some tree planting on the Tor at an earlier date. Beeches planted at the top of the south facing slope could have been part of the massive tree planting operation in the valley commissioned by Richard Arkwright junior and undertaken by John Webb before 1802.

[25] *HPN* 24/4/1880. This may have meant Edward Milner who was born locally but

practised in London or his partner and son Henry Ernest Milner.

[26] *HPN* 4/4/1903. A further footbridge from the Dale close to the Matlock Bath entrance to High Tor was constructed in 1915. This was not built primarily as an access route but rather as a neat solution to the problem of how to carry a sewer - slung beneath it - across the river for the Matlock sewerage scheme.

[27] *HPN* 2/4/1921.

[28] The High Tor grounds are included in Historic England's Register of Historic Parks and Gardens. The base station for the Heights of Abraham cable car was built on the disused tennis court in 1984.

[29] *HPN* 12/2/1881.

[30] Thomas Rawson, a lime burner and quarry owner, is listed in directories from 1862 to 1881. The Ordnance Survey map published in 1880 shows a lime burning kiln to the right of the Boathouse. At this date there were two separate quarries behind the buildings. Holt Quarry on the right and Harveydale Quarry to the left. In 1921 Alfred Shaw who ran Holt Quarry bought the rock which separated them. Harveydale was run by Alfred Greatorex at that time.

[31] Wheatcroft was making and supplying ginger beer somewhere in the village in 1870.

[32] A member of a later generation in the family believed that she bought it from her father. His entry in the 1891 census records him 'living on own means' and supports the suggestion.

[33] When Mary Whittaker died in 1920 the business was sold but it continued to trade as Whittaker's (Matlock Bath) Ltd.

[34] In 1966 the works escaped the fate of the two pairs of semi-detached houses at Hazel Bank which stood close by to the north. They were damaged by a rock fall and demolished soon after along with the cottage accommodation which stood over Tor Hill's former coach house and stables. The coach house survives marking the site today. At about this time Whittaker's was taken over by new owners. The works closed in the 1970s and the site was cleared.

CHAPTER NINE
PAGES 113-124

[1] *Matlock Companion,* 1837, A. Jewitt, page 11.

[2] Head, op. cit., pages 115-117.

[3] Adam, op. cit., 1838, page 30.

[4] Adam op. cit., page 36.

[5] *DM* 9/5/1844.

[6] Order of Partition, 16 July 1863, DRO D3415/1/1.

[7] *Sale notice,* DRO 1859M/E11-12.

[8] *DT&ChH* 16/7/1870.

[9] As named in the advertisement announcing its reopening in the *DT* 31/8/1878.

[10] Warings Caler, by 1906, becoming Waring and Gillow, manufacturers of fine furniture and specialist furnishing. *DA* 1/6/1906. The Ritz Hotel in London was among their clients.

[11] Bryan, op. cit., page 206.

[12] Wieland had big plans for the progress of the resort but he became frustrated by his failure to persuade Matlock Bath to embrace them. He proposed a crescent in place of the stabling near the fish pond, a promenade along the river and the introduction of drinking fountains. In the event the only drinking fountain to appear was the one he built into the roadside wall below the Royal Hotel (now moved to the side of the shelter opposite the Pavilion). Disappointed, Wieland left in 1891 and died two years later. *HPN* 22/7/1893.

[13] This call from Mr Bryan, the draper in Matlock Bath. *DT&ChH* 14/1/1888.

[14] *The Alcester Chronicle* July 18, 1891. The same article appeared in numerous local papers.

[15] *DT&ChH* 19/4/1902.

[16] *DDT* 26/9/1904.

[17] *DA* 3/2/1905; *DT&ChH* 22/4/1905.

[18] *SDT* 30/1/1905.

[19] *DDT* 8/2/1905.

[20] *DT&ChH* 2/4/1905.

[21] *DA* 3/2/1905.

[22] All this in addition to a new gas works and sewerage scheme. *SDT* 6/7/1905.

[23] It consisted of only 337 acres with a rateable

value of £11,092 and a debt of £25,451, much of it derived from the purchase of the gas works in 1896.

[24] *LG* 4/8/1905.

[25] In November the price to be paid for some of the land facing the Parade was settled by arbitration, Herbert Buxton receiving £425 and Mrs Greenhough £225. *SDT* 14/4/1906.

[26] Comment on the choice of this name included that it dissociated it from the original Pavilion; it was mysterious; catchy; people would be intrigued as to what one is. *HPN* 14 and 21/11/1908.

[27] *SI* 16/7/1908.

[28] The Matlock Bridge and Matlock Bath District Councils were under notice from Derbyshire County Council to carry out a joint sewerage scheme by 1907. *DT&ChH* 10/3/1906.

[29] For once the resort was abreast of current fashion joining seaside and inland resorts across the United Kingdom which were emulating their German neighbours by building Kursaals. The literal translation would be Cure Rooms but they are perhaps best described as places of healthy amusement. These varied in size and in the range of facilities they provided. The Harrogate Kursaal for example offered daily orchestral musical performances, cinematograph shows, vocal and variety programmes and, in the season, a weekly symphony concert; in Southend the Kursaal was in effect a large amusement park; and in Bognor the principal attraction was a roller skating rink though it also housed the Constitutional Club and contained a theatre and assembly room. In Harrogate it was the Corporation that funded the new development obtaining loan sanction for the estimated cost of £40,000. *Buxton Advertiser* 2/5/1901. By 1912 described as 'indisputably the finest building of its kind in the United Kingdom' the Harrogate Kursaal was said to have cost nearly £70,000. *Health Resorts of the British Isles*, 1912, page 67. Bognor, *The Stage*, 9/2/1911.

[30] *SDT* 6/11/1908, published a photograph of the proposed design; a massive structure of domes and projecting towers at least four times the size of the building eventually erected.

[31] *MC&LGA* 22/3/1909.

[32] Nuttall, an architect and surveyor, had worked for the Council before and was in effect the Council's architect; Francis William Ackland Hodge (1876-1921) had become known in Matlock Bath through his work on the Royal in 1904 and 1908. In census and other records he is variously described as a furniture salesman, surveyor and representative furnishing decorating and building [sic] CER 1901; freemason membership list, Eton lodge 1901; CER 1911; *DA* 8/7/1910; *DDT*. 1/12/1910.

[33] White announced about a score of tenders had been received. The successful bid was from Fords of Derby with a price of £8,694; the work to be completed in 7 months. *Ripley and Heanor News* 10/12/1909.

[34] *DA* 21/1/1910.

[35] *MC&LGA* 22/3/1909.

[36] In its first year the revenue of £375 set against the loan charges and other costs left a deficiency of £1,095. *MC&LGA* 23/9/1911. The building carried the name Kursaal until sometime between 1915 and 1917 when anti German feeling was at its height and the name was dropped in favour of the Grand Pavilion.

[37] Close by, Pearsons had a petrifying well under Temple Road, which was visited by Princess Victoria in 1832.

[38] Obelisks were widely used as garden features in the first half of the eighteenth century and became fashionable again in the nineteenth. Ornamental obelisks shaped from a variety of stones were a stock item in the lifetime of Matlock Bath's spar shops.

[39] *Gentlefolk and the Great North Magazine* Sept.1905, page 2079 and advertising leaflets.

[40] The billeting officer, Major Johnson of Aldershot housed 28 officers there with 200 men in the Royal Pavilion in the grounds Figures 93 and 300 in the present Pavilion building. Provision was also made for 130 horses. John Boden and Son of South Parade, Matlock Bath provided the army rations and William Barker, the corn miller at Cromford, feed for the horses.

[41] As in 1904 this was the work of F. W. Ackland Hodge. *HPN* 18/8/1908. The newly erected wing was inspected by guests at the British Medical Association conference.

[42] The wing survived, was later converted into flats and demolished in the 1960s.

[43] *HPN* 24/3/1917 and *DAJ* 28/10/1916.

[44] Croston, op. cit., page 228.

[45] The sale particulars explained that the large room on the side of Fishpond Hill, had been the sleeping accommodation for postilions in the coaching era and that the hotel still had stalls for eighteen horses. Pearson's petrifying well was derelict in 1919 when the brewers, Messrs Bass Ltd bought it with the Fishpond Hotel from Pearson's daughter Agnes Sellors. Three years later the brewery gave the land on which the well stood to the village for the erection of toilets. It is now a shelter. In the 1880s the several attempts made to limit the use of Fishpond Hill to pedestrian traffic by inserting a post or steps at the top were met with defiance by a public claiming long held rights for its use as a bridle road - and so for wheeled traffic. The post persistently and mysteriously disappeared, dynamite being used for the purpose on one occasion.

[46] *HPN* 30/5/1908.

CHAPTER TEN
PAGES 125-140

[1] Bryan, op. cit., pages 162-166.

[2] Croston, op. cit., page 226.

[3] Jewitt, 1837, op. cit., page 42.

[4] The photographer William Godber advertised The Rink Studio in late 1889.

[5] *HPN* 9/4/1892. In 1898 William Wyvill built Rockvale Villas and, a year later, Rockvale Terrace, on the site.

[6] Bryan, op. cit., page 205. Letter from visitor, *DT* 15/2/1883.

[7] This condition, was no doubt to safeguard trade at the two nearby licensed properties which Wheatcroft had built, the George Vaults, indicated by the oval hanging sign seen in the background of this view and the building which became the County and Station, now unoccupied. Wheatcroft may have planned the latter as his residence but by 1868, in the hands of his son Sidney Frederick Wheatcroft, it was the Palatine Dining and Refreshment Rooms serving 'Hot Dinners every Day in the Season'.

[8] Frances or Fanny may be remembered by some local people as the infant class teacher at Cromford School.

[9] The bath is now a fish pool at the Matlock Bath Aquarium.

[10] The Local Board and Urban District Council used it for their meetings. In February 1891 there was a proposal that the Local Board should purchase the Assembly Rooms and bath to use as offices; but it came to nothing. *DT&ChH* 7/2/1891.

[11] Bryan op. cit., page 205.

[12] Smedley Brothers of the Eagle Iron Works, Belper produced the ironwork. It stood in 15 acres of grounds landscaped by Edward Speed, the council's Surveyor, ('brother of Thomas Speed, successor to Mr Paxton at Chatsworth').

[13] *SI* 29/7/1884.

[14] *HPN* 4/8/1886.

[15] Accounts occasionally refer to the cottages as Stonniswood. Stonnis was a name which was used for Black Rock, the gritstone outcrop at the edge of Cromford Moor.

[16] *Nottingham Journal* 26/7/1882; *DT&ChH* 2/8/1884.

[17] *HPN* 17/3/1888.

[18] *DT&ChH* 1/3/1890.

[19] *DT&ChH* 12/3/1887.

[20] The promenade in the context of the Jubilee celebration was said to have been first proposed by the Hon. C.W. Trollope who spent much of his time as a resident of the New Bath Hotel. *DT* 10/7/1897.

[21] *DC* 21/8/1852. At the time Paxton was busy at Sydenham. *DM* 21/8/1852. Recall of the proposal more than 40 years later suggests that Paxton's idea was for a walk much higher on the hillside, to form 'one of the finest parades in Europe'. *HPN* 11/5/1895.

[22] Bryan, op. cit., page 191.

[23] *HPN* June 1897.

[24] *DT&ChH* 12/3/1887.

[25] *DM* 11/1/1888.

[26] *DT&ChH* 13/8/1887.

[27] MeasuringWorth.com

[28] *HPN* 12/11/1907. Decision taken. 14/1/1908 T.W. Ward tender for iron work £35-10s accepted. Completed for Easter 1908 and in need of repair by July, it was declared a white elephant in April the following year. In 1910 it was leased for cinematograph shows and later for many years used as a store. In 1927 it reverted to its original purpose – offering shelter for visitors. Matlock Bath Parish Council restored the building in the 1990s. It was restored again in 2017.

[29] *MG* 28/7/1906.

[30] *MBUDC minutes*, 29/1/1906. Turnstiles and fencing from Bayliss, Jones and Bayliss of Wolverhampton and the kiosks from Knutsford. 19/3/1906; two turnstiles were purchased from the Royal Hotel. The open fencing which had been removed was reused at Scarthin when its promenade was built in 1908.

[31] *DT&ChH* 1/6/1898.

[32] *HPN* 8/9/1906.

[33] *HPN* 11/7/1908. For the first time in July 1908, a daytime Floral Carnival was held with flower-decorated boats. A battle of flowers, a clown canoe tournament and a water polo match were held and the programme was punctuated by auxeto-phone (amplified gramophone) concerts presented by a local resident, Mr Fred Dalton. This new invention was described as so powerful it could take the place of a band at such events.

[34] The Orchard Holme was described as woodland when allotted to the proprietors of the Old Bath at Matlock Enclosure in 1784 but by 1848 the ground was largely cleared. It became the property of the Royal Hotel and part of it was used as its rubbish tip.

[35] *Edwardian Amusement Parks: the Pleasure Garden Reborn? Josephine Kane; in The Pleasure Garden from Vauxhall to Coney Island* edited by Jonathan Conlin, 2013, page 221. Once again Matlock Bath was abreast with the latest fashion. Roller coasters reached Britain from the United States in 1885 with the first one being installed in Skegness in that year.

[36] For a short time he fabricated fairground equipment in the former Rowing Club clubhouse. In World War II, the land was requisitioned for the army and afterwards some of the former army buildings housed new attractions. An advertisement of about 1950 shows an aquarium and aviary, a children's playground, a miniature railway, miniature racing cars and woodside walks.

[37] This had been focused on the Promenade but a new venue had to be found when the Promenade was reduced to a fragment of its former size by the A6 road-widening scheme.

[38] The derelict wooden bungalow which much earlier had been occupied by Ethel Wyrill, one of Herbert Buxton's married daughters was replaced by storage sheds. The Gardens were included in the Derbyshire Dales District Council's Matlock Parks Project, another refurbishment scheme which was completed in 2008.

[39] Advertisements for it claimed that 'Dr Cullimore, the well-known Physician, has declared not only that the use of the Switchback had a distinctly medical effect upon the liver, but that in order to get proper amount of benefit out of it, one ought not to confine oneself to "One Returned Course" but should take half a dozen such courses.' *Abel Heywood & Son's Guide*, Matlock, 1904.

[40] Mr Walker's production site for petrified objects is today visible as a dark recess in the bank on the opposite side of the river. It used water from the Old Bath spring which later served the paddling pool, (now a water feature) on the level above it.

[41] Audubon J. J. op. cit., page 210.

[42] The long considered sewerage scheme which had been designed to address the problem was not even begun and would not be completed for another 20 years.

CHAPTER ELEVEN
PAGES 141-166

[1] DR0 D7573.

[2] Lawton giving evidence before the arbitrator appointed to adjudicate over the price to be paid for the purchase of the Matlock Bath gasworks stated 'I came as manager for the first twelve months simply to grip the situation, and then became a partner. I did not put any money into the concern till 1880.' *DT&ChH* 25/11/1896.

[3] The agreement was to run from April 1st 1883 for 21 years. DRO D7573. In fact the partnership was dissolved in March 1899. *DM* 29/3/1899.

[4] The three youngest of the eight Lawton children were born in Dukinfield between 1883

and 1888.

[5] DRO D7573.

[6] The main doorway has a surround consisting of large blocks of stone interrupting the architrave, a form named after the architect James Gibbs (1682-1754). *Encyclopedia of Architectural Terms,* James Stevens Curl, 1992.

[7] He may have used brick earlier at Cromford when he built the second mill there in 1776. The architectural and archaeological evidence at Cromford is inconclusive but in 1890 one of the newspaper descriptions of the fire which destroyed the second mill draws attention to it being built of brick. *HPN* 15/11/1890.

[8] Machinery at Masson and Cromford described as useless consisted of 42 throstle frames of 192 spindles each, 2 single winding frames of 50 spindles each and 23 doubling frames of 144 spindles each. Though it is impossible to date this machinery the throstles could have been in use since the early years of the century.

[9] *MBA* 30/9/1865.

[10] *Derby & Chesterfield Reporter* 15/8/1884.

[11] *Manchester Guardian* 15/11/1890.

[12] See Chapman, op. cit., page 33; *Nottingham Review* 25/5/1832; CER 1841; *Electoral Registers* and *London Gazette* 4/8/1846. After the termination of the partnership with William Melville the business continued in J. C. Arkwright's name into the 1850s though by 1857 he was no longer living in Cromford and the company was now referred to as Arkwright & Co, cotton spinners, Cromford and Masson Mills. During the years 1846-1850 Richard Hackett (c. 1795-1862) was the manager of the mills. He was a member of the Hackett family which owned the tape mills in Tansley, and had begun working for the Arkwrights as a bookkeeper about 1815. By 1841 he was described as agent, and soon after, manager. See *Freebody's Directory,* 1852, *White's Directory,* 1857 and CER 1841.

[13] For example in May 1886 there was too much water; in August a year later a drought. In each case the workforce suffered. In November 1890 300-400 were out of work. *Nottingham Journal* 17/5/1886, *DT&ChH* 13/8/1887, *DC* 25/11/1890. In October 1885 Lawton used the pretext of a summer drought necessitating extra night working to explain to the magistrates how he had come to employ three 16 year olds for more than the twelve hours permitted by the factory legislation. Messrs Arkwright and Co were fined 6d with 14/6d costs. *DA&J* 2/10/1885.

[14] *DT* 15/9/1888.

[15] In September his new machinery was nearly lost when a fire broke out in the third floor of the mill. It was believed to have begun in the engine room chimney. In the event children spotted the danger, raised the alarm, and the fire was put out with buckets of water. *MC&LGA* 1/10/1888.

[16] *DT&ChH* 15/9/1888.

[17] Another of Lawton's innovations was the gassing process which he introduced in 1886 achieving full production in 1888. The process singed fine hairs from the thread achieving a smoother product. *DT&ChH* 25/11/1896.

[18] *DT&ChH* 10/11/1883.

[19] First while the 'large wheel' was fitted with new brackets and then through the breakage of the 'very old Driving wheel on the main upright shaft.' This system of transmitting power from the wheel via an upright shaft to the floors of the mill housing the textile machinery would have been as old as the mill itself. Transmission from the new steam engine was via a rope drive the technology which was universally adopted in the UK from the late 1860s. This and the information which follows is from the Masson Mills Report on the work during the year 1890. Private archive.

[20] Spooling. Winding the thread onto a wooden spool which is then labelled and boxed for despatch. *Seams Sewn Long Ago,* 2013, Brian Coats, page 61. The Stott survey of October 1897 records 3 self-acting spooling machines as dating from 1887.

[21] The doubling frames needed respindling and 'Black enamelled Brass headed bobbins' provided in every process. We have found no details of this major reorganisation of the mill but clearly the space previously occupied by the spinning processes would have provided accommodation for the new spooling department and allow the finishing previously done on the Cromford mills site to move to Masson so marking the end of the Arkwright's use of that site for textile production, an association that had begun in August 1771. We believe that it was in this

period of reorientation that spinning at Masson was given up to be replaced by yarn imported from Lancashire so providing the finer spun cotton required to make the new sewing threads. A consequence of this period of transition with so many trainee staff was 'the enormous difficulty' of disposing of the quantities of thread of second and third rate quality that were being produced.

[22] The 'Masson Mills of Sir Richard Arkwright & Co are in full working order and the new departure in sewing cottons has met with an inordinate demand for the goods.' *DA* 9/5/1890.

[23] Six cord sewing thread consisted of two ply and three-ply threads twisted together. Coats, op. cit., page 63.

[24] Mr George Tissington was described as 'foreman and manager of the extensive cotton factory of F. C. Arkwright Esq' in the notice recording his sudden death. *Sheffield & Rotherham Independent* 11/12/1877.

[25] These finishing processes consisted of winding the yarn produced at Masson into hanks and then packing the hanks into bundles. Each bundle of coarse cotton yarn weighed 10lb. Details of the work carried on at Cromford has been derived from a valuation of the machinery at Cromford and Masson, March 1872. DRO D7573.

[26] J. Pilkington, op. cit., page 301 quotes 800 for two mills at Cromford. He offers no figure for the mill [Masson] he mentions in Matlock Dale; J. Britton and E W. Brayley, op. cit., page 517 quote 1150 for 'two mills at Cromford and a third at Masson'; Buxton & Charlton op. cit., page 82 gives the figure for Cromford in 1816 as 725 (*Enquiry into State of Children employed in Manufactories,* page 277) and for Masson only in 1833 as 350; Chapman op. cit., page 33 notes 156 for Masson in 1865. Peter Arkwright's pocket book for 1866, DRO D7573, gives a figure of 241; the 1868 evidence presented to a House of Commons Committee considering Derby's water supply, *DA&J* 12/6/1868 for Masson alone offers 186 and in 1883 from *DT&ChH* 10/11/1883, Mr Young quotes 200 for Masson and Cromford together.

[27] During this period some of Derbyshire's millworkers were better served than many elsewhere. Peter Arkwright, and in Wirksworth, Tatlow and Wheatcroft, kept hands at work

running their mills at a loss. *DM* 12/12/1862.

[28] *London Daily News* 10/9/1850; William Dodd, *The Factory System Illustrated,* 1842 page 209. Dodd had also visited Belper noting that the wages paid by the Strutts though low were higher than in Matlock. He learned that the son of the eldest of the partners was 'popularly called the God of Belper' and that his smile [could] make, and his frown un-make or ruin any tradesman, or workman in the town.'

[29] Stott and Sons valuation 20/10/1897.

[30] Though even by 1897 there were only 92 incandescent lamps and the 300 gas lights predominated. Stott survey.

[31] Chapman, op. cit., page 35.

[32] Stott survey; *DT* 27/1/1904; *DA* 2/7/1910.

[33] *HPN* 11/11/1899, reported local contractors being appointed, Messrs W. Farnsworth and Sons and subcontractors Messrs F. Higton for joinery, Newton for the plumbing and Bunting for the blacksmithing.

[34] *HPN* 19/5/1900.

[35] The Manlove businesses, though consistently profitable in the years 1898-1901, were less fortunate. Unity Mill in Belper closed in 1900 and the Holymoorside complex near Chesterfield at the end of February 1902. *DT&ChH* 1/3/1902 and 10/5/1902.

[36] Warping. The winding of the warp thread onto the beam (a cylinder) from which it will be taken in the process of weaving. Mercerising, a process invented by John Mercer to give cotton threads a fine grained density and lustre.

[37] The hours worked were ten for women; twelve for men and 'by diligence – the system being piece-work – good wages might be earned.' *DA* 2/7/1910.

[38] A four storeyed building, it is of fire proof construction employing brick arches supported on cast iron pillars. The staircase tower is topped by a large water tank feeding a sprinkler system. From road level the lower parts of the building are unseen reducing the visual impact of the large block. The *Matlock Guardian* while welcoming the investment regretted the loss of the mill manager's house and its well-kept garden. *MG* 27/5/1911.

[39] *MG* 28/9/1911. Chapman, op. cit., page

38 states that 'it originally housed a vastly increased spinning capacity.' We have been unable to verify this information and have found no other evidence that spinning was reintroduced to Masson at this time.

40 By 1843 two cottages had been sold to Charles Clarke. They were later pulled down to make way for a carriage drive to Masson House.

41 *DC* 5/9/1914.

42 *DC* 19/7/1919.

43 *DDT* 10/9/1929.

44 A lady who worked at Masson from leaving school and again from 1970 after raising a family remembers talk of a strike; but it came to nothing.

45 In conversation with one of the present authors. *Through the Eye of the Needle,* 1947, page 56.

46 *Through the Eye...'* op. cit., page 57.

47 The well-known Saturday night dances to Glen Nash's band, half a crown, workers free.

48 *Belper News* 1/10/1920.

49 *Through the Eye...* op. cit., page 56. Personal communication.

50 The first synthetic corespun thread was developed by English Sewing in 1957. From Masson, the grey twisted thread, wound onto paper covered stainless steel springs, went to Milford to be dyed and then to Belper for lubrication and winding, and into stock. Notes for visitors to the Belper mills and *Derwent Valley News,* English Sewing, 1977.

51 *Through the Eye...* op. cit., suggests none of the old mill was in use but this is surely an error. The ground floor was in use together with the large area of what had once been the mill yard, until the end of production.

52 This was followed by a further exhibition in 1983-4 celebrating the 150th anniversary of Arkwright's birth.

53 ICOMOS, International Council on Monuments and Sites. UNESCO, United Nations Educational Scientific and Cultural Organisation.

54 Coats, op. cit., page 222.

55 *DT&ChH* 13/8/1898.

56 *Illustrated Sporting and Dramatic News* 11/11/1897.

57 It has to be admitted this remark was made in a speech at the wedding of Lawton's daughter May, an occasion when extravagant pleasantries were exchanged with a generosity that may seem excessive. Lawton, returning the compliment described Dewhurst as 'the keystone of the arch by which the Strutts and the Arkwrights after a lapse of a century, had again become partners.' *DT&ChH* 29/1/1898.

58 DT 27/11/1897.

59 There was a fourth Derbyshire company Wigleys of Derby and there might have been a fifth. In September 1897 the *LM* had reported negotiations with Walter Evans, the thread maker at Darley Abbey; but they remained independent. *LM* 9/9/1897.

60 The share offer was the most largely oversubscribed industrial flotation of that period apart from Liptons. Investors were encouraged by the support Coats gave the new company agreeing to invest £200,000. *Irish Independent* 21/12/1897 and *DT* 13/8/1898.

61 'nearing completion'. *DA&J* 27/12/1901.

62 *HPN* 13/5/1910 and 8/7/1911.

63 *The Trust Movement in British Industry,* H. W. Macrosty, 1907, page 129. The accountants, Ernest Crewdsons of Manchester, stated in the prospectus 'the profits earned during recent years have been taken into account; but the difficulty of arriving at a reliable figure on a common basis is so great, and the fluctuations owing to the excessive under-cutting...are so considerable that the Directors decline the responsibility of putting forward a detailed statement...the average profits of the past ten years have been comparatively small.' *The Globe,* 1/12/1897.

64 The *DT* was ecstatic. 'J and P Coats and the English Sewing Cotton Company will now control the sewing cotton trade of the world.' By January 1899 the company's 20/- shares had risen to 35/-. *DT&ChH* 19/11/1898 and 7/1/1899.

65 The network extended still further if the trustees for the debenture holders are included, amongst whom were F. C. Arkwright and G. H. Strutt. *DT* 7/1/1899.

[66] John Randolph Dos Passos (1844-1917), eminent criminal lawyer and expert on commercial trusts, who had already organised the sugar trust. A proud anglo saxon and advocate for joint anglo-american citizenship, he is best remembered now in the United States as the father of the celebrated novelist John Dos Passos (1896-1970). Melvin Landsbery, *John R. Dos Passos; his influence on the novelist's early political development.*

[67] *DT* 7/1/1899.

[68] Earlier in the year they had met Mr Philippi, a director of Coats, at the mills of the Willimantic Linen Company, the largest of the companies joining the new combine, and seemingly secured his support. *HPN* 9/4/1898.

[69] *DT&ChH* 10/5/1902.

[70] *DA* 30/12/1899. Yet less than a year later, at the end of the summer, 1900, the Manlove business in Belper closed. *DT&ChH* 1/3/1902.

[71] Macrosty, op.cit., page 132.

[72] Macrosty, op.cit., page 134 citing the *Financial Times* August 30, 1901. Lawton may have achieved some success in reshaping the management. In August 1901 the three managing directors were replaced by an executive chaired by Lawton. *DDT* 30/8/1901.

[73] *MC* 4/6/1873; *Hyde and Glossop Weekly,* 29/3/1873; Haynes, *Dukinfield Cotton Mills,* 1993, page 45; *Ashton Reporter,* 10/3/1883; CER, 1881; *Lloyd's List* 17/9/1879; *MC* 13/11/1883; *MC* 16/6/1885; *Staleybridge Reporter,* 13/2/1915, *DA* 12/2/1915 and *HPN* 13/2/1915. In 1871 Lawton was evidently still working for his uncle, his occupation in the census of that year described him as an accountant's clerk. This description may understate his actual status for two years later he was company secretary of a new cotton spinning company. Both he and John Buckley Kynder were involved in launching the Shaw Hall Spinning Co which would purchase an existing mill at Newton Moor, near Hyde; the one as company secretary, the other as a director. It was also in this period that Lawton took over the Union Mill which had been run by his wife's family since 1850. The precise date of the takeover has not been identified. The mill closed in 1883 and the machinery was sold.

[74] *Irish Times* 10/4/1902.

[75] *MC& LGA* 17/1/1903. Charles Diamond (1858-1934), member of parliament, (1892-1895), prolific founder of weekly newspapers – lifetime total 37; and an outspoken and controversial figure. See Wikipedia.

[76] By March 1902 he was known in some quarters as 'Diamond cut Diamond'. *DT&ChA* 22/3/1903.

[77] Diamond had relocated from London to Manchester and was eventually devoting 4 or 5 days a week to the company. *MC&LGA* 17/1/1903.

[78] *LM* 18/3/1902.

[79] *DT&ChH* 21/1/1898.

[80] A full account of this meeting appeared in the *DT&ChH* 10/5/1902.

[81] Diamond also identified Dewhurst and Manlove as particularly culpable.

[82] This was the second mill on the Cromford site built by Richard Arkwright in 1776-7 which burned down in 1890; the laundry was housed in its annexe which had largely escaped damage in the fire.

[83] Increasing it from £1000 to £2000, half of it paid by the American Thread Company.

[84] The figures for Strutts were 1898 3%, 1899 1%, 1900 4.3%, 1901 (4.5%); and for Manloves in the same years, 4.2%, 4.1%, 4.8%, 4.6%

[85] Letters were also sent to Messrs Ermen, Dewhurst and Strutt.

[86] £43,580; about a third of the total valuation. *Auditors Report,* July 1903.

[87] Diamond's assertion that Masson Mill had been barely profitable and did not warrant the value placed on it in 1897 and his evidence of poor returns in the years 1898-1901, casts doubt on the scale of what Chapman describes as Lawton's 'remarkable achievement' in regenerating the mills in the years between 1879 and 1897. Chapman, op. cit., page 35. Further evidence of the precarious state of the business in the 1890s emerges from Joseph Reed's evidence in the Board of Trade, Matlock Bath Gas Enquiry. He had been managing director of Matlock Bath gas company for ten years and said he had suggested more than once providing a larger gas main to Masson mill and would have done so 'but for Mr Lawton – [who] always held

out so little hope of the mill going on any longer, as the cotton trade was so bad.' *DT* 21/3/1896.

[88] The water rights the company purchased had some value. It lay in the control ownership offered of water flowing into the river Derwent from the Cromford Sough and the Bonsall Brook. Had the rights been purchased by the Cromford Canal Company it would have been possible for it to increase the flow of water into the canal (which was limited by the amended Canal Act to 24 hours per week) so diminishing the volume of water available to the English Sewing Cotton Company downstream in Belper and Milford.

[89] Otto Ernst Philippi (1847-1917) born of a German family but who took British citizenship; he is credited with masterminding the Coat's textile concerns international expansion through his exceptional grasp of administrative detail and leadership. Phillippi's contribution to the survival of the English Sewing Cotton Company at this juncture is difficult to judge. Otto Ernst Phillippi, *Dictionary of Scottish Business Biography,* vol.1. By making him available to the failing enterprise had Coats, for a brief period, taken it under their wing, see *Seams sewn long ago,* page 226 or simply facilitated a report which led to a radical administrative reorganisation see J. H. Clapham, *An Economic History of Modern Britain,* vol 3, page 226?

[90] With power to co-opt 2 more members. *YP* 7/10/1902.

[91] Ibid.

[92] *DT&ChH* 29/11/1902.

[93] Manlove had died in June 1902 so the case was to be brought against his executors. *DT&ChH,* 14/6/1902.

[94] *Sheffield Telegraph* 28/2/1903.

[95] *MC* 8/8/1903 and *YP&LI* 3/8/1903.

[96] The report is dated 29/7/1903.

[97] He had in fact been nominated to fill a vacancy on the board but had declined. *MC* 13/8/1903.

[98] *LM* 8/8/1903.

[99] *MC* 30/7/1904.

[100] The Ermen and Roby offer was £10,000 in stocks and shares but it was conditional on the other constituent businesses contributing and as this condition was not met the deal may not have been consummated. *MC* 3/7/1904 and 5/10/1904.

[101] Some, perhaps all, of Mellor mill had been destroyed by fire in November 1892 but it was sold in the expectation of a new mill being built on the site. *Ripley and Heanor News* 18/11/1892.

[102] The agreement reached with the Manlove family involved Unity Mill at Belper, the former Manlove property, which had been standing empty for four years after ESCC closed the business there. The Manloves sold it to G. H. Strutt which suggests the outcome of the deal with the Manloves was similar to the arrangement made with F. C. Arkwright; the building was returned to the original owner and an adjustment made to the debentures held in the company.

[103] The arrangements were approved at a meeting of the debenture holders in October 1904. Six months later ESCC sought sanction in Chancery for the cancellation of £50,000 of debenture stock arising from these repurchases. *DC* 21/3/1905.

[104] *DC* 29/5/1905.

[105] *YP&LI* 28/7/1905. The vote was 13-11.

[106] *DDT* 8/8/1905.

[107] *The Scotsman* 4/8/1905.

[108] During the meeting Lawton attacked Coats accusing them of failing to honour their commitment in the 1897 prospectus not to interfere in the running of the company. Previously conspicuously supportive of Coats his criticism may have been in retaliation for their refusal to endorse his candidacy. Coats responded to his comments in a letter to the ESSC board defending their conduct. They were, they said used to ill -informed criticism but could not ignore remarks from a previous vice-chairman who, though he had attacked them, had sought their support. Their letter was made public at their annual meeting in November 1905. If Lawton harboured thoughts of a further attempt at election this surely put the idea beyond reach. *Irish Times* 10/11/1905 and *The Times* 10/11/1905.

CHAPTER TWELVE
PAGES 167-184

[1] Words spoken at a dinner in honour of Robert Chadwick, Chairman of the Local Board, January

1867. *DM* 23/1/1867.

[2] An edited account from *DC* 17/6/1871.

[3] Effectively 1895; the council was not elected until December 1894.

[4] In 1905 Lawton giving evidence to a committee of the House of Lords estimated as many as 30,000 visitors in one day and a total of 250,000 during the season, 20/5/1905. At Easter 1895 he claimed there had been more than 50,000. *DT&ChH* 27/4/1895.

[5] In modern value about £1,500.

[6] He also said Mr Buxton had called him 'a cantankerous despicable humbug' for calling the meeting of ratepayers. *DC* 19/12/1885.

[7] The three retiring members up for re-election Lawton, Cardin and Cubley were defeated and replaced by White, Martin and Leggoe. *HPN* 16/2/1907 and 30/3/1907.

[8] *DT&ChH* 27/4/1895.

[9] *HPN* 23/3/1907.

[10] *DC* 6/5/1882.

[11] An edited extract from the *DT&ChH* 6/6/1891.

[12] Mr Leggoe who described himself as an accountant was also an officer in the Salvation Army. *DT&ChH* 11/1/1894.

[13] Such as John Burgess who Police Inspector Sims, the Board's Inspector of Nuisances, found to be keeping five pigs under his house. *DT&ChH* 5/11/1870.

[14] *DT&ChH* 30/4/1887.

[15] *DT&ChH* 18/6/1892.

[16] The plan to supplement the supply with the purchase of a spring was to cost a further £1,500. The ratepayers wanted an improved supply but were alarmed by the cost. *DC* 8/11/1883 and 19/12/1885.

[17] *DT&ChH* 8/11/1890, report of Mr W. H. Radford of Nottingham.

[18] *HPN* 24/9/1904.

[19] *DT&ChH* 28/3/1890 and 5/4/1890.

[20] *DT&ChH* 23/4/1893.

[21] *SI* 6/12/1894.

[22] This technique was once known in local government administrative circles (and perhaps still is) as the arsenic sandwich.

[23] *DC* 1/9/1900.

[24] *SI* 3/7/1897. His son Arthur was also for a time an elected member of the Council.

[25] *DT&ChH* 11/6/1898.

[26] The case turned on whether the footpath was part of the highway. It was resolved in Matlock Bath's favour after the County Council's appeal to the House of Lords failed. *DT&ChH* 20/11/1895.

[27] *National Gas Archive.*

[28] In 1887 the Matlock & District Gas Company was incorporated to manage this site. Four years later it was empowered to supply Wensley, Snitterton and Tansley.

[29] *HPN* 2/1/1897.

[30] The auditor rejected the claim; but it was approved on appeal. *DT* 18/11/1899.

[31] *HPN* 16/4/1904. It would appear the ratepayers' association formed earlier had been dissolved.

[32] *HPN* 2/7/1904.

[33] By 1905 the total debt was £25,451and rates 6/- in the £. *DC* 20/5/1905.

[34] The Reverend Richard Nicholson (1842-1916) a Congregational minister, was adopted by the Matlock Bath Ratepayers' Association for election to the Local Board in March 1890 but was not elected until 1891. He had become a Matlock Bath ratepayer in 1887 with the purchase of Clarence House Hydro. He already owned the Matlock Hall Hydro in Matlock Bridge which he had acquired in 1880. His membership of the Local Board ended abruptly in March 1894 when, unable to repay the loan he had received from Mrs Donkin, a local resident, he became insolvent and was obliged to resign. He left the district, moving to Liverpool where he died in 1916. Both his hydro properties were put up for sale by auction in June 1894. *DT* 29/3/1890; *SI* 8/3/1893, *DT&ChH* 9/6 1894.

[35] *DC* 18/2/1888; *HPN* 18/2/1888; *DA* 24/2/1888 published details of the proposed sewerage scheme including sites for septic tanks.

[36] One advantage of Speed's recommendation to install earth closets, not immediately apparent,

was that it would not impose additional strain on Matlock Bath's precarious water supply.

[37] The sanitation in Scarthin was particularly deficient. An earlier investigation had revealed the majority of the houses emptied their sewage into the mill dam. The stench was so bad that in March 1893 it prompted F. C. Arkwright to write to the Matlock Board urging it to make the funding available as soon as it could so the Cromford sewerage scheme could be completed. *DT&ChH* 7/4/1883; 11/3/1893; 11/11/1893.

[38] Based on *DC* 12/8/1890.

[39] *DT&ChH* 5/11/1892.

[40] Despite recognising that the problem could only be solved if the three settlements Matlock, Matlock Bath and Cromford worked together, in 1900-01 Matlock Bath spent £600 successfully opposing a sewerage scheme which had been proposed by Matlock in 1898 on much the same lines as Parkin's scheme had proposed in 1891.

[41] *DC* 31/10/1908.

[42] They were probably illiterate. At the time of their marriage neither was able to sign their name. The father, Frederick White (1838-1913), was a gardener.

[43] What brought him to Bonsall remains unclear. Genealogical research by David Hool proves that the account of this part of his life which appeared in the *HPN* 8/12/1923 was incorrect. This described his mother, a native of Bonsall taking him there on the death of her husband. In fact his mother Ruth had been born in Malmesbury and predeceased her husband, dying in 1870.

[44] The 1906 electoral register places him in Bonsall but by March 1907 he was in Matlock Bath canvassing voters for election to the Matlock Bath UDC.

[45] *DA* 7/12/1923.

[46] Particularly in Bonsall and the Matlocks.

[47] The offices from which he resigned were; membership of the County Council; membership and chairmanship of Matlock Bath UDC; membership of Belper, Matlock and Wirksworth Education Committees; membership of the Matlock Old Age Pension Committee; his position as a manager of the Church of England Schools in Matlock Bath; and as manager of the

Council Schools in Darley Dale. He also lost his employment with the Liberal Association.

[48] Among those who contributed was J. B. Marsden-Smedley of Lea Green previously an adversary both politically and, as the owner of Lea Mills, in the strike of 1911-12 see *Cromford Revisited,* pages 159-164, which White is believed to have instigated. J. B. Marsden-Smedley had also paid £150 towards the legal expenses of Mr Rose, one of the defendants in the slander trial thus ultimately supporting each side in the dispute. He and White worked together as magistrates and again during the war and a mutual respect seems to have developed between them. John Smedley Archive.

[49] Lord Kerry, the Cavendish nominee, was the brother of the Duchess of Devonshire. The family had never before lost control of the seat.

[50] He was there by March 1918. Correspondence, John Smedley Archive.

[51] For example the water supply for housing in Bakewell; the need for housing in North Darley; management behaviour in dismissing men at D. P. Battery Works; or the closure of the school at Atlow.

[52] This brief account of Charlie White's career is based on a range of sources which include census and registration material; electoral rolls; Hansard; and a number of newspaper articles in particular *DC* 26/11/1910; *DDT* 8/3/1913; 14/8/1918; 4/12/1923; *Sheffield Daily Independent,* 16/5/1914; *DA* 13/12/1918; 14/12/1923; 15/12/1923; *HPN* 8/12/1923.

[53] *DC* 8/3/1913.

[54] Mr Justice Darling (1849-1936), later the first Baron Darling, once described by a contemporary journalist as 'the impudent little man in horsehair', was renowned for his wit rather than for his legal acuity. *Henry Brooke Musings, Memories and Miscellanea,* 2017.

CHAPTER THIRTEEN
PAGES 185-198

[1] MBUDC minutes, 27/7/1912. New Head Post Office to be opened on September 1st. The demotion of Matlock Bath's post office to a branch office had to be made when the Post Office began to use motor vehicles; there was no room to house them at the Matlock Bath office on Derwent Parade.

[2] *HPN* 13 and 20/2/1915. Nearly 600 men were billeted in the Pavilion, where the Pump Room served as their canteen, and in the Royal Pavilion; their officers were lodged in the Royal Hotel. Provision was also made for 130 horses. The soldiers enjoyed the use of the Fountain Baths and the Day School was opened in the evenings for billiards etc. They declared themselves very well treated but units were often quickly moved on to camp at Darley Dale.

[3] The 1881 census refers to Museum Parade; the 1891 census to South Parade.

[4] Caudwell's Mill accounts, Caudwell's Mill Trust.

[5] The club was founded in 1878. Local residents formed their own club the Matlock Bath and District's Cycling Club. This held its first annual dinner in 1891.

[6] Howe's shop helps to date the picture. In 1856 W. E. Howe became manager of Bemrose's shop seen on the left in this view. He later took over the business though retaining the Bemrose agency. William Bemrose & Son, printers from Derby had opened a shop in Matlock Bath in 1851 and in September 1854 published the *Matlock Bath Advertiser*. In 1865 they combined it with their longer established rival newspaper, the *Matlock Bath Telegraph* which had begun life in 1853 then published by T. H. Holmes. In common with the fashion in spa resorts it published a weekly list of visitors to Matlock Bath. From 1854 to 1863, the firm shared premises with the Mechanics Institute and Mr Dakin, the lapidary before taking a 14 year lease of the whole premises.

[7] The 'tin hut' which stood beside Temple Walk opposite the entrance to the Royal Hotel is the small building visible here immediately above the Fishpond roof. The site had a long commercial use. A spar sales booth is shown on the site in a pen and wash drawing by Nicholas Pocock dated 1794; around 1900 a member of the Seaman family of photographers had a photographic studio there, later it was used by Percy Rowbottom for the same purpose.

[8] *HPN* 25/2/1921.

[9] Letter from Ken Smith collection.

[10] The memorial was supplied by Messrs Jas. Berresford of Belper.

[11] *HPN* 20/5/1922.

[12] *HPN* 19/2/1922.

[13] *HPN* 19/3/1921.

[14] 1922 was the year in which the only significant twentieth century building was added to the Parades. Williams Deacon's Bank Ltd had bought the corner property at the bottom of the Pitchings in 1919 and 3 years later demolished it to build new premises Figure 133. The building of the Parochial Hall at the north end of the village the following year and beside it Ardean House and garage some ten years later did not have the same architectural impact though Fred Greatorex's three year toil to single-handedly dig out the site for his garage does merit admiration.

[15] There was also the stream of commuting 'Derby clerks' who made the daily trip out of Matlock Bath on the busy ten to eight train (its precise departure governed by the guard Mr Wright 'following the right time not the Wright time') and back at 6pm.

[16] The Pavilion meanwhile had seen various attempts to manage its balance sheet including opening, closing and re-opening the cinematograph and in 1917 planning the introduction of industry to part of its ground floor then being used as the cinema. The opportunity to set up a business there was advertised but in the absence of any response, the Council Chairman, George Henry Key leased space and opened a glove factory which traded as the Spa Glove Company. It continued to trade under that name after it was sold in 1922. Then or soon after, in the hands of Mr Perry, the operation was moved into the former Boden's Restaurant building Figure126.

[17] On May 27th, 1937 the Royal Hotel Estate was put up for sale by auction. The sale catalogue confirmed that some work had begun on one of the considered new plans for the site. It included the cleared site of the hotel with excavations which could be used as the basis for a swimming pool; the surviving West Wing, formerly the ballroom of the hotel, partially reconditioned with a large Assembly Hall; the Palais Royal with seating for 800-1,000; 20 acres of land and the mineral rights and royalties. Fluor spar mining had already begun on the western boundary of the property providing an income of £100 per annum. Offered first as one lot, the property was withdrawn at £3,200. It was

then split into two lots but offers for the two combined failed to reach that figure and both lots were withdrawn. Ultimately it became Council property. Catalogue, private collection.

[18] *HPN* 30/1/1932.

[19] *Sheffield Daily Independent* 20/8/1936.

[20] He produced hair tonics which he promoted in a full page advertisement in the *Radio Times* in 1932 under the banner headline 'Remarkable effects of radio-activity on hair growth'. We do not know who owned this property between Howe and Godfrey.

[21] Miss Farnsworth was born in 1890 and this account was re-published in the local paper the *Matlock Mercury* on November 25th, 1994, some 30 years after it was first written.

[22] The former Hartle's Museum for example.

[23] Mount View was built on the Wapping sometime between 1784 and 1810 by Thomas Boden who acquired the land at Matlock Enclosure. From the 1820s until the 1860s it was an inn, the King's Head where The Firm and Friendly Society was formed in September 1834. Next to it were two cottages, the prominent one, Weirside stood on the site of the first Warmwalls toll-house of 1759 which was sold in 1820 when the new toll-house Figure 14 came into use.

[24] Probably built by the Skidmore family as cottages but when Samuel Skidmore sold the property in 1923, the family hosiery business founded there in 1784, occupied most of the ground floor. Soon after it was transferred to Matlock, the premises were converted to the café shown in this view. Skidmore built the house, Rock Weir, behind these properties in or soon after 1900.

[25] This twentieth century view shows a very much larger building than the one built by Richard Arkwright on this site sometime after 1784. Francis Shore purchased it in 1824 and bequeathed it to Miss Brace in 1852. The Post office was housed in the building during their ownerships. George Withers Saxton bought the house in 1856 and ran it as a lodging house after his retirement from the New Bath. It was probably at this date that the house became known as Woodland House and the Post office moved to the recently completed Woodland Terrace on the other side of the main road. In the 1860s it was moved to a more central position in the resort, the newly built Derwent Parade now No 62 North Parade.

[26] It was fed from the spring which supplied the New Bath pool and was advertised as the Original Well. It is probable that the bakehouse had been Boden's original sales-shop or Boden's Spar Manufactory as *Brewer's Directory* described it in 1823. Long after it was closed to the public, the well was used as a production well for other businesses, including Smith's Royal Well, the last well to close. The edge of Beck's sales shop is visible on the left.

[27] Guy Le Blanc Smith started the garage business in a wooden shed on this site in the early 1920s; he sold it to Dyson and Clough in 1930.

[28] The business was moved to Museum Parade in 1812. The building here continued in use as Hartle's Bazaar and later as Bath Terrace Museum and was in residential use before demolition.

[29] Jewitt described it as adding nothing beautiful to the view. It was run as a public house and, later, as a restaurant until it was demolished in 1967-8, see picture right. In the background behind the walkers the sign Victoria Hotel and Restaurant draws attention to Victoria House. With its matching neighbour Albert House it was built in the large garden adjacent to Rose Cottage in 1861 by William Pearson. Pearson lived behind Rose Cottage at The Mount, (sometimes called Mount Pleasant), which was built in the 1830s.

[30] The Green was part of the land which William Smedley bought from the Vernon estate in 1805. His will of 1816 bequeathed it to his daughter Ann and her husband James Pearson who built a house on it in which subsequently their daughter Jemima and her husband Edward Wheatcroft lived. Edward owned two houses there in 1848 so it seems likely that he built the additional dwelling; perhaps his first foray into speculative building. Mrs Francis Frost added a third storey to the one she purchased in 1902. The view from the back of the houses to the river might now be promoted as a picturesque selling point; for her neighbour William King the draper, it was an invitation to catch fish from his balcony.

[31] *DC* 30/10/1869.

[32] *LM* 7/4/1883.

[33] *DT&ChH,* 12/1/1878.

[34] The Board was proud of its handling of the local cabmen telling a neighbouring authority which had invited them to participate in a joint scheme 'they had now got their cabmen into an orderly condition and if they joined with other districts it would undoubtedly increase their difficulties.' *DT&ChH* 5/7/1884.

[35] Sir George Head, op. cit., page 118.

[36] The creation of Lover's Walk might be an example from an earlier period. It depends on the view taken of its creation.

APPENDIX
PAGES 203-204

[1] The census enumerator attributes the increase in 1841 to visitors in Matlock Bath; in 1861 due to 115 receiving hydropathic treatment; and in 1871 to hydropathy.

[2] The National Archives' figures for Midland Railway ticket bookings at Matlock Bath and Matlock stations illustrate the comparative growth of the two settlements in a different way. Figures for the number of tickets issued to passengers at Matlock Bath station are 66,664 in 1885 and 69,247 in 1920. For Matlock over the same 35 years the figure more than doubled from 82,810 in 1885 to 168,115 in 1920. Eventually express trains no longer stopped at Matlock Bath.

Index

Other Publications from the Trust

The Derwent Valley Mills and their Communities
ISBN 978-0-9541940-3-1, 115 pages, paperback, Price £18

A lavishly illustrated full colour exploration of the Derwent Valley Mills World Heritage Site and its architectural heritage providing an historical background to many of the key buildings, streets and houses within the World Heritage Site.

The Strutts and the Arkwrights
RS Fitton and AP Wadsworth
IBSN 978-0-9541940-5-5, 361 pages, paperback, Price £18

First published in 1958 this is the classic account of the birth of the factory system in the Derwent Valley in the late eighteenth century. Out of print for more than forty years the Trust has now made it available once again.

The Arkwrights Spinners of Fortune
RS Fitton
IBSN 978-0-9541940-4-8, 321 pages, paperback, Price £18

A detailed account of the careers of Sir Richard Arkwright and his son Richard Arkwright junior describing their technological breakthrough, their entrepreneurial genius and fabulous financial success which led the family in due course, to a secure place amongst the English gentry.

Cromford Revisited
Doreen Buxton and Christopher Charlton
IBSN 978-0-9541940-6-2, 192 pages, paperback, Price £18

This new study of Cromford, the Arkwright family's factory village, uses watercolours, drawings and photographs and previously unexplored archive material, to present an authoritative account of the origins and growth of this iconic settlement. The book includes descriptions of many of the village's key features, the several mills and their watercourses, Willersley Castle, Cromford Church, the Canal Wharf and the village schools. It concludes with the discovery of Cromford as a heritage destination and inscription within the Derwent Valley Mills World Heritage Site.

These books are available from the Derwent Valley Mills World Heritage Site Educational Trust, registered charity number 1099279.

To order email DVMWHS.EducationTrust@gmail.com
or by telephone 07784 875 333

MATLOCK BATH
KEY SITES

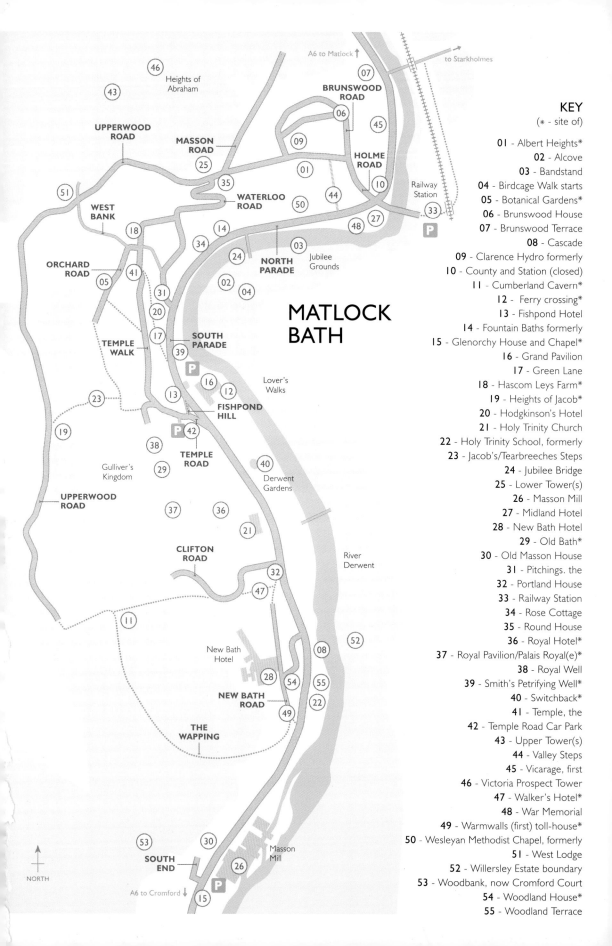

MATLOCK
BATH

NORTH

A6 to Matlock ↑
to Starkholmes

BRUNSWOOD ROAD
HOLME ROAD
Railway Station

Heights of Abraham
UPPERWOOD ROAD
MASSON ROAD
WATERLOO ROAD
WEST BANK
NORTH PARADE
Jubilee Grounds
ORCHARD ROAD
SOUTH PARADE
TEMPLE WALK
Lover's Walks
FISHPOND HILL
TEMPLE ROAD
Gulliver's Kingdom
Derwent Gardens
UPPERWOOD ROAD
CLIFTON ROAD
River Derwent
New Bath Hotel
NEW BATH ROAD
THE WAPPING
SOUTH END
Masson Mill
A6 to Cromford ↓